PENGUIN BOOKS

TITANIC

John Wilson Foster was born and raised in Belfast. He holds a B.A. and M.A. in literature and philosophy from the Queen's University of Belfast and a Ph.D. in English literature from the University of Oregon. He is a Professor of English at the University of British Columbia, Vancouver. In 1986–7 he was Senior Research Fellow at the Institute of Irish Studies, Queen's University, Belfast. Among his books are *Fictions of the Irish Literary Revival* (1987), *Colonial Consequences: Essays in Irish Literature and Culture* (1991), *The Achievement of Seamus Heaney* (1995) and *The* Titanic *Complex: A Cultural Manifest* (1997). He is Senior Editor of *Nature in Ireland: A Scientific and Cultural History* (1997). He plies between homes in Vancouver and Portaferry, Co. Down, enjoying the bird life of the Fraser River delta and Strangford Lough.

TITANIC

Edited by
JOHN WILSON FOSTER

PENGUIN BOOKS

PENGUIN BOOKS
Published by the Penguin Group
Penguin Putnam Inc., 375 Hudson Street,
New York, New York 10014, U.S.A.
Penguin Books Ltd, 27 Wrights Lane,
London W8 5TZ, England
Penguin Books Australia Ltd, Ringwood,
Victoria, Australia
Penguin Books Canada Ltd, 10 Alcorn Avenue,
Toronto, Ontario, Canada M4V 3B2
Penguin Books (N.Z.) Ltd, 182–190 Wairau Road,
Auckland 10, New Zealand

Penguin Books Ltd, Registered Offices:
Harmondsworth, Middlesex, England

First published in Penguin Books (U.K.) 1999
First published in Penguin Books (U.S.A.) 2000

10 9 8 7 6 5 4 3 2 1

Pages 361–2 constitute an extension of this copyright page.

ISBN 0 14 11.8483 3

Printed in the United States of America
Set in Adobe New Caledonia

Contents

Illustrations

Acknowledgements

Friends, acquaintances and strangers too numerous to mention have generously provisioned me over the years with *Titanic* literature, leads and lore. But some individuals and organizations must be acknowledged by name, else some of this anthology would constitute intellectual theft or serious ingratitude: from the University of British Columbia, Philip J. Thomas (and his Popular Song Collection lodged with Special Collections, Main Library), Daniel O'Leary, Bridget Donald, Leslie Arnovick, Geoffrey Winthrop-Young, Resource Sharing Services (Koerner Library), the staff of the English department and the Hampton Fund Grants Committee; from the Vancouver Public Library, Janet Tomkins; from the Vancouver Maritime Museum, James Delgado (Director); from Linenhall Library, Belfast, John Gray and his staff; from Belfast, Allison Murphy; from The Library of Congress (Washington, D.C.), the American Folklife Center; and from Penguin Press, Paul Keegan. I thank these and the unnamed others who survived my temporary mania.

The book is dedicated to Gail, my 'bright incipience'.

Introduction

Titanic – greatest ship ever was born
Frank Hutchison (blues singer),
'The Last Scene of the *Titanic*' (1927)

The accidental collision of Royal Mail Steamer *Titanic* with an iceberg at twenty minutes before midnight on the evening of 14 April 1912 occurred during a night of unusual quiet in a North Atlantic hardly disturbed by the fleet passage of the ship. 'She seemed to swim in oil, so smooth the sea', a Canadian poet wrote a quarter century later. Reporting Lord Mersey's British enquiry into the disaster, the magazine *Engineering* told its readers that 'The air was absolutely calm and the sea absolutely flat, a condition which Sir Ernest Shackleton said he had only experienced once or twice in twenty years.' It transpired that this calm had ironically made the passage more hazardous, there being no waves to throw cautionary glints off icebergs ahead. The calm must also have lent a benign stage-set surrealism to what passengers late to bed saw before the iceberg loomed. What followed must have composed its own horrific surrealism.

But it was chillingly real in the most literal sense. The collision shocked into motion an almost three-hour sequence of scenes aboard ship of curiosity, alarm, nervous jocularity, mobilization, reassurance, insouciance (real or feigned), terror, bravery, despair, stoicism. The drama of the sinking (the real time of which was roughly that of a theatrical performance) has retained for some the ambiguous appeal of stage tragedy. Yet one wonders if the appeal isn't deeper than that, rather medieval than modern. To some survivors, it was the name and spirit of Dante, the great Italian poet of the Middle Ages, author of *The Divine Comedy*, that seemed to preside over the tragedy. One might peruse the ledger of the lost and think, following Dante (in the translation of T. S. Eliot, evoking doomed crowds and the water beneath them): 'I had not thought death had undone so many'.

Like the bookish on board we see allegory. In our minds' eyes and in motion picture enactments we see struggle that resolves itself into the procession of human life towards the fatal destination of water. For here was enacted with an indifferent simplicity 'the state of manne, and how he is called at uncertayne tymes by death, and when he thinkest least thereon'. That one was called in company must have helped to muffle at first the sound of death's summoning voice. 'It all seemed like a play, like a drama that was being enacted for entertainment,' one woman survivor recalled, 'it did not seem real.' Fellow-passengers, after all, had the appearance of a holiday crowd, some in casual dress, some in tuxedos or evening gowns; Mrs Stengel wore a kimono, Officer Charles Lightoller wore a jumper and trousers over pyjamas, J. Bruce Ismay wore carpet slippers while he impatiently shepherded starboard passengers into the lifeboats.

Then the possible terrible outcome of what was happening must have intruded. As the sinking continued, the familiar options, potential and variety of one's life dwindled fast. All became foreground and the present distending moment. The sound of death must have grown less disregardable, the company less reassuring and at last comfortless, even hostile and alien.

When the great ship disappeared, it must have seemed to those in the boats that she was faithlessly abandoning them to their own frail devices. (Those in the water were quickly beyond metaphor and even thought, expelled from their previous land lives, creatures now, out of their element and in the final battle for survival.) The cruelly clear night and calm sea must have resembled to the saved in the boats a resort playground in hell, the manly and womanly voices raised not in cheer and sport but in summons and petition and in the end in abjection and mercifully diminishing terror. Unbearable to us is the thought of those still alive on the ship, borne under the waves, departing on that interminable voyage into the abyss.

In those short hours there must have been innumerable acts of compassion, selfishness, courage, failure of nerve. The situation must have released unfamiliar and surprising strength in some, unfamiliar and surprising weakness in others. Some became people they had not known in a lifetime – changed utterly; some proved to themselves what they had always known they were, good, bad or indifferent as that was. Many survivors must in later years have relived the experience in nightmare, some remembering their behaviour during the sinking with regret, or dubious satisfaction, perhaps painful self-reproach. Like the trenches three years later, *Titanic* was a breeding-ground for a lifetime's excruciation.

Lives were sea-changed by the disaster. Girls (like young widows and bereaved sweethearts from the Great War) lived on to become elderly witnesses and moral commentators, celebrities and cherished links with a time before the War, that uniquely mourned era we call the Edwardian summer (flexing our historical dates a little). But in that twilight of public chivalry, shame would have been the immediate portion for men (especially first-class men) who survived, and for other survivors that mingling of guilt and relief that is said to attend such good fortune.

Lives of those not on board were changed too. Should we mislay the reality of the disaster's consequences, we need only read the letter Third Engineer Herbert Jupe's father wrote to the authorities in Halifax, Nova Scotia where the bodies were brought.

> Dear Sir I have been inform by Mr F Blake Superintendent Engineer of the White Star Line Trafalgar Chambers on the 10th that the Body of my Beloved Son Herbert Jupe which was Electrical Engineer No. 3 on the ill-Fatted Titanic has been recovered and Burried at Sea by the Cable Steamer 'Mackey-Bennett' and that his Silver Watch and Handkerchief marked H. J. is in your Possession. He bought him half a doz of the same when he was at Belfast with the R.M.S. Olympic to have a new blade put to one of her Perpellors we are extremely oblidged for all your Kindness to my Precious Boy He was not married and was the Love of our Hearts and he loved his Home But God gave and God has taken Him Blessed be the Name of the Lord. He has left an Aceing Void in our Home which cannot be filled. Please send along the Watch and Handkerchief marked H. J.
>
> Yours Truly C. Jupe.
> His Mother is 72 Last april 4th.
> His father is 68 Last Feb 9th.

The theatrical illusion that the saved and the lost quickly outgrew that night was resumed by commentators. The editorialist in the London *Daily Mirror* of 17 April 1912 saw in the tragedy a sensation that outdid the romance-writers at their own game: it was one of the 'true romances'; in its account of the career of Thomas Andrews, the ship's designer who went down, the *Belfast News-Letter* of 20 April described what happened as 'a disaster that has thrilled and startled the world'. Joseph Conrad dismissed 'the false, written-up, Drury Lane aspects' of the event, which was 'neither drama nor melodrama'; but the thrill of the affair has been great enough to sustain two revivals (1950–60s, 1980–90s) and innumerable novels (mostly middlebrow romances) as well as plays, films, paintings, dance, opera, musicals. The modest number of serious artists who have tackled the subject suggests that many have been deterred by both the Dantean simplicity of the disaster and its popularity among poetasters, writers of novelettes, makers of Hollywood films.

Popular romance has fastened on the ship's real first class and imaginary third class and has preferred to ignore second class. The excluded class in popular memory and depiction is one of the true but overlooked episodes in the career of *Titanic* and says a great deal about our society and our popular art. The exclusion is a perspective that cannot bear very much reality and prefers comforting simplicities, such as a jolly, musical, bibulous steerage (some of whose members are venturesome enough to hurdle the class barriers to find love) and an effete, corrupt first cabin.

H. G. Wells's analysis of British Edwardian society in *Anticipations* (1901) is far more illuminating of life and death on board *Titanic* and the class system the ship has often been taken to embody or symbolize. He saw the new Urban Poor as, 'to borrow a popular phrase, the "submerged" portion of the social body, a leaderless, aimless multitude of people drifting down towards the abyss'. It is hard when reading this not to think of the fate of *Titanic*'s steerage. Immediately above these hapless, he saw the remnants of the old middle class,

> a vast intricate confusion of different sorts of people, some sailing about upon floating masses of irresponsible property, some buoyed by smaller fragments, some clinging desperately enough to insignificant atoms, a great and varied multitude swimming successfully without aid . . . and an equally varied multitude of less capable ones clinging to the swimmers, clinging to the floating rich, or clutching empty-handed and thrust and sinking down.

The most striking of the new classes he saw emerging was the shareholding class, a development of 'irresponsible wealthy people'. Little wonder that Wells had sympathy only for the submerged poor of *Titanic* and her sturdy engineers who stood by their post.

Wells is a reminder that shipwrecks and drowning were a floating

contemporary metaphor waiting for *Titanic*. The graphic confirmation
Titanic provided was part of its lure. Wells referred to the 'drowning
existences' of the unemployed, while E. M. Forster in his novel, *Howards
End* (1910), had admonished his better-off fellow citizens to 'remember
the submerged'. In his 1890 exposé of London poverty, *In Darkest
England*, General William Booth (whose daughter was among the
Titanic saved), devoted a chapter to those 'On the Verge of the Abyss'
and referred to the 'sinking classes'; Booth's answer was the 'Salvation
Ship', of which *Titanic* could be seen as a sad travesty. The answer is
certainly not, he argued, *laissez-faire*, the laws of human supply and
demand. How do these principles look 'when we apply them to the
actual loss of life at sea? Does "Let things alone" man the lifeboat? . . .
We want a Social Lifeboat Institution, a Social Lifeboat Brigade, to
snatch from the abyss those who, if left to themselves, will perish as
miserably as the crew of a ship that founders in mid-ocean.'

The class and economic meanings of the disaster – quickly grasped
by commentators – complicated the dreadful fascination with shipwrecks
in what was the climactic age of ships. Max Beckmann's huge canvas
of 1912, *The Sinking of the* Titanic, echoed Géricault's famous and
disturbing painting, *The Raft of the* Medusa, which depicted events
after the wrecking of the French frigate *Medusa* in 1816 when there
were insufficient boats and the shipwreck became, as a result, 'la théâtre
de scènes épouvantables'. The human scramble at *Titanic*'s end generated in listeners and readers a vicarious dread and prurient humility
that work their power even today and help make of the tragedy itself
some vast admonitory and exemplary work of art or portion of the Bible.

The enduring appeal of the ship (poetized by the mythic resonance
of her name) has to do with these and other contemporary themes she
illustrated. *Titanic* sailed and sank at the very centre of contemporary
cultural preoccupations. Many of the themes are, however, perennial
and cannot rust with age. Among them are those of luxury; of the double
hubris, in building such a leviathan, of humankind's emulating God and
his science defying Nature; and of the proper relations between men
and women, in crisis and in calm. As far as hubris is concerned, an entire
essay could be written about the infamous (and frequently misquoted)
phrase 'practically unsinkable' and its passage from its innocent and
justified use in the *Shipbuilder* in 1911 to its flourish (without the
adverb) as proof of divine retribution.

Before her maiden voyage, *Titanic* seemed to be the culmination of

Victorian mechanical genius; but after the sinking she seemed, as the Great War would do, more like the disastrous culmination of the pre-occupations and pathologies of the Victorian age. Either way, she helped to usher in the modern age, a role that was recognized at the time, for example by Rev. R. M. Ker who when preaching in Belfast on 21 April saw *Titanic* sinking in the cross-currents between two eras. The first revival of *Titanic* enthusiasm was a wave of nostalgia for the alleged certainties before the modern age, since the anxieties of modernism had grown acute by the 1950s. The second revival, triggered by the discovery of the wreck in 1985, began as technological admiration but has largely declined into a plethora of saleable trivialism, an assortment of association items sailing under the false colours of memorabilia, the virtual ship kept afloat by the independent momentum of commercial-ism. The larger cultural pattern underlying the commerce is that of spectacle and replication during which history is replaced by the eternal present of museums, theme parks, exhibits; depth by surface; reality by simulation. The shorthand among cultural historians for the prevailing philosophy of our own era is 'postmodernism' and *Titanic* once again sails and sinks at its centre.

In the summer of 1912, a writer in the *Literary Digest*, noting the publication of Lawrence Beesley's *The Loss of the S.S.* Titanic, Filson Young's *Titanic* and J. Bernard Walker's *An Unsinkable* Titanic, remarked: 'There seems to be no abatement in the production of books about the ill-fated *Titanic*'. Little did he know. The other important books of the year were *Wreck and Sinking of the* Titanic by Marshall Everett (Henry Neil), *The Truth about the* Titanic by Archibald Gracie, *Sinking of the* Titanic *and Great Sea Disasters* by Logan Marshall, *Sinking of the* Titanic by Jay Henry Mowbray.

After forty years of leisurely flow (during which *Titanic* fitfully excited the artistic imagination), literature of the ship quickened after Walter Lord's *A Night to Remember* (1956) signalled the first revival. From the 1960s interest ebbed until discovery of the wreck opened the sluice-gates for *Titanic* writing.

The *Titanic* corpus of books, articles, poems, plays, novels, stories, screenplays is now vast enough to provide its own stimulus for enlarge-ment. Much of it is local history, technical opinion, trivial pursuit, coffee-table divertissement; but much of it is of genuine historical and literary interest and the best non-fictional accounts to which I have had pleasant recourse are those by Lord, Wyn Craig Wade, Geoffrey Marcus, Michael Davie, Paul Heyer, Steven Biel and Daniel A. Butler – accounts by non-specialists. (Among the specialist *Titanic* historians, Eaton and Haas are readable and reliable.) Excerpting the corpus is a difficult task, one which I have tried to simplify by retelling in this anthology the cultural story of *Titanic*, though it implicates a daunting fraction of the cultural story of the twentieth century.

What explains, it is often asked, the enduring popularity of this one ship and this one shipwreck? I have suggested some answers above, to which I would add the persistence of questions still to be answered satisfactorily: the ship, even in its wrecked form at the bottom of the ocean, is still a nursery for puzzles.

A profounder answer, though, may lie in the fact that *Titanic* was not only a notable production of its culture but also for a few days composed a small moving culture of its own. Of interest to the cultural historian is the jewelled *Rubáiyát of Omar Khayyám* that reportedly sank with the ship. The binding by the British binders Sangorski and Sutcliffe was studded with precious stones and said to be the most remarkable specimen of binding ever produced. The book was on its way to the United States and could not be replicated as the binder worked to no plan and kept no record.

Another rarity was a 1598 edition of Francis Bacon's essays recently purchased in London by Harry Widener, a twenty-seven-year-old biblio-phile and heir to part of a vast fortune amassed by the Widener and Elkins families; Harry and his father perished, his mother and maid were saved. Harry sailed for Europe on *Mauretania* but expected to return on *Titanic* in time to attend the latter half of the Robert Hoe library sale at which he hoped to buy the Caxton edition of John Gower's *Confessio Amantis*, but feared Henry E. Huntington (whose name graces a famous research library) would thwart him. Before *Titanic* sank, Harry was reported to have said goodbye to his mother and told her: 'Mother, I have placed the volume in my pocket – the little "Bacon" goes with me.' And so it did. Harry had left his collection to Harvard University and his mother commemorated him by funding a library to house it – the Widener Library, that was dedicated in 1915.

The connection between *Titanic* and cultural institutions is oddly rich. An ancestor of John Jacob Astor had left the Astor library to New York City where it became the nucleus of the New York Public Library.

The smelting millionaire Benjamin Guggenheim, lost with honour, was of the family behind the Guggenheim Museum in New York; the name Guggenheim is now associated with prestigious grants for research. J. Pierpont Morgan by good fortune did not travel on the great ship he effectively owned; he was founder of the Pierpont Morgan Library in New York City which grew out of his opulent collections of books and manuscripts.

Morgan might have been interested in a manuscript on board his ship that was on its way to John Quinn, the celebrated New York collector. This was the manuscript to Joseph Conrad's story 'Karain' which the writer – who was to interest himself greatly in the tragedy – posted himself. Quinn's biographer tells us that also on board were a seal ring and rosary belonging to Lady Gregory, the confidante and collaborator of W. B. Yeats.

In another sense, too, was *Titanic* a vehicle for culture. On board was Lady Duff Gordon. As 'Lucile' the notorious couturière, she had been commissioned in 1897 to design *The Liars*, a play by Henry Arthur Jones, the playwright who would later greet *Carpathia* at New York with *Titanic* survivors. The California actress Margaret Graham was at first reported missing but turned up safe, as did the serial movie star Dorothy Gibson: indeed, she survived to star in a movie, *Saved from the* Titanic, released on 14 May, one month after the disaster!

A weightier cultural presence was Henry B. Harris, the Broadway producer who was returning from Europe with film versions of Max Reinhardt's story 'The Miracle' that he had acquired for £10,000. Henry Sleeper Harper, who unlike Harris survived, represented the world of journalism, being of the famous New York publishing family. The foremost journalist of the day, W. T. Stead, was also on board; amidst his other tireless activities, Stead was rumoured to have ghost-written Booth's *In Darkest England*.

One of the two distinguished artists on board, Francis Millet (b. 1846) had also been a journalist, who included spells as war correspondent. He found time to study at the Royal Academy of Fine Arts in Antwerp, and settled in England where he enjoyed the company of J. S. Sargent, Alma Tadema and other painters. At the request of Pierpont Morgan he became Director of the American Academy of Arts in Rome and was returning with Major Archibald Butt, President Taft's military aide. His work hung in the Tate Gallery.

Millet went down with *Titanic* but Paul Chevré survived. This French sculptor obtained commissions from an office in Quebec City and executed them in a studio in Paris. Making its way to New York on *Bretagne* was Chevré's huge marble bust of the Canadian Prime Minister Sir Wilfrid Laurier. Like Archibald Gracie, Chevré never truly recovered from his ordeal; he never sailed again and died at the age of forty-seven.

One survivor who remembered the kindness of Millet before she got away in one of the boats was the American writer Helen Churchill Candee. Her description in her short story inspired by the tragedy, 'Sealed Orders', of scenes on board the sinking liner as 'a fancy-dress ball in Dante's Hell' might have brought the Italian poet to the mind of her friend Gracie when he wrote his book of reminiscence and investigation.

The American detective writer Jacques Futrelle was one of 'God's noblemen', as Candee defined them. 'Futrelle Refused to Enter Lifeboat', the newspaper headlines said. He too had been a journalist and a theatre manager before turning his hand to fiction. Inspired by Conan Doyle and Edgar Allan Poe, he invented a super-sleuth, Professor Augustus S. F. X. Van Dusen, whom he introduced in *The Thinking Machine* (1907) as an intellectual escape artist and code-breaker. How he would have escaped the sinking *Titanic* must surely have flitted through his creator's mind, but Van Dusen was mind in action without the cultural impediments of social value, and chivalry was one code Futrelle could not break.

Futrelle struck up a shipboard acquaintance with an Irish priest. Frank Browne S.J. was a keen photographer and snapped Futrelle outside the ship's gymnasium. Browne's photographs on board *Titanic* are a notable cultural legacy and an essential part of the ship's memory. Browne sailed from Southampton and disembarked at Queenstown (Cobh) by order of his Provincial Superior; he was later to joke that it was the only time Holy Obedience had saved a man's life. He remembered his time on *Titanic* in the *Belvederian* for 1912, the annual magazine he had founded in Belvedere College, Dublin. At Belvedere and then Royal University he was an exact contemporary of James Joyce the future great novelist whom he beat in the Honours B.A. examinations in 1912 in both English and Latin.

Every large steamer in 1912 published a daily newspaper which included the important Stock Exchange quotations. *Titanic* passengers read the *Atlantic Daily Bulletin*. Geoffrey Marcus tells us that 'In addition to the news, the *Atlantic Daily Bulletin* contained articles of literary, artistic, and scientific interest, the latest social and theatrical gossip from London and Paris, and a good many advertisements, together with the menu of the day's dinner, and the previous day's run.' The newspaper is a reminder of the vivid way in which life on *Titanic* was a cross-section of the broader culture. It is hardly surprising, then, that the ship realized certain cultural forces that required the disaster. If her fate was, because of this, anticipated, then it is no more surprising that her fate in turn anticipated greater disasters that would befall England, Europe and America.[1]

---

[1] When I have provided my own title for an extract, it appears without quotation marks.

1
Leviathan of the Year

The press, the machine, the railway, the telegraph are premises whose
thousand-year conclusion no one has yet dared to draw.

Friedrich Nietzsche (1878)

The quarter century before the launch of RMS Titanic *saw a striking
sequence of technological discoveries and inventions, including the pneu-
matic tyre, electromagnetic waves (by Hertz) and the combustion engine.
In 1897 Marconi transmitted his first radio signals; three years after
that he made his first transatlantic radio communication. Powered flight
succeeded in 1903, and in 1909 Louis Blériot flew a monoplane across
the English Channel.*

*The famous biologist and controversialist T. H. Huxley had claimed in
1887 that 'the most obvious and the most distinctive feature of the History
of Civilization, during the last fifty years, is the wonderful increase of
industrial production by the application of machinery, the improvement
of old technical processes and the invention of new ones, accompanied by
an even more remarkable development of old and new means of locomotion
and intercommunication'. The machine troubled the nineteenth century,
and an agenda of anxiety was established in Britain by Thomas Carlyle
in 1829. Samuel Butler in* Erewhon *(1872) was exercised by machines,
musing on their superior speed of development compared to organic
forms, and their superior powers of calculation as well as stamina.*

*More than twenty years later, H. G. Wells created startling fictions
out of Butler's concerns. Yet like Carlyle, the writers Wells, Rudyard
Kipling and Joseph Conrad saw virtue in the kind of work that discovered,
invented and applied: work was a bulwark against introspection and
doubt. The engineering staff aboard* Titanic, *all of whom went down
with the ship, Wells saw as an island of efficiency amidst a sea of
slapdashery on board the liner that fateful night.*

According to Carlyle, Captains of Industry could display the old heroic force and energy that was largely gone from civilization. A Captain of Industry of whom Carlyle might have approved was W. J. Pirrie (later Lord Pirrie), the Canadian-born Ulsterman at the helm of Harland & Wolff shipyard that designed and built Titanic. The journalist, peace activist and spiritualist W. T. Stead praised Pirrie's foresight, incessant industry and unique powers of organization that built up 'the greatest business of the kind that has existed in the world since men first began to go down to the sea in ships'.

The engines of that business, the ships themselves, were culminations of the nineteenth-century preoccupation with mechanism and machinery. In prose as rich as that of the imaginative literature of the period, textured by fluent argot and technical nomenclature, the anatomy and physiology of Titanic and other engineering marvels were described in Scientific American, International Marine Engineering and Engineering. The midsummer 1911 souvenir number of the Shipbuilder is an essential Titanic text and a significant cultural document.

Carlyle's essay, with its gulf between the 'dynamics' and 'mechanics' of human nature, anticipates that between the 'two cultures' of science and literature championed respectively by T. H. Huxley and Matthew Arnold later in the century. The concentration of wealth and the chasm between the rich and the poor that Carlyle sees as the result of 'Mechanism' graphically became an issue when Titanic *went down.*

THOMAS CARLYLE
'The Mechanical Age'

(*Edinburgh Review*, 1829)

Were we required to characterize this age of ours by any single epithet, we should be tempted to call it, not an Heroical, Devotional, Philosophical, or Moral Age, but, above all others, the Mechanical Age. It is the Age of Machinery, in every outward and inward sense of that word; the age which, with its whole undivided might, forwards, teaches and practises the great art of adapting means to ends. Nothing is now done directly, or by hand; all is by rule and calculated contrivance. For the simplest operation, some helps and accompaniments, some cunning abbreviating process is in readiness. Our old modes of exertion are all discredited, and thrown aside. On every hand, the living artisan is driven from his workshop, to make room for a speedier, inanimate one. The shuttle drops from the fingers of the weaver, and falls into iron fingers that ply it faster. The sailor furls his sail, and lays down his oar; and bids a strong, unwearied servant, on vaporous wings, bear him through the waters. Men have crossed oceans by steam; the Birmingham Fire-king has visited the fabulous East; and the genius of the Cape, were there any Camoens now to sing it, has again been alarmed, and with far stranger thunders than Gamas. There is no end to machinery. Even the horse is stripped of his harness, and finds a fleet fire-horse yoked in his stead. Nay, we have an artist that hatches chickens by steam; the very brood-hen is to be superseded! For all earthly, and for some unearthly purposes, we have machines and mechanic furtherances; for mincing our cabbages; for casting us into magnetic sleep. We remove mountains, and make seas our smooth highway; nothing can resist us. We war with rude Nature; and, by our resistless engines, come off always victorious, and loaded with spoils.

What wonderful accessions have thus been made, and are still making, to the physical power of mankind; how much better fed, clothed, lodged and, in all outward respects, accommodated men now are, or might be, by a given quantity of labour, is a grateful reflection which forces itself on every one. What changes, too, this addition of power is introducing into the Social System; how wealth has more and more increased, and at the same time gathered itself more and more into masses, strangely altering the old relations, and increasing the distance between the rich and the poor, will be a question for Political Economists, and a much more complex and important one than any they have yet engaged with . . .

To us who live in the midst of all this, and see continually the faith, hope and practice of every one founded on Mechanism of one kind or other, it is apt to seem quite natural, and as if it could never have been otherwise. Nevertheless, if we recollect or reflect a little, we shall find both that it has been, and might again be otherwise. The domain of Mechanism, – meaning thereby political, ecclesiastical or other outward establishments, – was once considered as embracing, as we are persuaded can at any time embrace, but a limited portion of man's interests, and by no means the highest portion.

To speak a little pedantically, there is a science of *Dynamics* in man's fortunes and nature, as well as of *Mechanics*. There is a science which treats of, and practically addresses, the primary, unmodified forces and energies of man, the mysterious springs of Love, and Fear, and Wonder, of Enthusiasm, Poetry, Religion, all which have a truly vital and *infinite* character; as well as a science which practically addresses the finite, modified developments of these, when they take the shape of immediate 'motives', as hope of reward, or as fear of punishment.

Author of one of the best books on Titanic, *editor and reporter Michael Davie sees the metaphoric birthplace of the great ship in the mid-Atlantic, between British technical know-how and industrial might and American venture capital and instinct for merger and monopoly.*

MICHAEL DAVIE
The Starting Point

(*The* Titanic: *The Full Story of a Tragedy*, 1986)

In the 1860s, British industry was entering the most expansive and prosperous era it has ever known, or is ever likely to know. In particular, shipbuilding and transatlantic traffic were growing in volume year by year. It is impossible to understand the genesis of the *Titanic* without looking at the men who conceived the idea of a giant ship; and impossible to understand them, and the reasons why they ever imagined such an extraordinary vessel, without some notion of the tortuous and ruthlessly competitive international shipping business – British, German, American – of which they were part.

The man behind the *Titanic*, as it happens, was Canadian. He was born in Quebec in 1847 as William James Pirrie, the son of A. J. Pirrie, an Ulsterman of Scottish descent. His mother was also from Ulster, a member of the Montgomery family. After the father died, mother and son returned to Ireland, where the boy was apprenticed at the age of fifteen to the shipbuilding and engineering firm of Harland & Wolff. Pirrie was a partner in Harland & Wolff by the time he was twenty-seven. During the next half century, largely thanks to his leadership, it became the greatest shipyard in the world, and the birthplace of the *Titanic*.

People these days are inclined to think that the *Titanic* was a freak; a huge ship of unique size and luxury. This misunderstanding underrates the scale of the enterprise. Pirrie's idea, conceived in 1907, was that his firm, in partnership with the White Star Line, would build not one but three monster transatlantic liners. They would sweep the opposition off the seas. The first would be named the *Olympic*; the second the *Titanic*; and the third – according to report – the *Gigantic*.

All three were built. The *Olympic* had an illustrious career, carrying more troops than any other vessel in World War I. The *Gigantic*, prudently renamed the *Britannic*, was sunk by a German mine in 1916. Nowadays, nobody outside the passionate fraternity of lovers of old ships remembers this useful pair. But the *Titanic* became, as she has remained, the best-known of all ships to the man in the street, her name springing to mind more readily than the *Golden Hind*, the USS *Arizona* or HMS *Victory*.

It is odd that Pirrie, the bold prime mover, has disappeared so completely from the story. Had he sailed in the *Titanic* on her maiden voyage, as he fully intended, he would have been better known. He would either have drowned, in which case he would have been as closely associated with the ship as her skipper, Captain Smith, and her richest passenger, Colonel J. J. Astor; or he would have escaped, in which case he would have been as universally reviled as the chairman of White Star who got away in one of the last lifeboats, J. Bruce Ismay. As it was, his doctor forbade him to take the trip because of prostate trouble; he was too ill to testify in the much-publicised official enquiries that followed; and after their reports came out it was too late for anyone to ask him awkward questions. His role receded into the past. His hair turned white during his illness, but he remained the great shipbuilder. Indeed the business done by his world-beating yards actually boomed, because they reconstructed many ships after the disaster to make them conform to the new rules officially imposed as a result of the defects exposed in their prize product. In World War I, Lord Pirrie was in charge of all British merchant shipbuilding. He was made a baron in [1906]; he became a viscount in 1921. He died at sea in 1924 from pneumonia in the Panama Canal, returning with his wife from a voyage on Harland & Wolff business to South America . . .

Harland and Wolff joined forces just before Pirrie arrived in their yards as an apprentice. With every year that passed, their business expanded. In 1864, the gross tonnage of the ships they built was 30,000 tons. In 1884, the figure was 104,000. Pirrie's career was contemporaneous with the development of steel shipbuilding, and he himself was in the forefront of all the important advances in naval architecture and marine engineering. He took over as chairman when Harland died in 1894; so he was thirty years under Harland, and thirty years on his own as chairman . . .

The verdict of the *Dictionary of National Biography* is that he was 'the creator of the big ship'.

How did this happen? The starting point may be said to have been the alliance between Harland & Wolff and White Star . . .

The whole secret of the growth of the shipping companies and the size of the ships they built is to be found in the extraordinary expansion, unparalleled in history, of the population of the United States. During the half century between 1840, when Samuel Cunard's *Britannia* inaugurated the first transatlantic steamship service, and 1890, trade between the United States and Britain rose sevenfold, in cotton, tobacco and wheat, with Liverpool as its focus. At the same time, the population of the United States quadrupled. Cunard were not slow to realize that their business could not expand by relying on mail, cargo and first-class passengers alone; so they also started to carry steerage passengers, cashing in on the flood of immigrants from Britain as well as continental Europe. Bigger ships and longer passenger lists were the keys to profit; but the expanding market also attracted competitors. Ismay's White Star, financed by [Gustavus] Schwabe and building all its ships at Harland & Wolff's yards, was challenging Cunard on the Atlantic routes by the early 1870s; and by the 1880s the great German shipowners joined the battle as well.

Then came the Americans and J. P. Morgan. The impact of American capital on the shipping business had been long delayed, partly because of the American Civil War, and partly because the new breed of industrialists and financiers had been fully occupied opening up the continent with oil, steel and railways. But when it came it was devastating. It started when a company that later became part of the Morgan combine acquired Inman Lines of Liverpool, which gave the Americans access to British shipbuilding technology. At White Star, correctly identifying the threat, T. H. Ismay attempted to assemble a consortium of British shipowners to save the ailing company, but the other shipowners would not listen to him . . .

Morgan's aim was to establish in the Atlantic the same sort of business that he was used to at home: a monopoly. With Pirrie's help, he forced through an amalgamation with the big German lines, North German Lloyd and Hamburg-Amerika. He then launched the most vicious fare war in shipping history, offering third-class transatlantic passages for as little as £2. His principal target was Cunard. Having driven the company into financial trouble by his price-cutting, he then tried to buy it, and was only repulsed when the British government, alarmed by the idea of a great British asset passing into foreign hands, came to the rescue with substantial and favourable subsidies. The condition of the subsidies was openly nationalistic. 'Under no circumstances shall the management of the company be in the hands of, or the shares of the company held by, other than British subjects.'

Pirrie had quickly seen the Morgan threat. The source of much of his business, White Star, was as vulnerable as Cunard; profits reduced by the fare war, short of capital for new ships. Schwabe had died in 1890, Ismay in 1899. Ismay's son, J. Bruce Ismay, was relatively inexperienced. Pirrie saw that unless drastic action was taken White Star would drop further and further out of the battle and build fewer and fewer ships in Pirrie's shipyards. His solution was unattractive, but practical. Instead of opposing Morgan's ambitions, he supported them. Three years after Ismay Senior died, Morgan with Pirrie as an intermediary swallowed White Star. The head of Cunard, Lord Inverclyde, acquired considerable prestige from the skilful way he exploited Morgan's bid in order to extract favourable loans from the government, while yielding none of his company's independence. But at the very time that Inverclyde was concluding these advantageous arrangements, J. Bruce Ismay was being forced to sell – not least by the pressure of his father's old ally, Pirrie.

The transaction was a financier's cat's-cradle. It had been the International Navigation Company of Philadelphia, with the Pennsylvania Railroad Company, that had acquired Inman Lines. In 1902, the International Navigation Company changed its name to the International Mercantile Marine Company. This company, with Pirrie on the British board, acquired practically all the shares in the Oceanic Steam Navigation Company, which had always owned the ships of the White Star Line, of which Ismay, Imrie & Co. were managers. Morgan then registered the Oceanic Company shares in the name of the International Navigation Company of Liverpool, a subsidiary of the International Mercantile Marine Company, which in its turn transferred the shares to two trust companies in the United States as security for certain bonds.

Given the intricate nature of Morgan's combine, it is not surprising that the absoluteness of his control of White Star was not fully appreciated. The *Titanic* was generally regarded as a British ship. Even Lord Mersey, with his Liverpool background, was taken aback in the Board of Trade enquiry into the *Titanic*'s sinking when he learned that the White Star Company's seagoing rules, under which the *Titanic*, like all other White Star vessels, had been operating, had been drawn up in the United States. Morgan had seen how his bid for Cunard had alarmed the British. With White Star, the appearance of control stayed firmly in Britain. All White Star ships were to be officered by British subjects and to fly the British flag. A majority of the directors were to be British. The original Ismay company of Ismay, Imrie & Co. became a shell, but Bruce Ismay remained chairman of White Star and was soon persuaded by Morgan to become president of International Mercantile. The appointment looked impressive on paper, but for J. Bruce Ismay it was a humiliation.

These were significant events in the tilting of industrial power away from Britain and towards the United States. One great British company, Cunard, had had to be baled out by the government – an early example of state intervention. Another equally prominent British company, virtually a national institution, had been taken over. The effect of the White Star deal was to bring together British technology, in the shape of Harland & Wolff, and American capital. This was the conjunction that produced the *Titanic*.

In his Presidential Address to the Institution of Naval Architects in 1912, the Marquis of Bristol judged Titanic *'the leviathan of the year'. Five weeks after its loss, the Hamburg-American Line launched the even more gigantic* Imperator. *Already by then, Cunard had announced that its* Aquitania *would be a foot longer than* Imperator, *causing consternation in Hamburg.*

'Atlantic Liners'

(*Shipbuilder*, 1911)

The evolution of the Atlantic liner of today has been one of the most remarkable achievements in the scientific progress and commercial activity of modern times. It is difficult to realize that only 73 years have elapsed since the Atlantic was first crossed by a vessel continuously under steam power. This pioneer steamer, the *Sirius*, was a small wooden paddle steamer 208ft. long overall and 178ft. along the keel. Her breadth was 25ft. and depth of hold 18ft. Upon her first transatlantic voyage, in April 1838, she carried 94 passengers and averaged about 7½ knots speed. What a contrast to the present-day *Kronprinzessin Cecilie*, *La France*, *Lusitania*, *Mauretania*, *Olympic* and *Titanic*, to mention but the most celebrated of recent ships!

It is impossible in this article to trace all the stages of development from the *Sirius* to the two latest White Star liners, and only the most important facts can be mentioned. The increase in size and speed has been continuous . . . The use of wood as the material for construction of the hulls was followed by the introduction of iron, which in turn was superseded by steel. Paddle wheels as a means of propulsion were abandoned in favour of the screw propeller driven by reciprocating engines. The reciprocating engine developed from the compound to the triple, and later to the quadruple-expansion type, two sets of engines, driving twin screws, being adopted as larger powers were required. The highest perfection of this type of engine was reached in the German record breakers *Kaiser Wilhelm II* and *Kronprinzessin Cecilie*, which have twin screws and four sets of engines, two sets being mounted on each shaft.

Turbine propelling machinery in conjunction with triple screws appeared on the Atlantic in 1904, when the Allan liners *Victorian* and *Virginian* entered upon service, and was also adopted for the Cunard liner *Carmania*, completed in 1906. The greatest triumphs of the turbine have been won by the quadruple-screw express Cunarders *Lusitania* and *Mauretania*, which now hold all the Atlantic speed records. But although the turbine has been eminently successful for the high-speed ship, at more moderate speeds its economy is not so marked, a fact which has led to the introduction of the latest type of propelling machinery, the combination of reciprocating engines with a low-pressure turbine. When considering the type of machinery to be adopted for the *Olympic* and *Titanic*, the White Star Line and Messrs Harland and Wolff . . . agreed to test the merits of the combination system compared with reciprocating engines of the ordinary type by building two vessels exactly similar except in regard to propelling machinery. These two vessels, the *Megantic*, fitted with reciprocating engines, and the *Laurentic*, fitted with combination engines, were completed in 1909. Their relative performances in the White Star Line's Canadian service completely justified the expectation regarding the superior economy of the combined type of machinery, and it was decided to adopt combined engines for the later and much larger vessels . . .

It may not be out of place at this stage to briefly indicate the many problems which beset the designer of an Atlantic liner and the main considerations determining the dimensions, form and arrangement of ships like the *Olympic* and *Titanic* which are intended to eclipse earlier vessels. The two most important factors of design are the speed and passenger accommodation to be aimed at, and it has always been the endeavour of the competing steamship companies on the Atlantic to possess vessels which excel in one or both of these respects. Both factors are favoured by increase in size of ship; hence the tendency to greater dimensions which has been so marked during the past few years. The maximum possible dimensions of a new vessel depend upon the dock and harbour accommodation available when the ship is completed; and it is for this reason that Lord Pirrie, among others, has devoted so much time and energy to the question of increased dock and harbour facilities.

Reverting to the subject of speed, high speed is a very costly require-ment, not only owing to the great initial cost of the propelling machinery and the heavy cost of fuel on service, but also on account of the necessary fineness of the ship, which limits the earning power as regards cargo-carrying and the extent of passenger accommodation. In a high-speed Atlantic liner, the difficulties of design are greatly increased, as the designer is handicapped by the limited draught of water available at the terminal ports, and very careful consideration has to be given to the question of weight, any saving which can be effected being of great value. If, on the other hand, a more moderate speed is aimed at, the problem of weight is much simplified, as the vessel can be built to a fuller model and a greater displacement secured, without exceeding the draught available. It has been the custom of the White Star Line to strive for pre-eminence in passenger accommodation in conjunction with a speed which can be obtained without too great a sacrifice of cargo capacity, and the *Olympic* and *Titanic* have been designed in accordance with that policy. Although a passenger on one of these vessels will not have the honour of crossing in the fastest ship on the Atlantic, he will have many compensating advantages as regards increased comfort at sea and the greater extent and variety of the accommodation provided.

Young, a prolific journalist, wrote his book with such expedition that it appeared in the bookshops three weeks after the ship sank. One of the liveliest of the early books, it occasionally chooses instant legend over fact in order to keep the literary temperature high. The ship as cathedral and the scaffolding as forest (the grey horses are the lively currents of the waterways) are an early context for the later claim that Titanic had defied God and Nature.

FILSON YOUNG
The Miracle

(Titanic, 1912)

For months and months in that monstrous iron enclosure there was nothing that had the faintest likeness to a ship; only something that might have been the iron scaffolding for the naves of half-a-dozen cathedrals laid end to end. Far away, furnaces were smelting thousands and thousands of tons of raw material that finally came to this place in the form of great girders and vast lumps of metal, huge framings, hundreds of miles of stays and rods and straps of steel, thousands of plates, not one of which twenty men could lift unaided; millions of rivets and bolts – all the heaviest and most sinkable things in the world. And still nothing in the shape of a ship that could float upon the sea. The seasons followed each other, the sun rose now behind the heights of Carrickfergus and now behind the Copeland Islands; daily the ships came in from fighting with the boisterous seas, and the two grey horses cantered beside them as they slid between the islands; daily the endless uproar went on, and the tangle of metal beneath the cathedral scaffolding grew denser. A great road of steel, nearly a quarter of a mile long, was laid at last – a road so heavy and so enduring that it might have been built for the triumphal progress of some giant railway train. Men said that this roadway was the keel of a ship; but you could not look at it and believe them.

The scaffolding grew higher; and as it grew the iron branches multiplied and grew with it, higher and higher towards the sky, until it seemed as though man were rearing a temple which would express all he knew of grandeur and sublimity, and all he knew of solidity and permanence

– something that should endure there, rooted to the soil of Queen's Island for ever. The uproar and the agony increased. In quiet studios and offices clear brains were busy with drawings and calculations and subtle elaborate mathematical processes, sifting and applying the tabulated results of years of experience. The drawings came in time to the place of uproar; were magnified and subdivided and taken into grimy workshops; and steam-hammers and steam-saws smote and ripped at the brute metal, to shape it in accordance with the shapes on the paper. And still the ships, big and little, came nosing in from the high seas – little dusty colliers from the Tyne, and battered schooners from the coast, and timber ships from the Baltic, and trim mail steamers, and giants of the ocean creeping in wounded for succour – all solemnly received by the twin grey horses and escorted to their stations in the harbour. But the greatest giant of all that came in, which dwarfed everything else visible to the eye, was itself dwarfed to insignificance by the great cathedral building on the island.

The seasons passed; the creatures who wrought and clambered among the iron branches, and sang their endless song of labour there, felt the steel chill beneath the frosts of winter, and burning hot beneath the sun's rays in summer, until at last the skeleton within the scaffolding began to take a shape, at the sight of which men held their breaths. It was the shape of a ship, a ship so monstrous and unthinkable that it towered high over the buildings and dwarfed the very mountains beside the water. It seemed like some impious blasphemy that man should fashion this most monstrous and ponderable of all his creations into the likeness of a thing that could float upon the yielding waters. And still the arms swung and the hammers rang, the thunder and din continued, and the grey horses shook their manes and cantered along beneath the shadow, and led the little ships in from the sea and out again as though no miracle were about to happen.

A little more than its own length of water lay between the iron forest and the opposite shore, in which to loose this tremendous structure from its foundations and slide it into the sea. The thought that it should ever be moved from its place, except by an earthquake, was a thought that the mind could not conceive, nor could anyone looking at it accept the possibility that by any method this vast tonnage of metal could be borne upon the surface of the waters. Yet, like an evil dream, as it took the shape of a giant ship, all the properties of a ship began to appear and increase in hideous exaggeration. A rudder as big as a giant elm tree, bosses and bearings of propellers the size of a windmill – everything was on a nightmare scale; and underneath the iron foundations of the cathedral floor men were laying on concrete beds pavements of oak and great cradles of timber and iron, and sliding ways of pitch pine to support the bulk of the monster when she was moved, every square inch of the pavement surface bearing a weight of more than two tons. Twenty tons of tallow were spread upon the ways, and hydraulic rams and triggers built and fixed against the bulk of the ship so that, when the moment came, the waters she was to conquer should thrust her finally from earth.

And the time did come. The branching forest became clothed and thick with leaves of steel. Within the scaffoldings now towered the walls of the cathedral, and what had been a network of girders and cantilevers and gantries and bridges became a building with floors, a ship with decks. The skeleton ribs became covered with skins of wood, the metal decks clothed with planks smooth as a ballroom floor. What had been a building of iron became a town, with miles of streets and hundreds of separate houses and buildings in it. The streets were laid out; the houses were decorated and furnished with luxuries such as no palace ever knew.

And then, while men held their breath, the whole thing moved, moved bodily, obedient to the tap of the imprisoned waters in the ram. There was no christening ceremony such as celebrates the launching of lesser ships. Only the waters themselves dared to give the impulse that should set this monster afloat. The waters touched the cradle, and the cradle moved on the ways, carrying the ship down towards the waters. And when the cradle stopped the ship moved on; slowly at first, then with a movement that grew quicker until it increased to the speed of a fast-trotting horse, touching the waters, dipping into them, cleaving them, forcing them asunder in waves and ripples that fled astonished to the surrounding shores; finally resting and floating upon them, while thousands of the pigmy men who had roosted in the bare iron branches, who had raised the hideous clamour amid which the giant was born, greeted their handiwork, dropped their tools and raised their hoarse voices in a cheer.

The miracle had happened.

Preparation for launch of the (then) world's largest moving object.

*Amidst the journalese of the period that characterizes this account, the
'augury of the future' that* Titanic *'should be a huge success', proved a
dramatic irony. It seems difficult to avoid religious and sexual undertows
when writing about the birth and death of the great ship.*

Eager for the Baptism

(*Belfast News-Letter*, 1 June 1911)

In the presence of thousands of spectators, the S.S. *Titanic*,
which will share with the *Olympic* the distinction of being one of the
two largest vessels afloat, was launched from Messrs Harland & Wolff's
yard at the Queen's Island yesterday. When the *Olympic* was launched
on the 20th of October last there was considerable speculation as to
how the ceremony would pass off, as up to that time no ship of her
enormous dimensions had ever left the ways, and extraordinary precautions had to be taken in order to provide against any accident.
However, as matters turned out, it was proved that there was no cause
for anxiety. The builders had left nothing to chance, and the launch was
one of the most successful ever witnessed at the Island. The experience
gained on that occasion was very serviceable when applied to yesterday's
proceedings, and the certainty and smoothness with which the launch
was effected spoke volumes for the efficiency of the organization. No
one doubted for a single moment that the huge vessel would take the
water without any trouble occurring in regard to her departure from
the slips but they could hardly have anticipated that the scene presented
would be so inspiriting and impressive as it actually was. It was the
significance of the thing which struck their imagination, and caused
many of them to become very eager and excited as the time approached
for releasing the hydraulic apparatus which would set the vessel in
motion and send her gliding down the ways into the river.

It was a happy coincidence that on the day of the launch of the second
of the two liners Lord and Lady Pirrie were celebrating their birthday.
As the head of the firm of Messrs Harland & Wolff, Lord Pirrie has
naturally been keenly interested in the construction of these epoch-
making vessels, and he has personally supervised the building operations.
There is no detail either of machinery, decoration or equipment that

he has not made himself familiar with, and it is largely due to his courage and initiative together with his capacity for organization that the *Olympic* is now completed, while the *Titanic* has been safely launched and will in the course of a few months take her place in the White Star Line service. Both his Lordship and Lady Pirrie received many congratulations on the happy coincidence distinguishing the events of yesterday, amongst the wellwishers being Mr Pierpont Morgan, the American millionaire, who was one of the spectators at the launch. Mr Morgan occupied a place on the owners' stand, which had been erected under one of the huge gantries on the port side of the *Titanic* . . . Three other stands had been erected at the end of the yard opposite the bows of the vessel. One of these was reserved for the representatives of the Press, who numbered upwards of one hundred, whilst the others were for the accommodation of ticket-holders. The stands were by no means adequate for all who had assembled, and hundreds of people took up positions in various parts of the yard from where they could see the ship enter the water. The Lord Mayor and the Lady Mayoress (Mr and Mrs M'Mordie) were amongst the onlookers, and many other prominent citizens helped to swell the attendance.

Ladies formed a considerable proportion of the aggregate attendance, and even if their picturesque frocks appeared a trifle incongruous when contrasted with the surroundings of the shipyard itself they were unmistakably in harmony with the glow of the soft turquoise sky, from which the piercing rays of the sun descended, making the heat exceedingly trying to those who were exposed to it. Before eleven o'clock people were waiting to gain admission to the yard, and within half an hour from the gates being opened to ticket-holders both the public stands were filled with spectators.

. . . Many of the spectators had travelled from distant towns for the sole purpose of witnessing the ceremony, and if they saw the *Titanic* as she gracefully left the ways they must have felt amply repaid for all their trouble, as the spectacle was one which can never fade from the memory of those who witnessed it.

During the morning gangs of men were engaged in removing the heavy wooden posts which supported the vessel, a powerful ram being also used in the operation. The clanging of hammers was heard all over the ship as the preparations for the launch were developed, but the men using them were for the most part hidden from view. On the deck of the boat the figures of the workers whose duty it was to see to the drag ropes and cables were dwarfed and blurred by the distance which separated them from the people down below. About twelve o'clock Lord Pirrie left the owners' stand in order to make a last tour of inspection and to give final instructions, and responsible officials watched the movement of the hands on the hydraulic triggers as the supports were removed and the ship settled down on the launching ways. Every detail had to be judged with mathematical accuracy if accidents had to be averted, and the preparations had therefore to be made with great care and caution. Over the bows of the vessel the White Star Company's flag floated, and there was displayed a code signal which spelled the word 'success'. If the circumstances under which the launch took place can be accepted as an augury of the future, the *Titanic* should be a huge success. The weather was glorious, a multitude of people assembled to bid the vessel 'Godspeed', and it would be impossible to conceive of a launch for which the whole of the conditions could be more ideal.

The ceremony had been fixed for a quarter-past twelve, and ten minutes before that time a red flag was hoisted at the stern of the vessel. Five minutes later two rockets were discharged, shortly afterwards the explosion of another rocket was heard, and at 12.13 the spectators had the joy and satisfaction of seeing the vessel in motion. It was a wonderful and awe-inspiring sight, and a thrill passed through the crowd as their hopes and expectations were realized. The ship glided down to the river with a grace and dignity which for the moment gave one the impression that she was conscious of her own strength and beauty, and there was a roar of cheer as the timbers by which she had been supported yielded to the pressure put upon them. She took the water as though she were eager for the baptism, and in the short space of sixty-two seconds she was entirely free of the ways. The arrangements for checking her when once she had entered the river were similar to those adopted in the case of the *Olympic*. On each side of the ship anchors had been placed in the bed of the river, and to them were attached hawsers which were fastened to the eye plates on board. Cable drags, connected with the vessel in a similar fashion, were also used, and by means of them and the anchors the *Titanic* was pulled up in less than one-half of her own length. The men on board took off their caps and cheered lustily after the launch had been consummated, and the thousands of people in the yard and on the banks of the river promptly followed their example. For two or three minutes there were scenes of great enthusiasm. The tugs which were waiting close at hand to convey the vessel to the deep-water wharf, where she will receive her engines, sent up shrill sounds from their sirens, the ladies waved their handkerchiefs excitedly, and the men shouted themselves hoarse. But gradually the noise of the sirens and the cheers of the spectators died away, and a quarter of an hour after the vessel had been pulled up the crowd had melted away, and the yard was left in possession of the workmen who had for months been devoting their energies and talents to the building of the mighty leviathan.

The author was born in Belfast and his memory of the launch of Titanic *whetted his interest in producing a film of Walter Lord's 1955 book; many enthusiasts think* A Night to Remember *(1958) the best* Titanic *motion picture.*

WILLIAM MACQUITTY
A Launch to Remember

(*A Life to Remember*, 1991)

No. 89 Princetown Road, Bangor, overlooked Belfast Lough, where great steamers, coasters and the *Bangor Boat* paddle steamer came and went. Beyond the lough lay the Irish Sea, and beyond that the oceans of the world. Daily I walked round the rocky coast, searching the pools at low tide. After storms, conger eels and streamers of seaweed attached to huge mussels would be washed ashore to join the smaller creatures, crabs, prawns, sea anemones and little fish of the pools. Each day brought new discoveries. I learned to swim and my asthma melted away in the excitement of battling with this new element. I became hungry and started to grow; and I went to a small local school.

The whole of Ulster was at this time in a state of excitement at the final stages of the building of the largest ship in the world, the *Titanic*. Whenever I went to Belfast with Father, he would point out the huge vessel towering above the stocks of Harland & Wolff's vast shipyard. It seemed impossible to me that such a mountain of iron and steel could ever be placed in the sea and actually float. One day I watched teams of draught horses straining to haul just one of the ship's propellers from the foundry. 'How can they get it into the sea,' I asked Father.

'They lay the keel on a slipway leading to the sea,' he explained, 'and the ship is built on the keel. When everything is ready for the launch, tons of tallow, soft soap and train oil are used to grease the slipway. Hydraulic rams push the ship ever so slowly, and she begins to slide, going faster and faster until she reaches the water. You'll see for yourself when we go to the launch.'

The day of the launch was 31 May 1911, two weeks after my sixth birthday. The sun shone from a cloudless sky as we made our way to the press stand, which stood directly in front of the ship's bow. We could see Lord Pirrie, the chairman of Harland & Wolff, with his guests in a smaller stand to our left, the group including Pierpont Morgan, the American millionaire owner of the White Star Line. As well as the British Red Ensign, the ship therefore also flew the American Stars and Stripes. Signal flags reading 'Good Luck' fluttered above the throng of workers and spectators.

At five minutes past noon, a red flag was hoisted to warn the fleet of boats in the River Lagan to stand clear. Another five minutes went by before a rocket was fired and workers began to hammer at the restraining chocks. At 12.14 the firing of a second rocket reduced the vast crowd to silence. Would this huge vessel ever really move? All at once the workers on board gave a cheer in which the crowds on shore joined. The slide had begun. Every ship in the lough sounded its siren, the noise drowning the roar of the piles of restraining anchors as they were dragged along the ground. Slowly gathering speed, the *Titanic* moved smoothly down the ways, and a minute later was plunging into the water and raising a huge wave. I felt a great lump in my throat and an enormous pride in being an Ulsterman.

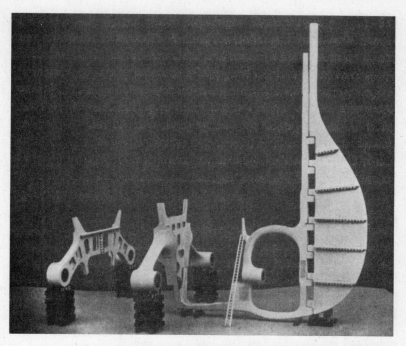

Machine art. Top: shipbuilder's arrangement (in model form) of *Titanic*'s propeller brackets and rudder; the rudder was 68 feet high and weighed 101 tons. Bottom: aft propeller brackets.

2
The Gilded Age

But the third went wide and far
Into an unforgiving sea
Under a fire-spilling star,
And it was rigged for a long journey.
    Philip Larkin, 'The North Ship'

Transatlantic liners – so-called because they made a 'line voyage' between points A and B – represented the latest conquest of the North Atlantic that had begun with early expeditions by European fishermen and the navigational achievements of European explorers in the late fifteenth and early sixteenth centuries, and had continued with regular traffic of emigrants and provisions to the colonies of the New World.

The Halifax businessman, Samuel Cunard, founded the first transatlantic steamship company in 1839, and the Britannia, his flagship, sailed from Liverpool to Halifax in 1840. Thereafter, rivalry between Cunard and other companies ensured that seductive comfort and competitive speed for passengers would be a priority.

Later, the rivalry became international with numerous British, German and French shipping lines ruthlessly vying for the lucrative North Atlantic passenger traffic. That traffic was a rich prize because of the money floating freely in the late Victorian and Edwardian periods, the springtime of American plutocracy as well as the Indian summer of British aristocracy.

Titanic in its first- and even second-class portions was a ship of almost unimaginable luxury. First-class staterooms were fitted with individually controlled electric heaters to allow Americans accustomed to more heat than Britons to supplement the warm-air system already in operation. Ten thousand lamps lit life on board Titanic; first-class staterooms had dimmer lights so that the nervous could sleep with less anxiety. Fifteen hundred bell pushes could summon help, necessaries or more luxury. Passenger elevators and service lifts conserved human energy. Titanic had its own fifty-line telephone exchange for inter-cabin communication and separate circuits for service communication, including that between the crow's nest and the bridge, which proved crucial on the evening of 14 April.

And as though the facilities and decor were not sufficient, a South-ampton florist provided fresh flowers for every White Star liner using the port. Lady Duff Gordon recalled her last meal on Titanic: 'We had a big vase of beautiful daffodils on the table, which were as fresh as if they had just been picked.'

R. A. Fletcher wrote in 1913: 'Luxury has been defined as the art of providing edibles out of season, and more things to use than anyone can possibly want combined with the least exertion and the utmost physical comfort if anyone should want to use them. If this definition be correct, then modern liners have certainly provided luxury.'

Titanic's Grand Staircase, with Honour and Glory crowning Time in the middle of the stairwell, are among the most famous steps in history.

The attention to detail and the cultural sophistication of Titanic's *interior decoration were remarkable, as this painstakingly rich description proves. Harland & Wolff had their own upholsterers and their own in-house decorators who worked in studios. One hundred and eighty-six men worked on the carved panelling on* Olympic *and* Titanic.

Accommodation of Unrivalled Magnificence

(*Shipbuilder*, 1911)

Full advantage has been taken of the great size of the *Olympic* and *Titanic* to provide passenger accommodation of unrivalled extent and magnificence . . . The arrangement has been most carefully considered from all points of view, and the excellent result achieved defies improvement. About 2,440 passengers can be accommodated in each ship, so that, with her crew of about 860, she carries a grand total of 3,300 persons.

First-class Accommodation
The accommodation for first-class passengers is placed amidships and extends over five decks, . . . the promenade (A), bridge (B), shelter (C), saloon (D) and upper (E) decks. Access from one deck to another is obtained by means of the two grand staircases, and other smaller stairways, and by three electric elevators adjacent to the forward staircase, which travel from the upper to the promenade deck. The first-class public rooms include the dining saloon, reception room, restaurant, lounge, reading and writing room, smoking room, and the verandah cafés and palm courts. Other novel features are the gymnasium, squash racket court, Turkish and electric baths, and the swimming bath. Magnificent suites of rooms, and cabins of size and style sufficiently diverse to suit the likes and dislikes of any passenger, are provided. There is also a large barber's shop, a dark room for photographers, a clothes-pressing room, a special dining room for maids and valets, a lending library, a telephone system and a wireless telegraphy installation. Indeed everything has been done in regard to the furniture and fittings to make the first-class accommodation more than equal to that provided in the finest hotels on shore.

Grand Entrances and Staircases

The forward main staircase is situated between the first and second funnels from forward, and extends from the middle to the boat decks, with large entrance halls at each level . . . It is over 60ft. in height and 16ft. wide. The style is early English of the time of William and Mary; but instead of the heavily carved balustrade usual at that period, wrought iron scroll work has been adopted, somewhat after the French style of Louis XIV, and occasionally seen in contemporary great houses in England. The ironwork is relieved by occasional touches of bronze in the form of flowers and foliage. The walls are covered with oak panelling, simple and dignified in character, but enriched in a few places by exquisite work reminiscent of the days when Grinling Gibbons collaborated with his great contemporary, Wren. The staircase is lighted by a large dome of iron and glass, beneath which, on the uppermost landing, a large carved panel gives a tone of richness to the otherwise plain and massive construction of the wall. The panel contains a clock, on either side of which is a female figure, the whole symbolizing Honour and Glory crowning Time. The three elevators . . . are placed just forward of this staircase . . . They are entered from the forward end, the entrance halls on each deck being extended in this direction to provide ample space for ingress and egress, and harmonize in design with their surroundings . . .

The after main staircase is situated between the third and fourth funnels from forward. It is in style exactly similar to the forward staircase, but extends only from the promenade to the shelter decks.

First-class Dining Saloon

The first-class dining saloon is situated upon the saloon deck amidships and is an immense room, by far the largest afloat, extending for the full 92ft. of the ship's width and 114ft. in length. The style adopted is Jacobean English of the early seventeenth century, for details the splendid decorations at Hatfield, Haddon Hall and other great houses of that period having been carefully studied; but instead of the sombre oak, which the sixteenth- and seventeenth-century builders would have adopted, the walls and ceiling have been painted white. The ceiling in particular is richly moulded in a manner characteristic of the plasterer's art of Jacobean times . . . A complete perception of its magnificence can only be obtained by actual presence on the ship when dinner is in progress. The sidelights in the shell of the vessel are in groups of six

and four lights alternately, each light being of large diameter. In front
of these lights inside the saloon large leaded glass windows have been
arranged . . . giving the effect of the windows in a large mansion. Dining
accommodation is provided for 532 passengers at the same time . . .
The saloon is arranged on the popular restaurant principle with small
tables. At the sides the tables are in recessed bays, which form in effect
a number of separate private dining rooms, where families or friends
can dine together practically alone, retired from the busy hum of
surrounding conversation. The furniture is of oak, designed to harmonize
with the surroundings and at the same time to avoid the austere disregard
for comfort which evidently proved no hindrance to the enjoyment of
a meal in Jacobean times. The sideboards are particularly handsome
and in keeping with the general character of the room, as is also the
piano. The floor is covered with linoleum tiles of a unique pattern. An
important point in connection with the dining of such a large number
of passengers, *viz.*, the service, has been carefully borne in mind, and
at the after end of the saloon, extending the full width of the vessel, are
two extensive pantries to ensure the maintenance of the traditions of
the White Star Line for quick and efficient service.

The Reception Room
The reception room, which adjoins the forward end of the dining saloon,
has a length of 54ft. and also extends the full width of the ship. The
style adopted is Jacobean English similar to the dining room, but the
furniture is, of course, different. The dignity and simplicity of the
beautifully proportioned white panelling, delicately carved in low relief,
will indeed form a fitting background to the brilliant scene when the
passengers forgather before dining. The main staircase rises directly
from this apartment, thus greatly increasing the palatial effect produced.
Facing the staircase is a large and very beautiful panel of French tapestry
adapted from one of a series entitled 'Chasse de Guise' at the National
Garde Meuble, and specially woven on the looms at Aubusson. The
floor is covered with a dark, richly coloured Axminster carpet. The
furniture includes capacious Chesterfields, grandfather chairs
upholstered in a floral pattern of wool damask, comfortable cane
chairs, and light tables distributed at intervals, and there is also a grand
piano.

Restaurant

The restaurant, situated on the bridge deck, will be considered by many competent judges the most enticing apartment in the vessel. It is 60ft. long and 45ft. wide. The style of decoration adopted is that of the Louis Seize period. The room is panelled from floor to ceiling in beautifully marked French walnut of a delicate light fawn brown colour, the mouldings and ornaments being richly carved and gilded. Large electric light brackets, cast and finely chased in brass and gilt, and holding candle lamps, are fixed in the centre of the large panels. On the right of the entrance is a buffet with a marble top of *fleur de pêche*, supported by panelling and plaster recalling the design of the wall panels. The room is well lighted by large bay windows, a distinctive and novel feature which creates an impression of spaciousness. The windows are divided into squares by ornamental metal bars, and are draped with plain fawn silk curtains having flowered borders and richly embroidered *pelmets*. Every small detail, including even the fastenings and hinges, has been carried out with due regard to purity of style. The ceiling is of plaster, in which delicately modelled flowers in low relief combine to form a simple design of trellis in the centre and garlands in the bays. At various well-selected points hang clusters of lights ornamented with chased metal gilt and crystals. The floor is covered with an elegant pile carpet of Axminster make, having a non-obtrusive design of the Louis Seize period. The colour is a delicate *vieux rose* of the shade known as *Rose du Barri*, in perfect harmony with the surroundings.

Comfort has been well considered in the arrangement of the furniture. Small tables have been provided to accommodate from two to eight persons, and crystal standard lamps with rose-coloured shades illuminate each table. The chairs have been well studied, and are made in similar light French walnut to the walls. The woodwork is carved and finished with a waxed surface. The upholstery covering is Aubusson tapestry in quiet tones, representing a *treillage* of roses. For convenience of service there are several dumb waiters encircling the columns and forming part of the decorative scheme. A bandstand, partly recessed and raised on a platform, is provided at the after end. On either side of the bandstand is a carved buffet, the lower portion of which is used for cutlery and the upper portion for the silver service, thus completing the necessities for a well-appointed restaurant to satisfy every requirement.

Lounge

The first-class lounge is situated upon the promenade deck A, and is a noble apartment in the Louis Quinze style, the details being taken from the Palace at Versailles. Here passengers will indulge in reading, conversation, cards, tea-drinking, and other social intercourse. The room is furnished, . . . and has a length of 59ft., a breadth of 63ft. and a height of no less than 12ft. 3in. The walls are covered with finely carved *boiseries* in which, without interfering with the symmetry of the whole, the fancy of the carver has shown itself in ever-varying detail. At one end is a large fireplace, and at the other a bookcase from which books can be borrowed.

Reading and Writing Room

Adjacent to the lounge is the reading and writing room, which is in the late Georgian style of about 1770–80 AD. The panelling is finished in white, as is also the ceiling. The room is 41ft. long, 41ft. wide and, like the lounge, is 12ft. 3in. high . . . On one side is the great bow window . . . from which an uninterrupted view of the horizon will be obtained. At the forward end is a large recess, slightly raised above the general level, which produces a most pleasing effect in the appearance of the room. The pure white walls and the light and elegant furniture will make this essentially a ladies' room.

Smoking Room

The smoking room is situated towards the after end of the promenade deck A, and is entered from the after main entrance. It is without doubt the finest apartment of its kind on the ocean. The length is 65ft., breadth 63ft. and height 12ft. 3in. The style is a free adaptation of early Georgian of about 1720 AD, and is based upon the decorations pertaining in various old English houses of that period. The walls are panelled with the finest mahogany, but the characteristic carving of the Georgian style has been largely replaced by inlaid work in mother-of-pearl . . . A large open fireplace is situated at the after end of the room, over which is placed a fine painting, the work of Mr Norman Wilkinson, entitled 'The Approach of the New World'. Light enters the room, tempered and softened, through large painted windows of remarkable size and beauty, upon which are depicted landscapes, ancient ships and other subjects.

Verandah Cafés and Palm Courts

A verandah and palm court is situated on each side of the deck house immediately abaft the smoking room, with an entrance from the latter on the port side only by a revolving draught-proof door. Each compartment is 30ft. long by 25ft. wide ... The verandahs are completely enclosed on all sides with the exception of the openings provided in the after end for access from the promenade space. With this arrangement the cafés are less liable to draughts and the effects of inclement weather than is the case with the wide open-ended cafés adopted in other vessels. To maintain the impression of sitting in the open, windows of exceptional size have been provided. The style is *treillage* of Louis Seize period; and to create the illusion that the cafés are on shore, ivy and climbing plants are trained up the green trellis-work panels. The furnishings consist of numerous little tables, comfortable cane settees and armchairs of elegant design.

Turkish Baths

The Turkish baths are situated on the middle deck F, conveniently adjoining the main companion-way. They include the usual steam, hot, temperate, shampooing, and cooling rooms ... The cooling room is in many respects one of the most interesting and striking rooms in the ship, and is appropriately decorated in the Arabian style of the seventeenth century. The portholes are concealed by an elaborately carved Cairo curtain, through which the light fitfully reveals something of the grandeur of the mysterious East. The walls from the dado to the cornice are completely tiled in large panels of blue and green, surrounded by a broad band of tiles in a bolder and deeper hue. The ceiling cornice and beams are gilt, with the intervening panels picked out in dull red. From the panels are suspended bronze Arab lamps. A warm coloured teak has been adopted for the dado, doors, and panelling, and forms a perfect setting to the gorgeous effect of the tiles and ceiling. The stanchions, also cased in teak, are carved all over with an intricate Moorish pattern, surmounted by a carved cap. Over the doors are small gilt domes, semi-circular in plan, with their soffits carved in a low-relief geometrical pattern. Low couches are placed around the walls with an inlaid Damascus table between each, upon which coffee and cigarettes or books may be placed.

Fletcher's list of ship's stores for Olympic *and* Titanic *has entered the legendry of the ill-fated liner. In popular imagination,* Titanic *is the Ship of Plenty. Fletcher's crockery and cutlery manifest is just as impressive: 8,000 dinner forks, 400 toast racks, 5,000 dinner spoons, 1,000 oyster forks, etc. Not to speak of the linen stores: 7,500 blankets, 6,000 tablecloths, 15,000 single sheets. etc.*

R. A. FLETCHER
The Commissariat

(*Travelling Palaces: Luxury in Passenger Steamships,* 1913)

The selection of the stores for an Atlantic liner has to be based on totally different considerations from those prevailing on a large passenger steamer going on a long voyage. In the North Atlantic palaces great numbers of passengers have to be catered for in large quantities for a few days only. The consumption of stores for one voyage of the *Olympic*, enumerated in the following particulars – the amounts given may be accepted as correct, as they were supplied me by the White Star line – may be considered as a fair average of what the company has to provide every time that steamer leaves Liverpool, and this statement does not include the replenishing stores embarked at New York: –

Fresh meats, 75,000 lb.; fresh fish, 11,000 lb.; salt and dried fish, 4,000 lb.; bacon and ham, 7,500 lb.; poultry and game, 8,000 head; fresh butter, 6,000 lb.; fresh eggs, 40,000; sausages, 2,500 lb.; sweetbreads, 1,000; ice cream, 1,750 quarts; coffee, 2,200 lb.; tea, 800 lb.; peas, rice, etc., 10,000 lb.; sugar, 10,000 lb.; jams, 1,120 lb.; flour, 200 barrels; potatoes, 40 tons; apples, 180 boxes; oranges, 180 boxes (36,000); lemons, 50 boxes (16,000); hothouse grapes, 1,000 lb.; fresh milk, 1,500 gals.; condensed milk, 600 gals.; grapefruit, 50 boxes; lettuces, 7,000; cream, 1,000 quarts; fresh asparagus, 800 bundles; onions, 3,500 lb.; fresh green peas, 1¼ tons; tomatoes, 2¾ tons; beer and stout, 20,000 bottles; mineral waters, 15,000 bottles; wines, 1,500 bottles; spirits, 850 bottles; cigars, 8,000 . . .

Certain articles obtainable in England are considered superior to those obtainable in America, and for this reason special supplies of

English grapes, nectarines, peaches, salmon, sole, turbot, mutton and lamb are shipped at Liverpool for the use of passengers on the return journey from America.

The foregoing may be regarded as the everyday necessities on the steamers of either of the great lines mentioned [Cunard and White Star]. To them must be added various extras such as about a ton of Christmas puddings, if the steamer is going to spend December 25th at sea, and perhaps half a ton of mince-meat for the mince-pies which will be cooked on board. Crabs, lobsters, and crayfish, varying in quantity according to the season; truffles, *pâté de fois gras*; the edible portion of French frogs and snails, for the delectation of cosmopolitan and continental travellers whose tastes lie in those directions; varieties of sausage to please German travellers: all these are added in their due season. Then on the American festival of Thanksgiving Day, when every good American in the United States and out of them thinks it his bounden duty to celebrate the event by eating roast turkey stuffed with oysters and served with cranberry sauce, the steamship companies add to the stores for that voyage a few hundred turkeys and the customary accompaniments.

These vessels each employ about fifty cooks to prepare the food, and this number would be ridiculously inadequate were it not for the many labour and time-saving appliances, worked by electricity, introduced on the steamers. Electricity, when suitably applied and treated as it should be, is a most accomplished scullery staff. There is hardly any of the rough or dirty work it will not do. It works the lifts by which the stores are conveyed from the storerooms in the lower part of the ship to the kitchen. It works ingenious little machines by which the potatoes are peeled better and quicker than a score of men could manage: other machines which revolve circular knives and cut loaves into slices of unvarying thickness for sandwiches, or thin bread and butter, or into slightly thicker slices for toast; these machines, also, will attack a side of bacon from which the bones have been removed and in a few seconds cut it into rashers all of the same thickness. Nor do the cooks have to make the toast. There are electrical toasters for this work. The slices are placed in the toaster, the current is switched on, if it is not on already, and in a few seconds there are some scores of slices ready for the passengers, and the machine rings the bell when they are done.

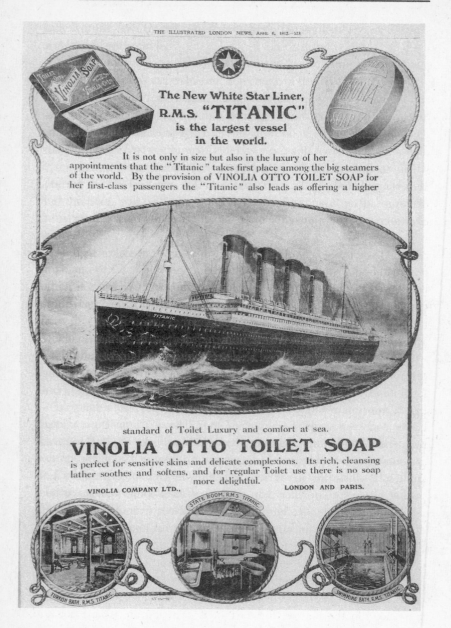

The New White Star Liner,
R.M.S. "TITANIC"
is the largest vessel
in the world.

It is not only in size but also in the luxury of her appointments that the "Titanic" takes first place among the big steamers of the world. By the provision of VINOLIA OTTO TOILET SOAP for her first-class passengers the "Titanic" also leads as offering a higher

standard of Toilet Luxury and comfort at sea.

VINOLIA OTTO TOILET SOAP

is perfect for sensitive skins and delicate complexions. Its rich, cleansing lather soothes and softens, and for regular Toilet use there is no soap more delightful.

VINOLIA COMPANY LTD.,   LONDON AND PARIS.

For sundry manufacturers, *Titanic* was an advertising dream that became a nightmare of bad associations and a fever of rewritten copy.

Seaborne hotels, travelling palaces, floating towns: these were early metaphors used to describe (and sometimes deplore) luxury liners of the period. The vastnesses between boat deck and stokehold included chefs, nurses, library stewards, orchestra members, page-boys, lift-boys, post-office clerks, bath attendants, barbers, butchers, bakers, window-cleaners, scullions, a ship's printer, interpreter, rackets professional, gymnasium instructor.

R. A. FLETCHER
A Floating Town

(*Travelling Palaces*)

There is no exaggeration in describing the steamship as a floating town. Perhaps a better description is that she is a travelling palatial hotel, combining the best features of the modern hotel with the comfort and luxury generally associated with the palace.

If the liner be described as a town, it can only be one in which the streets are built one above another, in which the co-operative principle of cooking is adopted, in which all the artificial light and heat required are obtained from common sources, in which the sanitation is as perfect as science can make it, in which the luxury provided is out of all proportion as a regular condition of life to the income of most of its dwellers, in which the minority work and the majority play, and in which the rent collector, tax-gatherer and 'men who come with nasty bills and always look so sleek' are conspicuous by their absence. The ship's community has no politics, no general elections, no canvassers for votes, no candidates enthusiastically making promises they know perfectly well they can never keep and no deluded electorate. There are no police, no law courts for the ventilation of moral unsavouries; the aggravations of the work-a-day world ashore are missing. The state, as epitomized by the liner, takes charge of the passenger; certain less fortunate persons minister to his or her wants; objectionable persons can be subjected to a rigid boycott, and their existence ignored; and beneath, above, and around is a system as perfect as skilled organization can make it for seeing that the floating city pursues the even tenor of its way until its destination is reached.

The names of the American rich or powerful who boarded Titanic *we have all learned to recite: Astor, Guggenheim, Straus, Widener, Butt, Hays, Roebling, Dodge, Ryerson, Case. 'A gay and distinguished company,' the rescuing captain, Arthur Rostron of* Carpathia, *later called first class. At the other end of the ship were the largely anonymous European emigrants in steerage.*

FILSON YOUNG
All the World in Little

(Titanic)

And who were the people who composed the population of this journeying town? Subsequent events made their names known to us – vast lists of names filling columns of the newspapers; but to the majority they are names and nothing else. Hardly anyone living knew more than a dozen of them personally; and try as we may it is very hard to see them, as their fellow voyagers must have seen them, as individual human beings with recognizable faces and characters of their own. Of the three hundred odd first-class passengers the majority were Americans – rich and prosperous people, engaged for the most part in the simple occupation of buying things as cheaply as possible, selling them as dearly as possible and trying to find some agreeable way of spending the difference on themselves. Of the three hundred odd second-class passengers probably the majority were English, many of them of the minor professional classes and many going either to visit friends or to take up situations in the western world. But the thousand odd steerage passengers represented a kind of Babel of nationalities, all the world in little, united by nothing except poverty and the fact that they were in a transition stage of their existence, leaving behind them for the most part a life of failure and hopelessness, and looking forward to a new life of success and hope: Jews, Christians and Mohammedans, missionaries and heathen, Russians, Poles, Greeks, Roumanians, Germans, Italians, Chinese, Finns, Spaniards, English and French – with a strong contingent of Irish, the inevitable link in that melancholy chain of emigration that has united Ireland and America since the Famine. But there were other differences, besides those of their condition and geographical distribution on the ship, that divided its inhabitants. For the first-class passengers the world was a very small place, about which many of them were accustomed to hurry in an important way in the process of spending and getting their money, taking an Atlantic liner as humbler people take a tramcar, without giving much thought to it or laying elaborate plans, running backwards and forwards across the Atlantic and its dangers as children run across the road in front of a motor car. They were going to America this week; they would probably come back next week or the week after. They were the people for whom the *Titanic* had specially been designed; it was for them that all the luxuries had been contrived, so that in their runnings backwards and forwards they should not find the long days tedious or themselves divorced from the kind of accompaniments to life which they had come to regard as necessities.

But for the people in the steerage this was no hurrying trip between one business office and another; no hasty holiday arranged to sandwich ten thousand miles of ozone as a refresher between two business engagements. This westward progress was for them part of the drift of their lives, loosening them from their native soil to scatter and distribute them over the New World, in the hope that in fresher soil and less crowded conditions they would strike new roots and begin a new life. The road they travelled was for most of them a road to be travelled once only, a road they knew they would never retrace. For them almost exclusively was reserved that strange sense of looking down over the stern of the ship into the boiling commotion of the churned-up waters, the maelstrom of snow under the counter merging into the pale green highway that lay straight behind them to the horizon, and of knowing that it was a road that divided them from home, a road that grew a mile longer with every three minutes of their storming progress. Other ships would follow on the road; other ships would turn and come again, and drive their way straight back over the white foam to where, with a sudden plunging and turning of screws in the green harbour water of home, the road had begun. But they who looked back from the steerage quarters of the *Titanic* would not return; and they, alone of all the passengers on the ship, knew it.

In the course of a scholarly and stylish account of the tragedy, Marcus sketches in the immediate cultural context of the ship's first-class American passengers, for whom the luxury transatlantic liner was a shuttle between the New World origins of their wealth and the Old World occasions for their enjoyment of it.

GEOFFREY MARCUS
The Gilded Age

(*The Maiden Voyage*, 1969)

Over on Platform 12 little groups of men and women stood chatting by the White Star Line Boat Train which was shortly to depart for Southampton. Occasionally porters wheeling their trolleys and other passers-by turned their heads at the sound of the nasal transatlantic accents and somewhat unfamiliar dress of most of these 'toffs' . . .

Taken all in all, these Americans travelling in the boat train to Southampton might be considered a fairly representative cross-section of the community which had nurtured them. It was the final phase of what Mark Twain, in a revealing phrase, had characterized as 'the Gilded Age'. In that hectic and often ruthless scramble for wealth not a few had amassed fortunes such as the world had never known before. Generally speaking, American plutocracy knew more about making money than spending it. The exuberance of some of the parties they had got up in the early part of this century had excited adverse comment even at home. 'They have given,' Caroline Astor had observed severely, 'entertainments which belonged under a circus tent rather than in a gentlewoman's house.' Of late they had been spending much of their time in Europe – particularly in London.

More and more the leisured classes of the United States felt themselves drawn towards the greatest city in the world, where, increasingly at home among a kindred people, they discovered what America could never give them – the impressive ceremonial which had grown up around the ancient monarchy, the companionship of men and women whose names were written in history, the order, grace and elegance of a mature civilization. Fresh in their memories was the wonderful London Season of 1911, which had witnessed, among other notable events, the coronation of King George V and Queen Mary, the stormy passage of the Parliament Bill, the first arrival in this country of Diaghilev's Russian Ballet led by Anna Pavlova, the conclusion of the long run of *The Arcadians* at the Adelphi Theatre and the first performances of *The Count of Luxemburg* and *The Quaker Girl*. They recalled those fashionable gatherings in the early evening by Stanhope Gate in Hyde Park, and the long procession of motor-cars and carriages pouring down Park Lane past the great houses with their green sunblinds and window-boxes overflowing with scarlet and pink geraniums. The drama of politics added zest to life. Party passion rose higher just then than at any time since Gladstone's Home Rule Bill. The country seemed to be on the brink of a social and economic revolution, and at times it sounded like civil war gathering up. But, outside political circles, the ordinary life of the country went on as usual.

From the opening night at the Royal Opera House, Covent Garden, in April, to Cowes Regatta in July, the various events of the Season had become almost as familiar to the rich of the United States as they were to their English friends and connections (the recent spate of international marriages had greatly assisted this *rapprochement*).

In this final phase of 'the Gilded Age' American society was dominated by a circle of immensely wealthy families who thought and spoke and acted as if the world had been made for them. They used their riches to acquire magnificent mansions in New York, Newport, Palm Beach and elsewhere; they crossed the ocean in the palatial ferries provided for them by the White Star, Cunard and Hamburg-Amerika Lines; they travelled about the Continent in trains-de-luxe several hundred feet long. They would reside at hotels like Claridge's and the Savoy in London; Hotel de Crillon, the Maurice, and the Ritz in Paris; the Adlon in Berlin; the Carlton in Cannes, and the Riviera Palace in Monte Carlo, 'the Most Luxurious Hotel in the World', as the advertisements claimed. World-famous yachts like Cornelius Vanderbilt's *Northern Star* and J. Pierpont Morgan's *Corsair* might be seen at Cowes and Kiel in company with the Royal Yacht *Victoria and Albert* and the German Emperor's *Hohenzollern*. Lapped in the accumulated treasures of the long peace and drugged by the widely accepted doctrine of universal and inevitable progress, the favoured few were rapidly losing touch with reality and existing almost in a dream-world of their own.

wHITE **STAR** LINE
TRIPLE SCREW STEAMER "TITANIC"

LUNCHEON

CONSOMME FERMIER   COCKIE LEEKIE
FILLETS OF BRILL
EGG A L'ARGENTEUIL
CHICKEN A LA MARYLAND
CORNED BEEF, VEGETABLES, DUMPLINGS

FROM THE GRILL

GRILLED MUTTON CHOPS
MASHED, FRIED & BAKED JACKET POTATOES
CUSTARD PUDDING
APPLE MERINGUE   PASTRY

BUFFET

SALMON MAYONNAISE   POTTED SHRIMPS
NORWEGIAN ANCHOVIES   SOUBED HERRINGS
PLAIN & SMOKED SARDINES
ROAST BEEF
ROUND OF SPICED BEEF
VEAL & HAM PIE
VIRGINIA & CUMBERLAND HAM
BOLOGNA SAUSAGE   BRAWN
GALANTINE OF CHICKEN
CORNED OX TONGUE
LETTUCE   BEETROOT   TOMATOES

CHEESE

CHESHIRE, STILTON, GORGONZOLA, EDAM, CAMEMBERT
ROQUEFORT, ST. IVEL, CHEDDAR

Iced draught Munich Lager Beer 3d & 6d a Tankard

1ST CLASS   APRIL 14, 1912

Titanic menu for first-class lunch.

Heading the deck officers brought alive by Marcus in this excerpt was Captain Edward J. Smith ('E. J.'), 'the beau ideal of a Western Ocean Mail Boat commander' who had commanded seventeen White Star ships, including Olympic. Despite the élite nature of the merchant marine officers on board Titanic, perfect discipline was not exhibited in the crisis of disaster, and Henry Sleeper Harper's eyewitness account was of inexpert fumbling by the crew around the lifeboats.

GEOFFREY MARCUS
The Elite of the Mercantile Marine

(*Maiden Voyage*)

Far removed from all that world of wealth and luxury was the little coterie of deck officers whose lives at sea revolved around the bridge and the officers' quarters at the forward end of the boat deck. There were seven of them all told, besides the Master – three watch-keepers (the Chief, First and Second Officers), and four juniors (the Third, Fourth, Fifth and Sixth Officers). Bred to the sea from their boyhood, they had mounted the ladder rung by rung, first in sail and then in steam, and had so far earned the approval of the ruling lights of the Line as now to be singled out for the high honour of serving as officers in the magnificent new liner on her maiden voyage.

Behind them lay the camaraderie of the half-deck with its memories of the seasick misery of their early days at sea; of the unforgettable thrill of going aloft for the first time, and of learning the ropes under the aegis of the Third Mate – traditionally the boys' mentor; of the halcyon experience of the Trades, with the ship snoring along with sails set and yards trimmed for days on end, in radiant 'flying fish weather'; of gathering in the second dog watch for the evening sing-song; of learning to prepare and enjoy those time-honoured confections of the half-deck, crackerjack and dandyfunk; of sweltering days in the Doldrums with the sails slatting idly against the masts and long weary spells of 'pulley-hauley'; of freshening winds and rising seas as they got down into the Forties and the ship laid her lee rail down to the water and the watch tailed on to the main topsail halyards to the chorus of 'Sally Brown'; of pitch-black nights off the Horn with the ship labouring in mountainous seas and men washed about the flooded decks, or clinging to the jackstay lashed by sleet and hail; of the peremptory cry of 'Wear ship!' and of the fearsome ordeal that would follow; of the favouring slant which finally enabled them to make their westing, and then to reach milder latitudes; of the open anchorage at Iquiqui, where the ships lay out in tiers loading nitrates for Europe; and of the ceremony of 'Hoisting the Southern Cross' and cheering the homeward-bounder as each ship in turn completed its lading and sailed for home.

Though textbooks like Lecky's *Wrinkles in Practical Navigation* and Todd and Whall's *Seamanship* would accompany their owner to sea, they usually lay about neglected in the half-deck until the apprentice's final voyage and the approach of the Second Mate's examination. Then would ensue furious spells of 'swatting up' mathematics, nautical astronomy, seamanship and navigation at some Navigation School ashore. After another year there would be similar preparation for the Mate's examination. And later still they would pass for Master, receiving the coveted slip of blue paper that qualified them to command at sea.

In the nineteen-hundreds an increasing number of young officers were also passing for Extra Master, which was of considerable advantage to those aspiring to an appointment in the Western Ocean mail boats, where it was essential, among other things, to have a thorough mastery of the spherical trigonometry underlying the solution of Great Circle problems.

The prestige and glamour of these great Atlantic liners drew the keenest, smartest men in the British merchant service like a lodestone. The short voyages, the regularity and frequency of shore leave (this was of particular importance to the family man), were powerful arguments in their favour; as were also the admirable living conditions, and the good and abundant food. With the long, gruelling years in sailing ships still fresh in their memory, it was as if they had entered the Elysian fields. 'This is the life!' the youthful James Bisset had whispered to himself on his first night on board an Atlantic mail boat; and then, with a contented sigh, turned his face to the bulkhead and fell fast asleep smiling . . .

The White Star Line demanded and secured some of the ablest officers, the best navigators, the finest seamen afloat. What was required of an applicant for one of these coveted mail boat berths was that he should have been trained in sail, gained all his certificates (including, if possible, the Extra Master's), and belonged to the Royal Naval Reserve.

The young men coming on in the Cunard and White Star Lines usually had these qualifications. They found the standard of discipline and navigation obtaining in the fast passenger steamships was something scarcely any of them could have dreamed of before. In effect, what the Masters and Mates of the famous China tea clippers had been in their day, so now, in the early nineteen-hundreds, were these officers of the North Atlantic mail boats – the élite of the British mercantile marine.

George Beedem was a bedroom steward on board Titanic. *He wrote to his wife and young son on 5 April (Good Friday) and 9 April (Easter Tuesday). Domestic concerns extend even to the ship – with dusters in short supply – and his lightly uttered cantankerous wish to see* Titanic *at the bottom of the sea came true; George Beedem went with her.*

GEORGE BEEDEM
Letters from *Titanic*

(Donald Hyslop *et al.*, *Titanic Voices: Memories from the Fateful Voyage*, 1994)

Southampton
5th April 1912
Titanic
Friday evening
Am enclosing card found in pocket

My Dearest Lill
Good Friday & I have been at work all day. I got on board yesterday about 9 o/c. The crowd here not started yet, they come tomorrow, there is very little difference between the two ships I have been 'standing by' today simply seeing the ship does not turn away, the others are not working, I signed on for rooms. It's been a lovely day today. Now how is your neck? Stick to that stuff my girl whatever you do. I cannot find any notepaper only this sheet in my bag so I must have another look. I have found a few sheets when I signed on. I found I had left my discharge book home on the dresser, please send it on to the *Titanic*. Now my girl I don't know what else to write about, I cannot get a stamp until tomorrow morning. I am going to take the pipe for a stroll somewhere or the other. I do like being here by myself so goodbye my little dears, hope Charlie sleeps alright now, so tata with love & kisses.

DaDa (George)

9th April 1912
On board RMS *Titanic*
Tuesday

My dear Lill & Charlie
This is the last night & thank goodness we are off tomorrow. I should never do another week along like I have this one. On Sunday I went all over the place house hunting. You had better let me know for certain at Plymouth what you are going to do in the way of coming down & going home. I don't suppose we shall leave the ship till 5 o/c on the Saturday night. I hope your neck is better, let me know all about it for certain at Plymouth. My cold has been rotten & I shall be glad to get away to have a good square meal. As usual I expect you will say I am wrong in my money. I have not been paid for Good Friday there were only 10 of us working & none have been paid through some fool leaving us off the list. I am sending 10/- that's 4/- short so I've managed to exist on about 8/- counting 2/- I had from you so it's a happy life. I have no news to tell you only the last 3 days. I've felt rotten & what with no dusters or anything to work with I wish the bally ship at the bottom of the sea. I heard from Mother today, Uncle John is a little better but cannot get up. Hope Charlie is having a nice holiday, so goodbye with love to both of you.

George

PS I have been thinking if it were possible to go right in for our own house, just think it over & see if anything can be done

Dad (George)

Cardsharps, or 'boat men', had already worked Olympic, *as the* San Francisco Examiner *reported on 10 April, winning $15,000 before smoking-room habitués realized they had been 'trimmed'.*

WALTER LORD
Alias *Titanic*

(*The Night Lives On*, 1986)

Sir Cosmo and Lady Duff Gordon were . . . names missing from the Passenger List but definitely on the *Titanic*. For some reason they were travelling as 'Mr and Mrs Morgan' – an odd decision, since Lady Duff Gordon was one of Society's most important couturières and lived by publicity.

More understandable was the decision of George Rosenshine and Maybelle Thorne to be listed as 'Mr and Mrs G. Thorne'. They were not married but travelling together, and in the Edwardian era, appearances were often more important than reality. Appearances also played a part in the case of 'Miss E. Rosenbaum'. She was a fashion stylist, and it simply seemed better business to anglicize her name. So although listed correctly, she was generally known as Edith Russell, and that is the way she has come down to us in most survivor accounts.

Three other passengers found it absolutely essential to travel incognito. They were professional cardsharps, hoping to make a maiden voyage killing. Obviously it was safer to use an assumed name; so George (Boy) Bradley was listed as 'George Brayton'; C. H. Romaine as 'C. Rolmane'; and Harry (Kid) Homer as 'E. Haven'. There's evidence that the well-known gambler Jay Yates was also on board, using the alias 'J. H. Rogers'. Neither name appears on the Passenger List, but a farewell note signed by Rogers was later handed to a survivor on the sloping boat deck.

One shady figure definitely not on the ship was Alvin Clarence Thomas, a con man later known as 'Titanic Thompson', who achieved a certain notoriety as a witness to the slaying of the gambler Arnold Rothstein in 1929. It was generally assumed that the alias came from Thompson's having plied his trade on the *Titanic*, but this is not so – he was only nine at the time. Actually, the name was an appropriate reference to several disastrous plunges taken when the stakes were high.

While the presence of this or that particular individual could be argued, there's no doubt that a number of cardsharps were indeed on the *Titanic*, and in fact on almost every express liner plying the Atlantic at the time. The combination of rich, bored passengers, easily made shipboard friendships and the ambience of the smoking room provided the perfect climate for 'sportsmen', as the gamblers were politely called.

The wonder is that the lines didn't do more to protect their ordinary passengers. The veteran gamblers were familiar figures to most of the pursers and smoking room stewards: were they being bribed to keep quiet? Undoubtedly there were occasional payoffs, but the real source of trouble seems to have been the steamship companies themselves. They didn't want to take any step that implied they might be responsible for their patrons' losses. Nor were all high-stake games dishonest; there was always the legal danger of a false charge. It was safer not to get involved.

On the *Titanic* there was only one low-keyed warning. This was a mild little insert, planted opposite the first page of the Passenger List:

SPECIAL NOTICE

The attention of the Managers has been called to the fact that certain persons, believed to be Professional Gamblers, are in the habit of travelling to and fro in Atlantic Steamships.

In bringing this to the knowledge of Travellers the Managers, while not wishing in the slightest degree to interfere with the freedom of action of Patrons of the White Star Line, desire to invite their assistance in discouraging Games of Chance, as being likely to afford these individuals special opportunities for taking unfair advantage of others.

Irish photographer Father Frank Browne captured *Titanic* as she left Queenstown on 11 April and sailed into history and myth.

Sailing day was almost ruined by a collision between Titanic *and the liner* New York, *loosed from her moorings by the backwash from the departing giant. After that, it was calm seas and plain sailing.*

GEOFFREY MARCUS
'Sailing Day'

(*Maiden Voyage*)

The principal Southampton hotels were crowded the previous night with passengers and their friends who had come down from London to see them off. At the South-Western Hotel, which stood just across the road from the long line of shipping offices, warehouses and other harbour buildings, a young London schoolmaster named Lawrence Beesley, who was going out to visit his brother in America, watched, as he sat at breakfast, the long straggling procession of firemen, trimmers, greasers, stewards and others which from very early in the morning had been slowly making its way through the streets of dockland to join the new ship. Hour after hour an apparently endless stream of people, both passengers and crew, filed across the gangways. From time to time a peremptory blast came from the ship's siren, warning all and sundry within a three-mile radius that it was sailing day. The deep, echoing vibrations scattered the seabirds, made all the windows rattle and eventually died away beyond the Bargate. Huge electric cranes dealt swiftly and dextrously with mounds of luggage. The last of the stores were being taken on board.

Also staying at the South-Western Hotel was Thomas Andrews, a managing director of Harland and Wolff, the great shipbuilding firm which had built the *Olympic*, the *Titanic* and all the other ships of the White Star fleet. Andrews, a master of everything relating to the construction and equipment of modern steamships, had been closely associated with his uncle and chief, Lord Pirrie, in the design of the *Titanic*, and in earlier years had supervised the construction of the *Baltic* and *Oceanic*. During the previous week Andrews had toiled early and late to get the mammoth liner ready for sailing day. On the 9th he had written home to Belfast: 'The *Titanic* is now about complete and will I think do the Old Firm credit tomorrow when we sail.' On the

10th he went on board at 6.30 a.m., and for nearly six hours moved about the great vessel as she lay ready to depart, searching, viewing, weighing and considering. The result of this final inspection satisfied Andrews. The *Titanic* was good – very good indeed. She would, he felt, always be remembered as one of the finest achievements of Harland and Wolff. Eight men from the Island Yard, including the chief draughtsman, were to sail in her to deal with any necessary alterations and repairs. Later in the morning he said goodbye to his secretary and the other officials. His last instructions to the former were, 'Remember now and keep Mrs Andrews informed of any news of the vessel.' He seemed in excellent health and spirits.

3
The Machine Stops

O Lord, methought what pain it was to drown!
What dreadful noise of waters in my ears!
What sights of ugly death within my eyes!
    William Shakespeare, *King Richard III*

Hear now the Song of the Dead – in the North
  by the torn berg-edges
    Rudyard Kipling, 'The Song of the Dead'

In 1909 E. M. Forster published a story called 'The Machine Stops'. In it, the 'Machine' controls our future subterranean world. But one day, after a gradual winding down, the Machine stops and the world as we understand it ends. Behind the uproar of humanity yelling and fighting when the Machine stops is 'silence, which is the voice of the earth'.

The first sign of something serious afoot was not the collision but the stopping of Titanic's *engines and the sudden silence. Survivors spoke later of the panic when the boats had departed and left hundreds still aboard and the irony of the starlit night, the silence of the earth that was panic's backdrop.*

And it was the earth that had inflicted the fatal damage. Sir James Bisset, Second Officer on the rescue ship Carpathia *and who went on to become wartime Captain of* Queen Mary *and* Queen Elizabeth, *wrote of the wayward behaviour of icebergs in his memoirs,* Tramps and Ladies *(1960), and of their progeny, 'growlers'. But as Richard Brown has remarked: 'There has only been one iceberg, and its history lasted for a minute.'*

Titanic *had been well warned of iceberg activity in her vicinity. Wireless telegraphy was highly developed by 1912; the Cunarder* Caronia *was 700 miles and Olympic 500 miles away from* Titanic *but heard the stricken liner clearly, though most steamers had wireless apparatus that allowed a range of* 200 *miles.* Geoffrey Marcus *in* The Maiden Voyage *has re-created the strange lives of shipboard wireless operators, their tense fraternity and their odd, contracted rhetoric that was both chivalrous and uncivil:* TU OM GN (Thank you, old man, good night!), GTH OM QRT (Get to hell, old man, keep quiet, I'm busy*).*

The unfolding drama that night had hundreds of surviving witnesses, but most kept their experiences to themselves or to family or, no doubt, wrote letters, by now destroyed or mislaid. Some told their story to newspaper reporters; or they told them at the official enquiries. Some published them as narratives, occasionally polished by hindsight or copy-editors. Although these are not rewarding to an equal degree as first-hand evidence, all are validated as presence in the neighbourhoods of terror and death.

Since November 1911, twenty sailing craft of from 100 to 300 tons had gone to the bottom of the sea in the vicinity of Newfoundland, seven of them with their entire crew.

RICHARD BROWN
An Appalling Winter

(*Voyage of the Iceberg*, 1983)

It has been an appalling winter, the worst in thirty years. One black storm after another comes howling off the coast of America and off toward Europe. Hurricane winds whip the spray off the enormous waves and hurl it at the ships struggling westward. The waves pound down on *Carmania*, a liner of 20,000 tons, and they toss her into a fifty-degree roll. They are death for anything smaller. They catch the schooners which ply up and down to Newfoundland, scatter them and break them. Some vanish without a trace. Some are blown south, dismasted, and drift derelict in the calms of the Sargasso Sea. One of them, *Maggie*, takes more than two months to cross from Portugal, battered, leaking, with one man dead, and after all that torture she never comes home. She is almost in sight of Newfoundland when the pack-ice catches her and crushes her, and *Sagona* arrives only just in time to rescue her crew. *Sagona* herself, brand-new and bound straight for the Seal Hunt, takes fifteen days to cross the Atlantic. *Erna*, the big ship everyone in St John's is waiting for, sinks in mid ocean. The North Atlantic is littered with spars, ropes, planking, derelict hulks, scraps of cargo – all of it pushed slowly toward Europe by the storms and the Gulf Stream.

By the beginning of April the worst is over, and as if to make up for the furious winter, the Atlantic falls into an unnatural calm. But the fine weather has come far too late to stop the drift of ice past Newfoundland. It is a rare berg that drifts as far south as the Grand Banks in most years, and often there are none at all. There are over a thousand of them in 1912. The Labrador Current takes them south, down the eastern edge of the Grand Banks, and a large sheet of pack-ice, 100 miles by 100, goes with them. This mass of ice drifts past the Tail of the Bank and on across the North Atlantic shipping lanes at an inexorable twenty-five miles a day.

Bergs, Growlers and Field Ice

(*Wireless messages to and from* Titanic)

Titanic *Time*
Friday April 12
Late forenoon.   *Officers and self send greetings and best of*
luck to the Titanic, her officers and
commander. Murray. Empress of Britain.
Many thanks for your kind message from
all here. Smith [Titanic]

About 7.00 p.m. G M T.   *My position 7pm, G M T, lat. 49°28', long.*
26°28'. Dense fog since this night. Crossed
thick ice field lat. 44°58', long. 50°40' Paris.
Saw another ice field and two icebergs lat.
45°20', long. 49°09' Paris. Saw a derelict lat.
40°56', long. 68°38' Paris. Please give me
position. Best regards and bon voyage.
Caussin.   [From Touraine, French]
Thanks for your message and information.
My position 7pm G M T. Lat. 49°45', long.
23°38' W. Greenwich. Had fine weather.
Compliments. Smith.

Saturday April 13
10.30 p.m.   *Have just passed through heavy field ice and*
several icebergs.   [Cargo steamer,
Rappahannock, bound for Liverpool from
Halifax, breaks free of pack ice in the early
evening and morses a warning on her signal
lamp to the passing *Titanic*. Message
acknowledged by lamp from *Titanic's*
bridge.]

Sunday April 14
9.00 a.m.   *Captain, Titanic. West-bound steamers*
report bergs growlers and field ice in 42° N

*to 51° W. 12th April. Compliments –
Barr.*   [From *Caronia*, Cunarder; Captain
Smith acknowledged this message; *Titanic*
then at lat. 43°35' N and long. 43°50' W.]

11.40 a.m.   *Congratulations on new command. Had
moderate westerly winds, fine weather, no
fog, much ice reported in lat. 42°24' to 42°45'
and long. 49°45' and long. 49°50' to
50°20'.*   [From *Noordam*, Dutch, via
Caronia; message formally acknowledged by
Captain Smith.]

12.55 p.m.   *Captain Smith, Titanic – Have had moderate,
variable winds and clear fine weather since
leaving. Greek steamer Athenai reports
passing icebergs and large quantities of field
ice today in lat. 41°51' N, long. 49°52' W.
Last night we spoke German oiltank steamer
Deutschland, Stettin to Philadelphia, not
under control, short of coal, lat. 40°42' N,
long. 55°11' W. Wishes to be reported to New
York and other steamers. Wish you and
Titanic all success. – Commander.*
    *Captain Ranson, Baltic – Thanks for your
message and good wishes. Had fine weather
since leaving. – Commander [Titanic]*

[Shortly after receiving this warning from a
fellow White Star liner, Captain Smith
passed it on to J. Bruce Ismay; *Titanic* then
at lat. 42°35' N, long. 45°50' W; Captain
Smith retrieved the message from Ismay
shortly before dinner.]

1.45 p.m.   *S S Amerika via Titanic and Cape Race.
Amerika passed two large icebergs in
41°27' N, 50°08' W, on the 14th of
April.*   [This message from a ship of the

Hamburg-Amerika Line to Cape Race via
Titanic was forwarded by Cape Race to
Hydrographic Office, Washington, D.C.]

7.30 p.m.

*To Captain, Antillian, 6.30pm [apparent
ship's time]. Lat. 42°03' N, long. 49°09' W.
Three large bergs five miles to the southward
of us. Regards – Lord* (signed)   [From
Californian, Leyland Line; message
intercepted and delivered to MGY bridge;
Captain Stanley Lord repeated the message
to *Titanic* which replied:]
*It is all right, I heard you sending it to the
Antillian and I have got it MGY.*

9.40 p.m.

*From Mesaba to Titanic and all east-bound
ships. Ice report in lat. 42° N to 41°25' N,
long. 49° to 50°30' W. Saw much heavy pack
ice and great number large icebergs. Also
field ice. Weather good, clear.*
    Received; thanks MGY.   [This message
from a ship of the Atlantic Transport
Company was not acknowledged by Captain
Smith – to the surprise of the *Mesaba*
wireless operator – and was probably not
delivered to an officer.]

11.00 p.m.

*Say, old man, we are stopped and
surrounded by ice MWL.*   [From
Californian.]
Shut up. I am busy. I am working Cape Race
[MCE].
    [To MCE:] *Sorry. Please repeat, jammed
MGY.*   [The message from the
Californian was not relayed to the bridge of
Titanic.]

[*Titanic* struck the iceberg at 11.40 p.m.]

Lord's remains the classic blow-by-blow account of the sinking. His technique of brisk sentences, multiple and rapidly shifting perspectives and refusals to theorize has kept his book in print after its publication generated the first wave of Titanic *enthusiasm since the tragedy itself. Yet by fastening on the high life aboard, the book manages to be elegiac as well as journalistic.*

WALTER LORD
The Collision

(*A Night to Remember*, 1955)

High in the crow's-nest of the new White Star Liner *Titanic*, Lookout Frederick Fleet peered into a dazzling night. It was calm, clear and bitterly cold. There was no moon, but the cloudless sky blazed with stars. The Atlantic was like polished plate glass; people later said they had never seen it so smooth.

This was the fifth night of the *Titanic*'s maiden voyage to New York, and it was already clear that she was not only the largest but also the most glamorous ship in the world. Even the passengers' dogs were glamorous. John Jacob Astor had along his Airedale Kitty. Henry Sleeper Harper, of the publishing family, had his prize Pekingese Sun Yat-sen. Robert W. Daniel, the Philadelphia banker, was bringing back a champion French bulldog just purchased in Britain. Clarence Moore of Washington also had been dog-shopping, but the fifty pairs of English foxhounds he bought for the Loudoun Hunt weren't making the trip.

That was all another world to Frederick Fleet. He was one of six lookouts carried by the *Titanic*, and the lookouts didn't worry about passenger problems. They were the 'eyes of the ship', and on this particular night Fleet had been warned to watch especially for icebergs.

So far, so good. On duty at 10 o'clock . . . a few words about the ice problem with Lookout Reginald Lee, who shared the same watch . . . a few more words about the cold . . . but mostly just silence as the two men stared into the darkness.

Now the watch was almost over, and still there was nothing unusual. Just the night, the stars, the biting cold, the wind that whistled through the rigging as the *Titanic* raced across the calm, black sea at 22½ knots. It was almost 11.40 p.m. on Sunday, the 14th of April 1912.

Suddenly Fleet saw something directly ahead, even darker than the darkness. At first it was small (about the size, he thought, of two tables put together), but every second it grew larger and closer. Quickly Fleet banged the crow's-nest bell three times, the warning of danger ahead. At the same time he lifted the phone and rang the bridge.

'What did you see?' asked a calm voice at the other end.

'Iceberg right ahead,' replied Fleet.

'Thank you,' acknowledged the voice with curiously detached courtesy. Nothing more was said.

For the next thirty-seven seconds, Fleet and Lee stood quietly side by side, watching the ice draw nearer. Now they were almost on top of it, and still the ship didn't turn. The berg towered wet and glistening far above the forecastle deck, and both men braced themselves for a crash. Then, miraculously, the bow began to swing to port. At the last second the stem shot into the clear, and the ice glided swiftly by along the starboard side. It looked to Fleet like a very close shave.

At this moment Quartermaster George Thomas Rowe was standing watch on the after bridge. For him too, it had been an uneventful night – just the sea, the stars, the biting cold. As he paced the deck, he noticed what he and his mates called 'Whiskers 'round the Light' – tiny splinters of ice in the air, fine as dust, that gave off myriads of bright colours whenever caught in the glow of the deck lights.

Then suddenly he felt a curious motion break the steady rhythm of the engines. It was a little like coming alongside a dock wall rather heavily. He glanced forward – and stared again. A windjammer, sails set, seemed to be passing along the starboard side. Then he realized it was an iceberg, towering perhaps 100 feet above the water. The next instant it was gone, drifting astern into the dark.

Meanwhile, down below in the first-class dining saloon on D deck, four other members of the *Titanic*'s crew were sitting around one of the tables. The last diner had long since departed, and now the big white Jacobean room was empty except for this single group. They were dining-saloon stewards, indulging in the time-honoured pastime of all stewards off duty – they were gossiping about their passengers.

Then, as they sat there talking, a faint grinding jar seemed to come from somewhere deep inside the ship. It was not much, but enough to break the conversation and rattle the silver that was set for breakfast next morning.

Steward James Johnson felt he knew just what it was. He recognized the kind of shudder a ship gives when she drops a propeller blade, and he knew this sort of mishap meant a trip back to the Harland & Wolff Shipyard at Belfast – with plenty of free time to enjoy the hospitality of the port. Somebody near him agreed and sang out cheerfully, 'Another Belfast trip!'

In the galley just to the stern, Chief Night Baker Walter Belford was making rolls for the following day. (The honour of baking fancy pastry was reserved for the day shift.) When the jolt came, it impressed Belford more strongly than Steward Johnson – perhaps because a pan of new rolls clattered off the top of the oven and scattered about the floor.

The passengers in their cabins felt the jar too, and tried to connect it with something familiar. Marguerite Frolicher, a young Swiss girl accompanying her father on a business trip, woke up with a start. Half-asleep, she could think only of the little white lake ferries at Zurich making a sloppy landing. Softly she said to herself, 'Isn't it funny . . . we're landing!'

Major Arthur Godfrey Peuchen, starting to undress for the night, thought it was like a heavy wave striking the ship. Mrs J. Stuart White was sitting on the edge of her bed, just reaching to turn out the light, when the ship seemed to roll over 'a thousand marbles'. To Lady Cosmo Duff Gordon, waking up from the jolt, it seemed 'as though somebody had drawn a giant finger along the side of the ship'. Mrs John Jacob Astor thought it was some mishap in the kitchen.

It seemed stronger to some than to others. Mrs Albert Caldwell pictured a large dog that had a baby kitten in its mouth and was shaking it. Mrs Walter B. Stephenson recalled the first ominous jolt when she was in the San Francisco earthquake – then decided this wasn't that bad. Mrs E. D. Appleton felt hardly any shock at all, but she noticed an unpleasant ripping sound . . . like someone tearing a long, long strip of calico.

The jar meant more to J. Bruce Ismay, Managing Director of the White Star Line, who in a festive mood was going along for the ride on the *Titanic*'s first trip. Ismay woke up with a start in his de luxe suite on B deck – he felt sure the ship had struck something, but he didn't know what.

Some of the passengers already knew the answer. Mr and Mrs George A. Harder, a young honeymoon couple down in cabin E-50, were still awake when they heard a dull thump. Then they felt the ship quiver, and there was 'a sort of rumbling, scraping noise' along the ship's side. Mr Harder hopped out of bed and ran to the porthole. As he looked through the glass, he saw a wall of ice glide by.

The same thing happened to James B. McGough, a Gimbels buyer from Philadelphia, except his experience was somewhat more disturbing. His porthole was open, and as the berg brushed by, chunks of ice fell into the cabin.

Like Mr McGough, most of the *Titanic*'s passengers were in bed when the jar came. On this quiet, cold Sunday night a snug bunk seemed about the best place to be. But a few shipboard die-hards were still up. As usual, most were in the first-class smoking room on A deck.

And as usual, it was a very mixed group. Around one table sat Archie Butt, President Taft's military aide; Clarence Moore, the travelling Master of Hounds; Harry Widener, son of the Philadelphia streetcar magnate; and William Carter, another Main Liner. They were winding up a small dinner given by Widener's father in honour of Captain Edward J. Smith, the ship's commander. The Captain had left early, the ladies had been packed off to bed, and now the men were enjoying a final cigar before turning in too. The conversation wandered from politics to Clarence Moore's adventures in West Virginia, the time he helped interview the old feuding mountaineer Anse Hatfield.

Buried in a nearby leather armchair, Spencer V. Silverthorne, a young buyer for Nugent's department store in St Louis, browsed through a new best-seller, *The Virginian*. Not far off, Lucien P. Smith (still another Philadelphian) struggled gamely through the linguistic problems of a bridge game with three Frenchmen.

At another table the ship's young set was enjoying a somewhat noisier game of bridge. Normally the young set preferred the livelier Café Parisien, just below on B deck, and at first tonight was no exception. But it grew so cold that around 11.30 the girls went off to bed, and the men strolled up to the smoking room for a nightcap. Most of the group stuck to highballs; Hugh Woolner, son of the English sculptor, took a hot whisky and water; Lieutenant Hokan Bjornstrom Steffanson, a young Swedish military attaché on his way to Washington, chose a hot lemonade.

Somebody produced a deck of cards, and as they sat playing and laughing, suddenly there came that grinding jar. Not much of a shock, but enough to give a man a start – Mr Silverthorne still sits up with a jolt when he tells it. In an instant the smoking-room steward and Mr

Silverthorne were on their feet . . . through the aft door . . . past the palm court . . . and out on to the deck. They were just in time to see the iceberg scraping along the starboard side, a little higher than the boat deck. As it slid by, they watched chunks of ice breaking and tumbling off into the water. In another moment it faded into the darkness astern.

Others in the smoking room were pouring out now. As Hugh Woolner reached the deck, he heard a man call out, 'We hit an iceberg – there it is!'

Woolner squinted into the night. About 150 yards astern he made out a mountain of ice standing black against the starlit sky. Then it vanished into the dark.

The excitement, too, soon disappeared. The *Titanic* seemed as solid as ever, and it was too bitterly cold to stay outside any longer. Slowly the group filed back, Woolner picked up his hand, and the bridge game went on. The last man inside thought, as he slammed the deck door, that the engines were stopping.

He was right. Up on the bridge First Officer William M. Murdoch had just pulled the engine-room telegraph handle all the way to 'Stop'. Murdoch was in charge of the bridge this watch, and it was his problem, once Fleet phoned the warning. A tense minute had passed since then – orders to Quartermaster Hitchens to turn the wheel hard a-starboard . . . a yank on the engine-room telegraph for 'Full-Speed Astern' . . . a hard push on the button closing the watertight doors . . . and finally those thirty-seven seconds of breathless waiting.

Now the waiting was over, and it was all so clearly too late. As the grinding noise died away, Captain Smith rushed on to the bridge from his cabin next to the wheelhouse. There were a few quick words:

'Mr Murdoch, what was that?'

'An iceberg, sir. I hard-a-starboarded and reversed the engines, and I was going to hard-a-port around it, but she was too close. I couldn't do any more.'

'Close the emergency doors.'

'The doors are already closed.'

They were closed, all right. Down in boiler room No. 6, Fireman Fred Barrett had been talking to Assistant Second Engineer James Hesketh when the warning bell sounded and the light flashed red above the watertight door leading to the stern. A quick shout of warning – an ear-splitting crash – and the whole starboard side of the ship seemed to give way. The sea cascaded in, swirling about the pipes and valves, and the two men leaped through the door as it slammed down behind them.

Barrett found things almost as bad where he was now, in boiler room No. 5. The gash ran into No. 5 about two feet beyond the closed compartment door, and a fat jet of sea water was spouting through the hole. Nearby, Trimmer George Cavell was digging himself out of an avalanche of coal that had poured out of a bunker with the impact. Another stoker mournfully studied an overturned bowl of soup that had been warming on a piece of machinery.

It was dry in the other boiler rooms farther aft, but the scene was pretty much the same – men picking themselves up, calling back and forth, asking what had happened. It was hard to figure out. Until now the *Titanic* had been a picnic. Being a new ship on her maiden voyage, everything was clean. She was, as Fireman George Kemish still recalls, 'a good job . . . not what we were accustomed to in old ships, slogging our guts out and nearly roasted by the heat'.

All the firemen had to do was keep the furnaces full. No need to work the fires with slice bars, pricker bars and rakes. So on this Sunday night the men were taking it easy – sitting around on buckets and the trimmers' iron wheelbarrows, shooting the breeze, waiting for the 12-to-4 watch to come on.

Then came that thud . . . the grinding, tearing sound . . . the telegraphs ringing wildly . . . the watertight doors crashing down. Most of the men couldn't imagine what it was – the story spread that the *Titanic* had gone aground just off the Banks of Newfoundland. Many of them still thought so, even after a trimmer came running down from above shouting, 'Blimey! We've struck an iceberg!'

In this account, Thomas Andrews explains 'quietly', Charles Hays replies 'placidly': the postponement of panic on board Titanic *was remarkable, in part professional response, in part official policy of withholding bad news from passengers, in part English coolness under fire.*

WALTER LORD
The Last Good News

(A *Night to Remember*)

The fifth watertight compartment from the bow contained boiler room No. 6. This was where Fireman Barrett and Assistant Second Engineer Hesketh jumped through the watertight door just as it slammed down after the collision. Others didn't make it and scrambled up the escape ladders that laced their way topside. A few hung on, and after a moment some of the others came down again.

Shouts of 'Shut the dampers!' and then 'Draw the fires!' came from somewhere. Fireman George Beauchamp worked at fever pitch as the sea flooded in from the bunker door and up through the floor plates. In five minutes it was waist deep – black and slick with grease from the machinery. The air was heavy with steam. Fireman Beauchamp never did see who shouted the welcome words, 'That will do!' He was too relieved to care as he scurried up the ladder for the last time.

Just to the stern, Assistant Second Engineer Hesketh, now on the dry side of the watertight door, struggled to get boiler room No. 5 back to normal. The sea still spouted through a two-foot gash near the closed door, but Assistant Engineers Harvey and Wilson had a pump going, and it was keeping ahead of the water.

For a few moments the stokers stood by, aimlessly watching the engineers rig the pumps; then the engine room phoned to send them to the boat deck. They trooped up the escape ladder, but the bridge ordered them down again, and for a while they milled around the working alleyway on E deck – halfway up, halfway down – caught in the bureaucracy of a huge ship and wondering what to do next.

Meanwhile the lights went out in boiler room No. 5. Engineer Harvey ordered Fireman Barrett, who had stayed behind, to go aft to the engine room for lanterns. The connecting doors were all shut; so Barrett had to climb to the top of the escape ladder, cross over, and go down the other side. By the time he retraced his steps, the engineers had the lights on again and the lanterns weren't needed.

Next, Harvey told Barrett to shut down the boilers – the pressure, built up while the ship was at full steam, now lifted the safety valves and was blowing joints. Barrett scrambled back up the ladder and drafted 15 or 20 of the stokers wandering around E deck. They all clattered down and began wetting the fires. It was back-breaking work, boxing up the boilers and putting on dampers to stop the steam from rising. Fireman Kemish still remembers it with feeling: 'We certainly had one hell of a time putting those fires out . . .'

Clouds of steam gushed through the boiler room as the men sweated away. But gradually order returned. The lights burned bright, the place was clear of water, and, in No. 5 at any rate, everything seemed under control. There was an air of cheerful confidence by the time word spread that the men on the 12-to-4 watch were dragging their beds to the recreation deck because their rooms were flooded. The men on the 8-to-12 watch paused in their work, thought this was a huge joke and had a good laugh.

Up on the bridge, Captain Smith tried to piece the picture together. No one was better equipped to do it. After thirty-eight years' service with White Star, he was more than just senior captain of the line; he was a bearded patriarch, worshipped by crew and passengers alike. They loved everything about him – especially his wonderful combination of firmness and urbanity. It was strikingly evident in the matter of cigars. 'Cigars,' says his daughter, 'were his pleasure. And one was allowed to be in the room only if one was absolutely still, so that the blue cloud over his head never moved.'

Captain Smith was a natural leader, and on reaching the wheelhouse after the crash, he paused only long enough to visit the starboard wing of the bridge to see if the iceberg was still in sight. First Officer Murdoch and Fourth Officer Boxhall trailed along, and for a moment the three officers merely stood peering into the darkness. Boxhall thought he saw a dark shape far astern, but he wasn't sure.

From then on all was business. Captain Smith sent Boxhall on a fast inspection of the ship. In a few minutes he was back: he had been as far forward in the steerage as he could go, and there was no sign of damage. This was the last good news Captain Smith heard that night.

Still worried, Smith now told Boxhall, 'Go down and find the carpenter and get him to sound the ship.' Boxhall wasn't even down the bridge ladder when he bumped into Carpenter J. Hutchinson rushing up. As Hutchinson elbowed his way by, he gasped, 'She's making water fast!'

Hard on the carpenter's heels came mail clerk Iago Smith. He too pushed on toward the bridge, blurting as he passed, 'The mail hold is filling rapidly!'

Next to arrive was Bruce Ismay. He had pulled a suit over his pyjamas, put on his carpet slippers, and climbed to the bridge to find whether anything was happening that the President of the line should know. Captain Smith broke the news about the iceberg. Ismay then asked, 'Do you think the ship is seriously damaged?' A pause, and the Captain slowly answered, 'I'm afraid she is.'

They would know soon enough. A call had been sent for Thomas Andrews, Managing Director of Harland & Wolff Shipyard. As the *Titanic*'s builder, Andrews was making the maiden voyage to iron out any kinks in the ship. If anybody could figure out the situation, here was the man.

He was indeed a remarkable figure. As builder, he of course knew every detail about the *Titanic*. But there was so much more to him than that. Nothing was too great or too small for his attention. He even seemed able to anticipate how the ship would react to any situation. He understood ships the way some men are supposed to understand horses.

And he understood equally well the people who run ships. They all came to Andrews with their problems. One night it might be First Officer Murdoch, worried because he had been superseded by Chief Officer Wilde. The next night it might be a couple of quarrelling stewardesses who looked to Andrews as a sort of Supreme Court. This very evening Chief Baker Charles Joughin made him a special loaf of bread.

So far, Andrews's trip had been what might be expected. All day long he roamed the ship, taking volumes of notes. At 6.45 every evening he dressed for dinner, dining usually with old Dr O'Loughlin, the ship's surgeon, who also had a way with the stewardesses. And then back to his stateroom A-36, piled high with plans and charts and blueprints. There he would assemble his notes and work out his recommendations.

Tonight the problems were typical – trouble with the restaurant galley hot press . . . the colouring of the pebble dashing on the private promenade decks was too dark . . . too many screws on all the stateroom hat hooks. There was also the plan to change part of the writing room into two more staterooms. The writing room had originally been planned partly as a place where the ladies could retire after dinner. But this was the twentieth century, and the ladies just wouldn't retire. Clearly, a smaller room would do.

Completely absorbed, Andrews scarcely noticed the jar and stirred from his blueprints only when he got Captain Smith's message that he was needed on the bridge.

In a few minutes Andrews and the Captain were making their own tour – down the crew's stairway to attract less attention . . . along the labyrinth of corridors far below . . . by the water surging into the mail room . . . past the squash court, where the sea now lapped against the foul line on the backboard.

Threading their way back to the bridge, they passed through the A deck foyer, still thronged with passengers standing around. Everybody studied the two men's faces for some sign of good news or bad; nobody could detect any clue . . .

Far above on A deck, second-class passenger Lawrence Beesley noticed a curious thing. As he started below to check his cabin, he felt certain the stairs 'weren't quite right'. They seemed level, and yet his feet didn't fall where they should. Somehow they strayed forward off balance . . . as though the steps were tilted down toward the bow.

Major Peuchen noticed it too. As he stood with Mr Hays at the forward end of A deck, looking down at the steerage passengers playing soccer with the loose ice, he sensed a very slight tilt in the deck. 'Why, she is listing!' he cried to Hays. 'She should not do that! The water is perfectly calm and the boat has stopped.'

'Oh, I don't know,' Mr Hays replied placidly, 'you cannot sink this boat.'

Others also felt the downward slant, but it seemed tactless to mention the matter. In boiler room No. 5, Fireman Barrett decided to say nothing to the engineers working on the pumps. Far above in the A deck foyer, Colonel Gracie and Clinch Smith had the same reaction. On the bridge the commutator showed the *Titanic* slightly down at the head and listing 5 degrees to starboard.

Nearby, Andrews and Captain Smith did some fast figuring. Water in the forepeak . . . No. 1 hold . . . No. 2 hold . . . mail room . . . boiler room No. 6 . . . boiler room No. 5. Water 14 feet above keel level in the first ten minutes, everywhere except boiler room No. 5. Put together, the facts showed a 300-foot gash, with the first five compartments hopelessly flooded.

What did this mean? Andrews quietly explained. The *Titanic* could float with any two of her 16 watertight compartments flooded. She could float with any three of her first five compartments flooded. She could even float with all of her first four compartments gone. But no matter how they sliced it, she could not float with all of her first five compartments full.

The bulkhead between the fifth and sixth compartments went only as high as E deck. If the first five compartments were flooded, the bow would sink so low that water in the fifth compartment must overflow into the sixth. When this was full, it would overflow into the seventh, and so on. It was a mathematical certainty, pure and simple. There was no way out.

But it was still a shock. After all, the *Titanic* was considered unsinkable. And not just in the travel brochures. The highly technical magazine *Shipbuilder* described her compartment system in a special edition in 1911, pointing out, 'The Captain may, by simply moving an electric switch, instantly close the doors throughout and make the vessel practically unsinkable.'

Now all the switches were pulled, and Andrews said it made no difference.

It was hard to face, and especially hard for Captain Smith. Over fifty-nine years old, he was retiring after this trip. Might even have done it sooner, but he traditionally took the White Star ships on their maiden voyages. Only six years before, when he brought over the brand-new *Adriatic*, he remarked:

'I cannot imagine any condition which would cause a ship to founder. I cannot conceive of any vital disaster happening to this vessel. Modern shipbuilding has gone beyond that.'

Now he stood on the bridge of a liner twice as big – twice as safe – and the builder told him it couldn't float.

At 12.05 a.m. – 25 minutes after that bumping, grinding jar – Captain Smith ordered Chief Officer Wilde to uncover the boats . . . First Officer Murdoch to muster the passengers . . . Sixth Officer Moody to get out the list of boat assignments . . . Fourth Officer Boxhall to wake up Second Officer Lightoller and Third Officer Pitman. The Captain himself then walked about 20 yards down the port side of the boat deck to the wireless shack.

Inside, First Operator John George Phillips and Second Operator Harold Bride showed no sign that they realized what was happening. It had been a tough day. In 1912 wireless was still an erratic novelty; range was short, operators were inexperienced, and signals were hard to catch. There was a lot of relaying, a lot of repeats and a lot of frivolous private traffic. Passengers were fascinated by the new miracle, couldn't resist the temptation of sending messages to friends back home or on other ships.

All this Sunday the messages had piled up. It was enough to fray the nerves of any man working a 14-hour day at 30 dollars a month, and Phillips was no exception. Evening came, and still the bottomless in-basket, still the petty interferences. Only an hour ago – just when he was at last in good contact with Cape Race – the *Californian* barged in with some message about icebergs. She was so close she almost blew his ears off. No wonder he snapped back, 'Shut up, shut up! I am busy; I am working Cape Race!'

It was such a hard day that Second Operator Bride decided to relieve Phillips at midnight, even though he wasn't due until 2.00 a.m. He woke up about 11.55, brushed by the green curtain separating the sleeping quarters from the 'office', and asked Phillips how he was getting along. Phillips said he had just finished the Cape Race traffic. Bride padded back to his berth and took off his pyjamas. Phillips called after him that he thought the ship had been damaged somehow and they'd have to go back to Belfast.

In a couple of minutes Bride was dressed and took over the head-phones. Phillips was hardly behind the green curtain when Captain Smith appeared: 'We've struck an iceberg and I'm having an inspection made to see what it has done to us. You better get ready to send out a call for assistance, but don't send it until I tell you.'

Then he left but returned again in a few minutes. This time he merely stuck his head in the doorway:

'Send the call for assistance.'

The double exposure in this Fr Browne photograph of Harold Bride in the Marconi room of *Titanic* (the only known photograph of the famous room) lends a fitting ghostly presence.

Come Quick – Danger

(Wireless messages)

Titanic *Time*
Monday April 15
12.15 a.m. *CQD CQD CQD CQD CQD CQD MGY Have
struck an iceberg. We are badly damaged. Titanic
Position 41°44' N, 50°24' W.*

[*La Provence*, French ship, receives signal; *Mount
Temple*, Canadian, replies, cannot be heard. Marconi
Wireless Station at Cape Race, Newfoundland, hears
CQD, calculates location 380 miles SSE of Cape Race.]

12.18 a.m. *CQD Position 41°44' N, 50°24' W. Require assistance
MGY.*   [Repeated about 10 times; received by
Ypiranga, Japanese.]
    [*Titanic* switches to combined SOS CQD call. DFT
(*Frankfurt*), German, first to respond audibly.]
    Titanic to DFT: *Come at once MGY.*
    Stand by DFT   [*Frankfurt* 172 miles from
Titanic.]

12.25 a.m. MPA (*Carpathia*), British Cunarder, to *Titanic*: *GMOM
(Good morning old man). Do you know that there are
despatches for you at Cape Cod?* . . .
    MGY to MPA, interrupting: *CQD CQD SOS SOS
CQD SOS Come at once. We have struck a berg. It's a
CQD OM. Position 41°46' N, 50°14' W. CQD SOS
MGY*
    Shall I tell my captain? Do you require assistance?
MPA.
    Yes. Come quick. MGY.

[Cape Race, hearing corrected position – location 5 or 6
miles different – replies, no answer.]

12.26 a.m.   *MGY CQD Position 41°46' N, 50° W. Require*
immediate assistance. We have collided with iceberg.
Sinking. Can hear nothing for noise of steam.   [Picked
up by *Ypiranga* 15 to 20 times.]

12.30 a.m.   *Titanic to DFT (Frankfurt): Position 41°46' N, 50°14' W*
Tell your Captain to come to our help. We are on the ice
MGY.
　What is the matter with you? DFT
　We have collision with iceberg. Sinking. Please tell
Captain to come MGY.
　OK Will tell DFT

　Caronia, Cunarder, to *Baltic,* White Star: *MGY struck*
iceberg, require immediate assistance.   [*Caronia,* 700
miles from *Titanic,* contented herself with distributing
information.]

　Mount Temple to Titanic: Our Captain reverses ship.
We are about fifty miles off.

12.36 a.m.   [*Prinz Friedrich Wilhelm,* German, replies and gives her
position.]

12.45 a.m.   *Carpathia to Titanic: We are coming as quickly as*
possible and expect to be there within four hours MPA.
　TUOM (Thank you, old man) MGY

　[*Titanic* sends SOS to sister ship *Olympic.*]

　[SOS call from MGY intercepted by *Birma* (SBA),
Russian, which requests more information; MGY
replies:]

　CQD SOS from MGY. We have struck iceberg
sinking fast come to our assistance. Position Lat.
41°46' N., Lon. 50°14' W. MGY.   [*Birma,* 100 miles
SW, estimates will reach *Titanic* at 6.30 a.m.]

12.50 a.m.   *C Q D I require immediate assistance. Position 41°46' N, 50°14' W M G Y.*   [Received by *Celtic*.]

12.53 a.m.   *Caronia to Baltic: M G Y C Q D in 41°46' N, 50°14' W. Wants immediate assistance.*

1.00 a.m.   *Olympic to Titanic* (having picked up her distress calls): *What's up old man? M K C.*

           We have struck an iceberg 41°46' N, 50°14' W M G Y.

1.02 a.m.   *Titanic to Asian: C Q D Want immediate assistance M G Y.*   [*Asian*, en route to Halifax towing disabled German oil tanker *Deutschland*, replies at once and receives *Titanic*'s position; *Asian* Captain wants operator to confirm *Titanic*'s position.]

           [*Virginian*, Canadian, calls *Titanic* but gets no reply; Cape Race tells *Virginian* to report to his Master M G Y has struck iceberg and requires immediate assistance.]

1.10 a.m.   *Titanic to Olympic: We are in collision with berg. Sinking Head down. 41°46' N, 50°14' W. Come as soon as possible M G Y.*
           [Again]: *Captain says get your boats ready. What is your position? M G Y*

1.15 a.m.   *Baltic to Caronia: Please tell Titanic we are making towards her M B C.*

1.20 a.m.   Cape Race to *Virginian: Titanic struck iceberg, wants immediate assistance, her position 41°46' N and 50°14' W M C E.*
           Virginian to Cape Race: *Inform M G Y that we are going to his assistance. Our position 170 miles N. of 'Titanic'.*   [*Virginian* hears Cape Race relay message.]

1.25 a.m.   *Caronia to Titanic: Baltic coming to your assistance.*

Commander, Titanic. [Answering request for position:]
*40°52' N, 61°18' W. Are you steering southerly to meet
us?* Haddock. [Captain, *Olympic*]
   Tell Captain we are putting women off in the boats
MGY.

1.35 a.m.   [*Baltic* hears *Titanic* say *Engine room getting flooded*]

   [*Olympic* to *Titanic:*] *What weather have you had?*
MKC.
   Clear and calm MGY.

   Frankfurt to *Titanic* [heard by *Mount Temple*]: *Are
there any boats around you already?* DFT.
   You fool, stand by and keep out MGY.

1.37 a.m.   *Baltic* to *Titanic: We are rushing to you MBC.*

1.40 a.m.   *Commander, Titanic. Am lighting up all possible boilers
as fast as can. Haddock.*

   Cape Race to *Virginian: Please tell your Captain this:
the Olympic is making all speed for Titanic but his
position is 40°32' N, 61°18' W. You are much nearer to
Titanic. The Titanic is already putting women off in the
boats, and he says the weather there is calm and clear.
The Olympic is the only ship we have heard say, 'Going
to the assistance of the Titanic. The others must be a long
way from the Titanic.'*

   *SOS SOS CQD CQD MGY We are sinking fast
passengers being put into boats MGY.*   [Received by
Birma.]

1.45 a.m.   *Titanic* to *Carpathia: Come as quickly as possible. Engine
room filling up to the boilers. TU OM GN (thank you
old man good night).*   [Last message from *Titanic* to
Carpathia.]

[*Mount Temple* hears *Frankfurt* calling M G Y. No reply.]

1.48 a.m.   [*Asian* hears *Titanic* S O S, answers but receives no reply.]

1.50 a.m.   [*Caronia* hears *Frankfurt* working *Titanic* to no avail.]

1.55 a.m.   Cape Race to *Virginian*: *We have not heard Titanic for about half an hour. His power may be gone M C E.*

2.00 a.m.   [*Virginian* hears *Titanic* call faintly.]

2.17 a.m.   [*Virginian* hears *Titanic* call C Q D, then signals end abruptly. Calls *Titanic* but no response.]

3.15 a.m.   *Mount Temple* hears *Carpathia* message *Titanic*: *If you are there we are firing rockets M P A.*

3.30 a.m.   [*Carpathia* calling *Titanic*.]

3.48 a.m.   *Birma* believes she hears *Titanic* and calls: *Steaming full speed for you. Shall arrive you 6.00 in morning. Hope you are safe. We are only 50 miles now S B A.*

[R M S *Titanic* foundered at 2.20 a.m.]

Young gave credence to the story of Captain Smith's saving of one baby while a stoker (who told the story) saved another. In another version of events, retailed by the New York Times *of 19 April, Captain Smith saved first a woman and then a baby but refused to be saved himself. In other versions, Captain Smith shot himself or was washed overboard when the ocean overwhelmed the forward superstructure.*

FILSON YOUNG
The End

(*Titanic,* 1912)

The end, when it came, was as gradual as everything else had been since the first impact. Just as there was no one moment at which everyone in the ship realized that she had suffered damage; just as there was no one moment when the whole of her company realized that they must leave her; just as there was no one moment when all in the ship understood that their lives were in peril, and no moment when they all knew she must sink; so there was no one moment at which all those left on board could have said, 'She is gone.' At one moment the floor of the bridge, where the Captain stood, was awash; the next a wave came along and covered it with four feet of water, in which the Captain was for a moment washed away, although he struggled back and stood there again, up to his knees in water. 'Boys, you can do no more,' he shouted, 'look out for yourselves!' Standing near him was a fireman and – strange juxtaposition – two unclaimed solitary little children, scarce more than babies. The fireman seized one in his arms, the Captain another; another wave came and they were afloat in deep water, striking out over the rail of the bridge away from the ship.

The slope of the deck increased, and the sea came washing up against it as waves wash against a steep shore. And then that helpless mass of humanity was stricken at last with the fear of death, and began to scramble madly aft, away from the chasm of water that kept creeping up and up the decks. Then a strange thing happened. They who had been waiting to sink into the sea found themselves rising into the air as the slope of the decks grew steeper. Up and up, dizzily high out of reach of the dark waters into which they had dreaded to be plunged, higher and higher into the air, towards the stars, the stern of the ship rose slowly right out of the water, and hung there for a time that is estimated variously between two and five minutes; a terrible eternity to those who were still clinging. Many, thinking the end had come, jumped; the water resounded with splash after splash as the bodies, like mice shaken out of a trap into a bucket, dropped into the water. All who could do so laid hold of something; ropes, stanchions, deck-houses, mahogany doors, window frames, anything, and so clung on while the stern of the giant ship reared itself towards the sky. Many had no hold, or lost the hold they had, and these slid down the steep smooth decks, as people slide down a water chute into the sea.

We dare not linger here, even in imagination; dare not speculate; dare not look closely, even with the mind's eye, at this poor human agony, this last pitiful scramble for dear life that the serene stars shone down upon. We must either turn our faces away, or withdraw to that surrounding circle where the boats were hovering with their terror-stricken burdens, and see what they saw. They saw the after part of the ship, blazing with light, stand up, a suspended prodigy, between the stars and the waters; they saw the black atoms, each one of which they knew to be a living man or woman on fire with agony, sliding down like shot rubbish into the sea; they saw the giant decks bend and crack; they heard a hollow and tremendous rumbling as the great engines tore themselves from their steel beds and crashed through the ship; they saw sparks streaming in a golden rain from one of the funnels; heard the dull boom of an explosion while the spouting funnel fell over into the sea with a slap that killed every one beneath it and set the nearest boat rocking; heard two more dull bursting reports as the steel bulkheads gave way or decks blew up; saw the lights flicker out, flicker back again and then go out for ever, and the ship, like some giant sea creature forsaking the strife of the upper elements for the peace of the submarine depths, launched herself with one slow plunge and dive beneath the waves.

There was no great maelstrom as they had feared, but the sea was swelling and sinking all about them; and they could see waves and eddies where rose the imprisoned air, the smoke and steam of vomited-up ashes and a bobbing commotion of small dark things where the *Titanic*, in her pride and her shame, with the clocks ticking and the fires burning in her luxurious rooms, had plunged down to the icy depths of death.

Marine Disasters from *City of Rio de Janeiro* to *Titanic*

1901, Feb. 22. – *City of Rio de Janeiro*, Pacific Mail Steamship Company, sunk at entrance to San Francisco Bay; 122 lives lost.

1904, June 15. – *General Slocum*, excursion steamboat with 1,400 persons aboard; took fire going through Hells Gate, East River; more than 1,000 lives lost.

1905, Sept. 12. – Japanese warship *Mikasa* sunk after explosion in Sasebo Harbour; 599 lives lost.

1906, Jan. 21. *Aquidaban*, Brazilian battleship, sunk near Rio de Janeiro by an explosion of the powder magazine; 212 lives lost.

1906, Jan. 22. – *Valencia*, steamship, Cape Beale, Vancouver Island, B.C.; 117 lives lost.

1906 – *Sirlo*, Italian emigrant ship, struck a rock off Cape Palos; 350 lives lost.

1907, Jan. – British steamship *Pengwern* foundered in the North Sea; crew and 24 men lost.

1907, Feb. 12. – Steamship *Larchmont* in collision with *Harry Hamilton* in Long Island Sound; 183 lives lost.

1907, Feb. 21. – English mail steamship *Berlin* wrecked off the Hook of Holland; 142 lives lost.

1907, Feb. 24. – Austrian Lloyd steamship *Imperatrix*, from Trieste to Bombay, wrecked on Cape of Crete and sunk; 137 lives lost.

1907, March – French warship *Jena* blown up at Toulon; 120 lives lost.

1907, July – Steamship *Columbia*, sunk off Shelton Cove, California, in collision with steamship *San Pedro*; 50 lives lost.

1908, Feb. 3. – Steamship *St Cuthbert*, bound from Antwerp to New York, burned at sea off Nova Scotia; 15 lives lost.

1908, March 23. – *Kutsu Maru*, Japanese steamer, sunk in collision near Hakodate; 300 lives lost.

1908, April 25. – British cruiser *Gladiator* rammed by American liner *St Paul* off Isle of Wight; 30 lives lost.

1908, April 30. – *Matsu Shima*, sunk off the Pescadores owing to an explosion; 200 lives lost.

1908, July – Chinese warship *Ying King* foundered; 300 lives lost.

1908, Aug. 24. – Steamship *Folgenenden* wrecked; 70 persons lost.

1908, Nov. 6. – Steamship *Taish* sunk in storm off Etoro Island; 150 lives lost.

1909, Aug. 1. – *Waratah*, British steamer, from Sydney via Port Natal for London, last heard from leaving Port Natal on July 26; 300 lives lost.

1910 – *General Chanzy*, French steamer, wrecked off Minorca; 200 lives lost.

1911, Feb. 2. – Steamship *Abenton* wrecked; 70 lives lost.

1911, April 2. – Steamship *Koombuna* wrecked; 150 lives lost.

1911, April 23. – Steamship *Asia* ran aground; 40 lives lost.

1911, Sept. 5. – Steamship *Tuscapel* wrecked; 81 lives lost.

1911, Sept. 25. – *Liberté*, French battleship, sunk by explosion in Toulon Harbour; 233 lives lost.

1911, Oct. 2. – Steamship *Hatfield* in collision and sunk; 207 lives lost.

Elizabeth Shutes was a governess who embarked at Cherbourg with her charge who was travelling first cabin with her mother; she was saved in boat no. 3. Shutes's exclamation, 'the horror, the helpless horror', echoes Joseph Conrad's Kurtz in Heart of Darkness (1902) as Charlotte Collyer's 'terrible beauty' (see below) anticipates W. B. Yeats's famous use of the phrase in 'Easter 1916'.

ELIZABETH W. SHUTES
The Blackest Night

(Colonel Archibald Gracie, *The Truth about the* Titanic, 1913)

Such a biting cold air poured into my stateroom that I could not sleep, and the air had so strange an odour, as if it came from a clammy cave. I had noticed that same odour in the ice cave on the Eiger glacier. It all came back to me so vividly that I could not sleep, but lay in my berth until the cabin grew so very cold that I got up and turned on my electric stove. It threw a cheerful red glow around, and the room was soon comfortable; but I lay waiting. I have always loved both day and night on shipboard, and am never fearful of anything, but now I was nervous about the icy air.

Suddenly a queer quivering ran under me, apparently the whole length of the ship. Startled by the very strangeness of the shivering motion, I sprang to the floor. With too perfect a trust in that mighty vessel I again lay down. Some one knocked at my door, and the voice of a friend said: 'Come quickly to my cabin; an iceberg has just passed our window; I know we have just struck one.'

No confusion, no noise of any kind, one could believe no danger imminent. Our stewardess came and said she could learn nothing. Looking out into the companionway I saw heads appearing asking questions from half-closed doors. All sepulchrally still, no excitement. I sat down again. My friend was by this time dressed; still her daughter and I talked on, Margaret pretending to eat a sandwich. Her hand shook so that the bread kept parting company from the chicken. Then I saw she was frightened, and for the first time I was too, but why get dressed, as no one had given the slightest hint of any possible danger? An officer's cap passed the door. I asked: 'Is there an accident or danger of any kind?' 'None, so far as I know,' was his courteous answer, spoken quietly and most kindly. This same officer then entered a cabin a little distance down the companionway and, by this time distrustful of everything, I listened intently, and distinctly heard, 'We can keep the water out for a while.' Then, and not until then, did I realize the horror of an accident at sea. Now it was too late to dress; no time for a waist, but a coat and skirt were soon on; slippers were quicker than shoes; the stewardess put on our life-preservers, and we were just ready when Mr [Washington Augustus H.] Roebling came to tell us he would take us to our friend's mother, who was waiting above . . .

No laughing throng, but on either side [of the staircases] stand quietly, bravely, the stewards, all equipped with the white, ghostly life-preservers. Always the thing one tries not to see even crossing a ferry. Now only pale faces, each form strapped about with those white bars. So gruesome a scene. We passed on. The awful good-byes. The quiet look of hope in the brave men's eyes as the wives were put into the lifeboats. Nothing escaped one at this fearful moment. We left from the sun deck, seventy-five feet above the water. Mr [Howard] Case and Mr Roebling, brave American men, saw us to the lifeboat, made no effort to save themselves, but stepped back on deck. Later they went to an honoured grave.

Our lifeboat, with thirty-six in it, began lowering to the sea. This was done amid the greatest confusion. Rough seamen all giving different orders. No officer aboard. As only one side of the ropes worked, the lifeboat at one time was in such a position that it seemed we must capsize in mid-air. At last the ropes worked together, and we drew nearer and nearer the black, oily water. The first touch of our lifeboat on that black sea came to me as a last good-bye to life, and so we put off – a tiny boat on a great sea – rowed away from what had been a safe home for five days. The first wish on the part of all was to stay near the *Titanic*. We all felt so much safer near the ship. Surely such a vessel could not sink. I thought the danger must be exaggerated, and we could all be taken aboard again. But surely the outline of that great, good ship was growing less. The bow of the boat was getting black. Light after light was disappearing, and now those rough seamen put to their oars and we were told to hunt under seats, any place, anywhere, for a lantern, a light of any kind. Every place was empty. There was no water – no stimulant of any kind. Not a biscuit – nothing to keep us alive had we drifted long. Had no good *Carpathia*, with its splendid Captain Rostron, its orderly crew, come to our rescue we must have all perished. Our men knew nothing about the position of the stars, hardly how to pull together. Two oars were soon overboard. The men's hands were too cold to hold on. We stopped while they beat their hands and arms, then started on again. A sea, calm as a pond, kept our boat steady, and now that mammoth ship is fast, fast disappearing. Only one tiny light is left – a powerless little spark, a lantern fastened to the mast. Fascinated, I watched that black outline until the end. Then across the water swept that awful wail, the cry of those drowning people. In my ears I heard: 'She's gone, lads; row like hell or we'll get the devil of a swell.' And the horror, the helpless horror, the worst of all – need it have been? . . .

Sitting by me in the lifeboat were a mother and daughter (Mrs Hays and Mrs Davidson). The mother had left a husband on the *Titanic*, and the daughter a father and husband, and while we were near the other boats those two stricken women would call out a name and ask, 'Are you there?' 'No,' would come back the awful answer, but these brave women never lost courage, forgot their own sorrow, telling me to sit close to them to keep warm. Now I began to wish for the warm velvet suit I left hanging in my cabin. I had thought of it for a minute, and then had quickly thrown on a lighter weight skirt. I knew the heavier one would make the life-preserver less useful. Had I only known how calm the ocean was that night, I would have felt that death was not so sure, and would have dressed for life rather than for the end. The life-preservers helped to keep us warm, but the night was bitter cold, and it grew colder and colder, and just before dawn, the coldest, darkest hour of all, no help seemed possible. As we put off from the *Titanic* never was a sky more brilliant, never have I seen so many falling stars. All tended to make those distress rockets that were sent up from the sinking ship look so small, so dull and futile. The brilliancy of the sky only intensified the blackness of the water, our utter loneliness on the sea. The other boats had drifted away from us; we must wait now for dawn and what the day was to bring us we dare not even hope. To see if I could not make the night seem shorter, I tried to imagine myself again in Japan . . .

Two rough looking men had jumped into our boat as we were about to lower, and they kept striking matches, lighting cigars, until I feared we would have no matches left and might need them, so I asked them not to use any more, but they kept on. I do not know what they looked like. It was too dark to really distinguish features clearly, and when the dawn brought the light it brought something so wonderful with it no one looked at anything else or anyone else. Someone asked: 'What time is it?' Matches were still left; one was struck. Four o'clock! Where had the hours of the night gone? Yes, dawn would soon be here; and it came, so surely, so strong with cheer. The stars slowly disappeared, and in their place came the faint pink glow of another day. Then I heard, 'A light, a ship.' I could not, would not, look while there was a bit of doubt, but kept my eyes away. All night long I had heard, 'A light!' Each time it proved to be one of our other lifeboats, someone lighting a piece of paper, anything they could find to burn, and now I could not believe. Someone found a newspaper; it was lighted and held up. Then I looked and saw a ship. A ship bright with lights; strong and steady she waited, and we were to be saved. A straw hat was offered (Mrs Davidson's); it would burn longer. That same ship that had come to save us might run us down. But no; she is still. The two, the ship and the dawn, came together, a living painting. White was the vessel, but whiter still were those horribly beautiful icebergs, and as we drew nearer and nearer that good ship we drew nearer to those mountains of ice. As far as the eye could reach they rose. Each one more fantastically chiselled than its neighbour. The floe glistened like an ever-ending meadow covered with new-fallen snow. Those same white mountains, marvellous in their purity, had made of the just ended night one of the blackest the sea has ever known.

The author, who became the modest hero of the 1979 motion picture S O S Titanic, had been a Cambridge-educated science master in England. He writes with the precision of a scientist and the equipoise of the second-class passenger, devoid of 'swank', yet can achieve poetry on occasion. Like Archibald Gracie, he pondered the event and published a book, The Loss of the R.M.S. Titanic *(1912). In it he adds literary touches, remembering now that after* Titanic *had gone down he had considered the aptness of Lorenzo's description of the heavens in* The Merchant of Venice. *Gracie's use of Dante is rather similar.*

LAWRENCE BEESLEY
An Ideal Night

(*New York Times*, 19 April 1912)

One by one the boats were filled with women and children, lowered and rowed away into the night. Presently the word went round among the men, 'the men are to be put in boats on the starboard side'. I was on the port side and most of the men walked across the deck to see if this was so. I remained where I was and presently heard the call:

'Any more ladies?'

Looking over the side of the ship, I saw the boat, no. 13, swinging level with B deck, half full of ladies. Again the call was repeated:

'Any more ladies?'

I saw none come on, and then one of the crew looked up and said:

'Any ladies on your deck, Sir?'

'No,' I replied.

'Then you had better jump.'

I dropped and fell in the bottom as they cried, 'Lower away.' As the boat began to descend two ladies were pushed hurriedly through the crowd on B deck and heaved over into the boat, and a baby of 10 months was passed down after them. Then we went, the crew calling to those lowering which end to keep her level. 'Aft', 'Stern', 'Both together', until we were some ten feet from the water.

Here occurred the only anxious moment we had during the whole of our experience from leaving the deck to reaching the *Carpathia*. Immediately below our boat was the exhaust of the condensers, a huge stream of water pouring all the time from the ship's side just above the water line.

It was plain that we ought to be smart away from this not to be swamped by it when we touched water. We had no officer aboard, nor petty officer or member of the crew to take charge. So one of the stokers shouted: 'Some one find the pin which releases the boat from the ropes and pull it up.' No one knew where it was. We felt as well as we could on the floor and sides but found no pin, and it was hard to move among so many people – we had 60 or 70 on board.

Down we went and presently floated with our ropes still holding us, the exhaust washing us away from the vessel and the swell urging us back against the sides again. The result of all these forces was a force which carried us parallel to the ship's side and directly under boat 14 [*sic* – it was 15], which had filled rapidly with men and was coming down on us in a way that threatened to submerge our boat.

'Stop lowering 14,' our crew shouted, and the crew of 14, now only twenty feet above, shouted the same. But the distance to the top was some seventy feet, and the creaking pulleys must have deadened all sound to those above, for down she came – fifteen feet, ten feet, five feet, and a stoker and I reached up and touched her swinging above our heads, but just before she dropped another stoker sprang to the ropes with his knife.

'One,' I heard him say; 'two', as his knife cut through the pulley ropes, and the next moment the exhaust steam had carried us clear, while Boat 14 dropped into the water, into the space we had the moment before occupied, our gunwales almost touching.

We drifted away easily as the oars were got out, and headed directly away from the ship. The crew seemed to me to be mostly cooks in white jackets, two to an oar, with a stoker at the tiller. There was a certain amount of shouting from one end of the boat to the other and discussion as to which way we should go, but finally it was decided to elect the stoker, who was steering, Captain, and for all to obey his orders. He set to work at once to get into touch with the other boats, calling to them and getting as close as seemed wise; so that when the search boats came in the morning to look for us there would be more chance for all to be rescued by keeping together.

It was now 1 a.m., a beautiful starlight night, with no moon and not very light. The sea was as calm as a pond, just a gentle heave as the boat dipped up and down in the swell: an ideal night, except the bitter cold for any one who had to be out in the middle of the Atlantic Ocean in an open boat, and if ever there was a time when such a night was needed surely it was now, with hundreds of people, mostly women and children, afloat hundreds of miles from land . . .

The Captain-stoker told us that he had been at sea twenty-six years and had never yet seen such a calm night on the Atlantic. As we rolled away from the *Titanic* we looked from time to time back to watch her, and a more striking spectacle it was not possible for any one to see. Only a short time before dinner I remarked that when we arrived at New York I should take an opportunity to get a look at her from a distance to realize something of her dimensions.

We did not think our desire was so soon to be granted. In the distance she looked an enormous length, her great hulk outlined in black against the starry sky, every porthole and saloon blazing with light.

It was impossible to think anything could be wrong with such a leviathan were it not for that ominous tilt downward in the bow, where the water was by now up to the lowest row of portholes. We were now about two miles from her, and all the crew insisted that such a tremendous wave would be formed by suction as she went down that we ought to get as far as possible away. The Captain agreed, and all lay on their oars and widened the gap.

Presently, about 2 a.m., as near as I can remember, we observed her settling very rapidly, with the bows and the bridge completely under water, and concluded it was now only a question of minutes before she went; and so it proved. She slowly tilted straight on end, with the stern vertically upward, and as she did the lights in the cabins and saloons, which had not flickered for a moment since we left, died out, came on again for a single flash, and finally went altogether.

At the same time the machinery reared down through the vessel with a rattle and a groaning that could be heard for miles, the weirdest sound, surely, that could be heard in the middle of the ocean, a thousand miles away from land. But this was not quite the end.

To our amazement she remained in that upright position for a time which I estimate as five minutes. Others in the boat say less, but it was certainly some minutes while we watched at least fifteen [150] feet of the *Titanic* above the sea and looming black against the sky.

Then with a quiet slanting dive she disappeared beneath the waters, and our eyes had looked for the last time on the gigantic vessel we had set out on from Southampton Wednesday. And there was left to us the gently heaving sea, the boat filled to standing room with men and women in every conceivable condition of dress and undress, above the perfect sky of brilliant stars with not a cloud in the sky, all tempered with a bitter cold that made us all long to be one of the crew who toiled away with the oars and kept themselves warm thereby – a curious, deadening bitter cold unlike anything we had felt before.

And then with all these there fell on us the most appalling noises that human being ever listened to. The cries of our fellow-beings struggling in the icy-cold water, crying for help with a cry that we knew could not be answered. We longed to return and pick up some of those swimming, but this would have meant swamping our boat and further loss of lives of all of us.

We tried to sing to keep the women from hearing the cries and rowed hard to get away from the scene of the wreck, but I think the memory of those sounds will be one of the things the rescued will find it difficult to efface from memory. We are all trying hard not to think of it.

We kept a lookout for lights, and several times it was shouted that steamer lights were seen, but they turned out to be either a light from another boat or a star low down on the horizon. About 3 a.m. we saw faint lights showing on the sky, and all rejoiced to see what we expected was the coming dawn, but, after watching half an hour and seeing no change in the intensity of the light, realized it was the northern lights.

Presently low down on the horizon we saw a light, which slowly resolved itself into a double light, and we watched eagerly to see if the two lights would separate, and so prove to be only two of our boats, or whether they would remain together, in which case we should expect them to be the masthead light and deck light of a rescuing steamer.

To our joy they moved as one and we swung the boat and headed for her. The steersman shouted: 'Now, boys, sing,' and for the first time the boat broke into song with 'Row for the Shore, Boys', and for the first time tears came to the eyes of us all as we realized that safety was at hand. The song was sung, but it was a very poor imitation of the real thing, for quavering voices make poor songs. A cheer was given next, and that was better – you needn't keep time for a cheer.

Harvey Collyer, a grocer from Hampshire, had bought a fruit-farm in Idaho and was on his way to take possession of it, travelling in second cabin with his wife Charlotte and their daughter. He wrote a letter to his parents from Titanic:

CHARLOTTE COLLYER
Charlotte Collyer's Story

(*Titanic Voices*, 1994, and *Semi-Monthly Magazine*, 26 May 1912)

My dear Mum and Dad   *Titanic* April 11th
It don't seem possible we are out on the briny writing to you. Well dears so far we are having a delightful trip the weather is beautiful and the ship magnificent. We can't describe the tables it's like a floating town. I can tell you we do swank we shall miss it on the trains as we go third on them. You would not imagine you were on a ship. There is hardly any motion she is so large we have not felt sick yet we expect to get to Queenstown today so thought I would drop this with the mails. We had a fine send off from Southampton and Mrs S and the boys with others saw us off. We will post again at New York then when we get to Payette. Lots of love don't worry about us. Ever your loving children
                                        Harvey & Lot & Madge

Harvey was lost, but Charlotte and her daughter survived. She wrote to her in-laws from New York on 21 April with the bad news:

                                        Brooklyn, New York
                                        Sun April 21st
My dear Mother and all,
I don't know how to write to you or what to say, I feel I shall go mad sometimes but dear as much as my heart aches it aches for you too for he is your son and the best that ever lived. I had not given up hope till today that he might be found but I'm told all boats are accounted for. Oh mother how can I live without him. I wish I'd gone with him if they had not wrenched Madge from

me I should have stayed and gone with him. But they threw her into the boat and pulled me in too but he was so calm and I know he would rather I lived for her little sake otherwise she would have been an orphan. The agony of that night can never be told. Poor mite was frozen. I have been ill but have been taken care of by a rich New York doctor and feel better now. They are giving us every comfort and have collected quite a few pounds for us and loaded us with clothes and a gentleman on Monday is taking us to the White Star office and also to another office to get us some money from the funds that is being raised here. Oh mother there are some good kind hearts in New York, some want me to go back to England but I can't, I could never at least not yet go over the ground where my all is sleeping.

Sometimes I feel we lived too much for each other that is why I've lost him. But mother we shall meet him in heaven. When that band played 'Nearer My God to Thee' I know he thought of you and me for we both loved that hymn and I feel that if I go to Payette I'm doing what he would wish me to, so I hope to do this at the end of next week where I shall have friends and work and I will work for his darling as long as she needs me. Oh she is a comfort but she don't realize yet that her Daddy is in heaven. There are some dear children here who have loaded her with lovely toys but it's when I'm alone with her she will miss him. Oh mother I haven't a thing in the world that was his only his rings. Everything we had went down. Will you, dear mother, send me on a last photo of us, get it copied I will pay you later on. Mrs Hallets brother from Chicago is doing all he can for us in fact the night we landed in New York (in our nightgowns) he had engaged a room at a big hotel with food and every comfort waiting for us. He has been a father to us. I will send his address on a card (Mr Horder) perhaps you might like to write to him at some time.

God bless you dear mother and help and comfort you in this awful sorrow. Your loving child

Lot

The lack of punctuation, the mark of a feminine hand (as James Joyce would have known), not that of an illiterate hand, does not conceal insight and sensitivity, but it does suggest that the editor of Semi-Monthly Magazine *may have come close to ghost-writing Charlotte's fine published account.*

Suddenly there was a commotion near one of the gangways, and we saw a stoker come climbing up from below. He stopped a few feet away from us. All the fingers of one hand had been cut off. Blood was running from the stumps, and blood was spattered over his face and over his clothes. The red marks showed very clearly against the coal dust with which he was covered.

I started over and spoke to him. I asked him if there was any danger.

'Dynger!' he screamed, at the top of his voice. 'I should just sye so! It's 'ell down below. Look at me! This boat'll sink like a log in ten minutes.'

He staggered away, and lay down, fainting, with his head on a coil of rope. And at that moment I got my first grip of fear – awful, sickening fear. That poor man with his bleeding hand and his speckled face, brought up a picture of smashed engines and mangled human bodies. I hung on to my husband's arm, and although he was very brave and was not trembling, I saw that his face was as white as paper. We realized that the accident was much worse than we had supposed; but even then I, and all the others about me of whom I have any knowledge, *did not believe that the* Titanic *could go down.*

The officers, now, were running to and fro, and shouting orders. I have no clear idea of what happened during the next quarter of an hour. The time seemed much shorter; but it must have been between ten and fifteen minutes. I saw First Officer Murdock [*sic*] place guards by the gangways, to prevent others like the wounded stoker from coming on deck. How many unhappy men were shut off in that way from their one chance of safety I do not know; but Mr Murdock was probably right. He was a masterful man, astoundingly brave and cool. I had met him the day before, when he was inspecting the second-cabin quarters, and thought him a bull-dog of a man who would not be afraid of anything. This proved to be true; he kept order to the last, and died at his post. They say he shot himself. I do not know.

Those in charge must have herded us toward the nearest boat deck;

for that is where I presently found myself, still clinging to my husband's arm, and with little Marjorie beside me. Many women were standing with their husbands, and there was no confusion.

Then, above the clamour of people asking questions of each other, there came the terrible cry: 'Lower the boats. Women and children first!' Some one was shouting those last four words over and over again! 'Women and children first! Women and children first!' They struck utter terror into my heart, and now they will ring in my ears until I die. They meant my own safety; but they also meant the greatest loss I have ever suffered – the life of my husband.

The first lifeboat was quickly filled and lowered away. Very few men went in her, only five or six members of the crew, I should say. The male passengers made no attempt to move themselves. I never saw such courage, or believed it possible. How the people in the first cabin and the steerage may have acted, I do not know; but our second-cabin men were heroes. I want to tell that to every reader of this article.

The lowering of the second boat took more time. I think all those women who were really afraid and eager to go had got into the first. Those who remained were wives who did not want to leave their husbands, or daughters who would not leave their parents. The officer in charge was Harold Lowe. First Officer Murdock had moved to the other end of the deck. I was never close to him again.

Mr Lowe was very young and boyish-looking; but some how, he compelled people to obey him. He rushed among the passengers and ordered the women into the boat. Many of them followed him in a dazed kind of way; but others stayed by their men. I could have had a seat in that second boat; but I refused to go. It was filled at last, and disappeared over the side with a rush.

There were two more lifeboats at that part of the deck. A man in plain clothes was fussing about them and screaming out instructions. I saw Fifth Officer Lowe order him away. I did not recognize him, but from what I have read in the newspapers, it must have been Mr J. Bruce Ismay, the managing director of the line.

The third boat was about half full when a sailor caught Marjorie, my daughter, in his arms, tore her away from me and threw her into the boat. She was not even given a chance to tell her father good-bye!

'You, too!' a man yelled close to my ear. 'You're a woman. Take a seat in that boat, or it will be too late.'

The deck seemed to be slipping under my feet. It was leaning at a sharp angle; for the ship was then sinking fast, bows down. I clung desperately to my husband. I do not know what I said; but I shall always be glad to think that I did not want to leave him.

A man seized me by the arm. Then, another threw both his arms about my waist and dragged me away by main strength. I heard my husband say: 'Go, Lotty! For God's sake, be brave, and go! I'll get a seat in another boat.' The men who held me rushed me across the deck, and hurled me bodily into the lifeboat. I landed on one shoulder and bruised it badly. Other women were crowding behind me; but I stumbled to my feet and saw over their heads my husband's back, as he walked steadily down the deck and disappeared among the men. His face was turned away, so that I never saw it again; but I know that he went unafraid to his death.

His last words, when he said that he would get a seat in another boat, buoyed me up until every vestige of hope was gone. Many women were strengthened by the same promise, or they must have gone mad and leaped into the sea. I let myself be saved, because I believed that he, too, would escape; but I sometimes envy those whom no earthly power could tear from their husbands' arms. There were several such among those brave second-cabin passengers. I saw them standing beside their loved ones to the last; and when the roll was called the next day on board the *Carpathia*, they did not answer.

The boat was practically full, and no more women were anywhere near it when Fifth Officer Lowe jumped in and ordered it lowered. The sailors on deck had started to obey him, when a very sad thing happened. A young lad, hardly more than a school boy, a pink-cheeked lad, almost small enough to be counted as a child, was standing close to the rail. He had made no attempt to force his way into the boat, though his eyes had been fixed piteously on the officer. Now, when he realized that he was really to be left behind, his courage failed him. With a cry, he climbed upon the rail and leaped down into the boat. He fell among us women, and crawled under a seat. I and another woman covered him up with our skirts. We wanted to give the poor lad a chance; but the officer dragged him to his feet and ordered him back upon the ship.

He begged for his life. I remember him saying that he would not take up much room; but the officer drew his revolver, and thrust it into his face. 'I give you just ten seconds to get back on to that ship before I blow your brains out!' he shouted. The lad only begged the harder, and I thought I should see him shot as he stood. But the officer suddenly changed his tone. He lowered his revolver, and looked the boy squarely in the eyes. 'For God's sake, be a man!' he said gently. 'We've got women and children to save. We must stop at the decks lower down and take on women and children.'

The little lad turned round and climbed back over the rail, without a word. He took a few uncertain steps, then lay face down upon the deck, his head beside a coil of rope. He was not saved.

All the women about me were sobbing; and I saw my little Marjorie take the officer's hand. 'Oh, Mr Man, don't shoot, please don't shoot the poor man!' she was saying; and he spared the time to shake his head and smile.

He screamed another order for the boat to be lowered; but just as we were getting away, a steerage passenger, an Italian, I think, came running the whole length of the deck and hurled himself into the boat. He fell upon a young child, I found out afterward, and injured her internally. The officer seized him by the collar, and by sheer brute strength pushed him back on to the *Titanic*. As we shot down toward the sea, I caught a last glimpse of this coward. He was in the hands of about a dozen men of the second cabin. They were driving their fists into his face, and he was bleeding from the nose and mouth.

As a matter of fact, we did not stop at any other deck to take on other women and children. It would have been impossible, I suppose. The bottom of our boat slapped the ocean, as we came down, with a force that I thought must shock us all overboard. We were drenched with ice-cold spray; but we hung on, and the men at the oars rowed us rapidly away from the wreck.

It was then that I saw for the first time the iceberg that had done such terrible damage. It loomed up in the clear starlight, a bluish-white mountain quite near to us. Two other icebergs lay close together, like twin peaks. Later, I thought I saw three or four more; but I cannot be sure. Loose ice was floating in the water. It was very cold.

We had gone perhaps half a mile when the officer ordered the men to cease rowing. No other boats were in sight, and we did not even have a lantern to signal with. We lay there in silence and darkness in that utterly calm sea.

I shall never forget the terrible beauty of the *Titanic* at that moment. She was tilted forward, head down, with her first funnel partly under water. To me she looked like an enormous glow worm; for she was alight from the rising water line, clear to her stern – electric lights blazing in every cabin, lights on all the decks and lights at her mast heads. No sound reached us, except the music of the band, which I seemed, strange to say, to be aware of for the first time. Oh, those brave musicians! How wonderful they were! They were playing lively tunes, ragtime, and they kept it up to the very end. Only the engulfing ocean had power to drown them into silence.

At that distance, it was impossible to recognize any one on board. But I could make out groups of men on every deck. They were standing with arms crossed upon their chests, and with lowered heads. I am sure that they were in prayer. On the boat deck that I had just left, perhaps fifty men had come together. In the midst of them was a tall figure. This man had climbed upon a chair, or a coil of rope, so that he was raised far above the rest. His hands were stretched out, as if he were pronouncing a blessing. During the day, a priest, a certain Father Byles, had held services in the second-cabin saloon; and I think it must have been he who stood there, leading those doomed men in prayer. The band was playing 'Nearer My God to Thee'; I could hear it distinctly. The end was very close.

It came with a deafening roar that stunned me. Something in the very bowels of the *Titanic* exploded, and millions of sparks shot up to the sky, like rockets in a park on the night of a summer holiday. This red spurt was fan-shaped as it went up; but the sparks descended in every direction, in the shape of a fountain of fire. Two other explosions followed, dull and heavy, as if below the surface. The *Titanic* broke in two before my eyes. The fore part was already partly under the water. It wallowed over and disappeared instantly. The stern reared straight on end, and stood poised on the ocean for many seconds – they seemed minutes to me.

It was only then that the electric lights on board went out. Before the darkness came, I saw hundreds of human bodies clinging to the wreck, or leaping into the water. The *Titanic* was like a swarming bee-hive; but the bees were men; and they had broken their silence now. Cries more terrible than I had ever heard rang in my ears. I turned my face away; but looked round the next instant and saw the second half of the great boat slip below the surface as easily as a pebble in a pond. I shall always remember that last moment as the most hideous of the whole disaster.

Titanic's *Second Officer, having cast adrift the last Engelhardt collapsible from the top of the officers' quarters, defied his instinct to clamber towards the stern ahead of the rising water. Of his testimony at the British Enquiry, Geoffrey Marcus writes: 'The audience craned forward in their seats to catch every syllable of the narration of this sturdy, bronzed, stern-faced sailor with his deep, powerful voice and confident air as he spoke of the grim realities of life and death.'*

CHARLES LIGHTOLLER
Only One Thing to Do

(Titanic *and Other Ships*, 1935)

I knew, only too well, the utter futility of following that driving instinct of self-preservation and struggling up towards the stern. It would only be postponing the plunge, and prolonging the agony – even lessening one's already slim chances, by becoming one of a crowd. It came home to me very clearly how fatal it would be to get amongst those hundreds and hundreds of people who would shortly be struggling for their lives in that deadly cold water. There was only one thing to do, and I might just as well do it and get it over, so, turning to the fore part of the bridge, I took a header. Striking the water, was like a thousand knives being driven into one's body, and, for a few moments, I completely lost grip of myself – and no wonder for I was perspiring freely, whilst the temperature of the water was 28°, or 4° below freezing.

Ahead of me the lookout cage on the foremast was visible just above the water – in normal times it would be a hundred feet above. I struck out blindly for this, but only for a short while, till I got hold of myself again and realized the futility of seeking safety on anything connected with the ship. I then turned to starboard, away from the ship altogether.

For a time I wondered what was making it so difficult for me to keep my head above the water. Time and again I went under, until it dawned on me that it was the great Webley revolver, still in my pocket, that was dragging me down. I soon sent that on its downward journey.

The water was now pouring down the stokeholds, by way of the fiddley gratings abaft the bridge, and round the forward funnel.

On the boat deck, above our quarters, on the fore part of the forward funnel, was a huge rectangular air shaft and ventilator, with an opening about twenty by fifteen feet. On this opening was a light wire grating to prevent rubbish being drawn down or anything else being thrown down. This shaft led direct to No. 3 stokehold, and was therefore a sheer drop of close on [a] hundred feet, right to the bottom of the ship.

I suddenly found myself drawn, by the sudden rush of the surface water now pouring down this shaft, and held flat and firmly up against this wire netting with the additional full and clear knowledge of what would happen if this light wire carried away. The pressure of the water just glued me there whilst the ship sank slowly below the surface.

Although I struggled and kicked for all I was worth, it was impossible to get away, for as fast as I pushed myself off I was irresistibly dragged back, every instant expecting the wire to go, and to find myself shot down into the bowels of the ship.

Apart from that, I was drowning, and a matter of another couple of minutes would have seen me through. I was still struggling and fighting when suddenly a terrific blast of hot air came up the shaft, and blew me right away from the air shaft and up to the surface.

The water was now swirling round, and the ship sinking rapidly, when once again I was caught and sucked down by an inrush of water, this time adhering to one of the fiddley gratings. Just how I got clear of that, I don't know, as I was rather losing interest in things, but I eventually came to the surface once again, this time alongside that last Engleheart [*sic*] boat which [Samuel] Hemming and I had launched from on top of the officers' quarters on the opposite side – for I was now on the starboard side, near the forward funnel.

There were many around in the water by this time, some swimming, others (mostly men, thank God), definitely drowning – an utter nightmare of both sight and sound. In the circumstances I made no effort to get on top of the upturned boat, but, for some reason, was content to remain floating alongside, just hanging on to a small piece of rope.

The bow of the ship was now rapidly going down and the stern rising higher and higher out of the water, piling the people into helpless heaps around the steep decks, and by the score into the icy water. Had the boats been around many might have been saved, but of them, at this time there was no sign. Organized help, or even individual help, was quite impossible. All one could do was just wait on events, and try and forget the icy cold grip of the water.

The terrific strain of bringing the after-end of that huge hull clear out of the water, caused the expansion joint abaft No. 1 funnel to open up. (These expansion joints were found necessary in big ships to allow the ship to 'work' in a seaway.) The fact that the two wire stays to this funnel, on the after-part, led over and abaft the expansion joint, threw on them an extraordinary strain, eventually carrying away the port wire guy, to be followed almost immediately by the starboard one. Instantly the port one parted, the funnel started to fall, but the fact that the starboard one held a moment or two longer, gave this huge structure a pull over to that side of the ship, causing it to fall, with its scores of tons, right amongst the struggling mass of humanity already in the water. It struck the water between the Engleheart and the ship, actually missing me by inches.

Amongst the many historic and, what in less tragic circumstances would have been humorous – questions, asked by Senator Smith at the Washington Enquiry was, 'Did it hurt anyone?'

One effect of the funnel crashing down on the sea, was to pick up the Engleheart, in the wash so created, and fling it well clear of the sinking ship.

When I again recognized my surroundings, we were full fifty yards clear of the ship. The piece of rope was still in my hand, with old friend Engleheart upturned and attached to the other end, with several men by now standing on it. I also scrambled up, after spending longer than I like to remember in that icy water. Lights on board the *Titanic* were still burning, and a wonderful spectacle she made, standing out black and massive against the starlit sky; myriads of lights still gleaming through the portholes, from that part of the decks still above water.

The fore part, and up to the second funnel was by this time completely submerged, and as we watched this terribly awe-inspiring sight, suddenly all lights went out and the huge bulk was left in black darkness, but clearly silhouetted against the bright sky. Then, the next moment, the massive boilers left their beds and went thundering down with a hollow rumbling roar, through the bulkheads, carrying everything with them that stood in their way. This unparalleled tragedy that was being enacted before our very eyes, now rapidly approached its finale, as the huge ship slowly but surely reared herself on end and brought rudder and propellers clear of the water, till, at last, she assumed *an absolute perpendicular position*. In this amazing attitude she remained for the space of half a minute. Then with impressive majesty and ever-increasing momentum, she silently took her last tragic dive to seek a final resting place in the unfathomable depths of the cold grey Atlantic.

Almost like a benediction everyone round me on the upturned boat breathed the two words, 'She's gone.'

Fortunately, the scene that followed was shrouded in darkness. Less fortunately, the calm still silence carried every sound with startling distinctness. To enter into a description of those heartrending, never-to-be-forgotten sounds would serve no useful purpose. I never allowed my thoughts to dwell on them, and there are some that would be alive and well today had they just determined to erase from their minds all memory of those ghastly moments, or at least until time had somewhat dimmed the memory of that awful tragedy.

This American first-class passenger also gained the roof of the officers' quarters but before he could get to his feet the ship took him down. Gracie's is an essential Titanic text for his grasp of shipboard life and its unfolding in the hours of crisis. Having survived, he stalked the disaster that nearly did for him, hunting down its details less in revenge than in a passion to set the record straight. But the effects of his ordeal at the age of fifty-four took their toll, and he died in December, as his book was going to press. In this excerpt he quotes Harold Bride to underline the error of Gracie and his friend Clinch Smith leaving the scene of the Engelhardt boat 'B', an error the author rectified only by an astonishing swim under water.

ARCHIBALD GRACIE
Out of the Deep

(Gracie, *Truth about the* Titanic)

'Out of the deep have I called unto Thee, O Lord.'
Psalm 130:1

'. . . I went to the place where I had seen the collapsible boat on the boat deck and to my surprise I saw the boat, and the men still trying to push it off. They could not do it. I went up to them and was just lending a hand when a large wave came awash of the deck. The big wave carried the boat off. I had hold of an oarlock and I went off with it. The next I knew I was in the boat. But that was not all. I was in the boat and the boat was upside down and I was under it . . . How I got out from under the boat I do not know, but I felt a breath at last.'

From this it appears evident that, so far as Clinch Smith is concerned, it would have been better to have stayed by this Engelhardt boat to the last, for here he had a chance of escape like [Harold] Bride and others of the crew who clung to it, but which I only reached again after an incredibly long swim under water. The next crisis, which was the fatal one to Clinch Smith and to the great mass of people that suddenly arose before us as I followed him astern . . . The simple expedient of jumping with the 'big wave' as demonstrated above carried me to safety, away from a dangerous position to the highest part of the ship; but I was the only one who adopted it successfully. The force of the wave that struck Clinch Smith and the others undoubtedly knocked most of them there unconscious against the walls of the officers' quarters and other appurtenances of the ship on the boat deck. As the ship keeled over forward, I believe that their bodies were caught in the angles of this deck, or entangled in the ropes, and in these other appurtenances thereon, and sank with the ship.

My holding on to the iron railing just when I did prevented my being knocked unconscious. I pulled myself over on the roof on my stomach, but before I could get to my feet I was in a whirlpool of water, swirling round and round, as I still tried to cling to the railing as the ship plunged to the depths below. Down, down, I went: it seemed a great distance. There was a very noticeable pressure upon my ears, though there must have been plenty of air that the ship carried down with it. When under water I retained, as it appears, a sense of general direction, and, as soon as I could do so, swam away from the starboard side of the ship, as I knew my life depended upon it. I swam with all my strength, and I seemed endowed with an extra supply for the occasion. I was incited to desperate effort by the thought of boiling water, or steam, from the expected explosion of the ship's boilers, and that I would be scalded to death, like the sailors of whom I had read in the account of the British battleship *Victoria* [*Pretoria*] sunk in collision with the *Camperdown* in the Mediterranean in 1893. Second Officer [Charles Herbert] Lightoller told me he also had the same idea, and that if the fires had not been drawn the boilers would explode and the water become boiling hot. As a consequence, the plunge in the icy water produced no sense of coldness whatever, and I had no thought of cold until later on when I climbed on the bottom of the upturned boat. My being drawn down by suction to a greater depth was undoubtedly checked to some degree by the life-preserver which I wore, but it is to the buoyancy of the water, caused by the volume of air rising from the sinking ship, that I attributed the assistance which enabled me to strike out and swim faster and further under water than I ever did before. I held my breath for what seemed an interminable time until I could scarcely stand it any longer, but I congratulated myself then and there that not one drop of sea water was allowed to enter my mouth. With renewed determination and set jaws, I swam on. Just at the moment I thought that for lack of breath I would have to give in, I seemed to have been provided with a second

wind, and it was just then that the thought that this was my last moment
came upon me . . .

With this second wind under water there came to me a new lease of
life and strength, until finally I noticed by the increase of light that I
was drawing near to the surface. Though it was not daylight, the clear
star-lit night made a noticeable difference in the degree of light immediately below the surface of the water. As I was rising, I came in contact
with ascending wreckage, but the only thing I struck of material size
was a small plank, which I tucked under my right arm. This circumstance
brought with it the reflection that it was advisable for me to secure what
best I could to keep me afloat on the surface until succour arrived.
When my head at last rose above the water, I detected a piece of
wreckage like a wooden crate, and I eagerly seized it as a nucleus of
the projected raft to be constructed from what flotsam and jetsam I
might collect. Looking about me, I could see no *Titanic* in sight. She
had entirely disappeared beneath the calm surface of the ocean and
without a sign of any wave. That the sea had swallowed her up with all
her precious belongings was indicated by the slight sound of a gulp
behind me as the water closed over her. The length of time that I was
under water can be estimated by the fact that I sank with her, and when
I came up there was no ship in sight . . .

What impressed me at the time that my eyes beheld the horrible
scene was a thin light-grey smoky vapour that hung like a pall a few feet
above the broad expanse of sea that was covered with a mass of tangled
wreckage . . . it produced a supernatural effect, and the pictures I had
seen by Dante and the description I had read in my Virgil of the infernal
regions, of Charon, and the River Lethe, were then uppermost in my
thoughts. Add to this, within the area described, which was as far as my
eyes could reach, there arose to the sky the most horrible sounds ever
heard . . . The agonizing cries of death from over a thousand throats,
the wails and groans of the suffering, the shrieks of the terror-stricken
and the awful gaspings for breath of those in the last throes of drowning,
none of us will ever forget to our dying day. 'Help! Help! Boat ahoy!
Boat ahoy!' and 'My God! My God!' were the heart-rending cries and
shrieks of men, which floated to us over the surface of the dark waters
continuously for the next hour, but as time went on, growing weaker
and weaker until they died out entirely.

As I clung to my wreckage, I noticed just in front of me, a few yards away, a group of three bodies with heads in the water, face downwards, and just behind me to my right another body . . . There was no one alive or struggling in the water or calling for aid within the immediate vicinity of where I arose to the surface. I threw my right leg over the wooden crate in an attempt to straddle and balance myself on top of it, but I turned over in a somersault with it under water, and up to the surface again . . .

. . . I espied to my left, a considerable distance away, a better vehicle of escape than the wooden crate on which my attempt to ride had resulted in a second ducking. What I saw was no less than the same Engelhardt, or 'surf-boat', to whose launching I had lent my efforts, until the water broke upon the ship's boat deck where we were. On top of this upturned boat, half reclining on her bottom, were now more than a dozen men, whom, by their dress, I took to be all members of the crew of the ship. Thank God, I did not hesitate a moment in discarding the friendly crate that had been my first aid. I struck out through the wreckage and after a considerable swim reached the port side amidships of this Engelhardt boat, which with her companions, wherever utilized, did good service in saving the lives of many others. All honour to the Dane, Captain Engelhardt of Copenhagen, who built them. I say 'port side' because this boat as it was propelled through the water had Lightoller in the bow and Bride at the stern, and I believe an analysis of the testimony shows that the actual bow of the boat was turned about by the wave that struck it on the boat deck and the splash of the funnel thereafter, so that its bow pointed in an opposite direction to that of the ship. There was one member of the crew on this craft at the bow and another at the stern who had 'pieces of boarding', improvised paddles, which were used effectually for propulsion.

When I reached the side of the boat I met with a doubtful reception, and, as no extending hand was held out to me, I grabbed, by the muscle of the left arm, a young member of the crew nearest and facing me. At the same time I threw my right leg over the boat astraddle, pulling myself aboard, with a friendly lift to my foot given by someone astern as I assumed a reclining position with them on the bottom of the capsized boat. Then after me came a dozen other swimmers who clambered around and whom we helped aboard. Among them was one completely exhausted, who came on the same port side as myself. I pulled him in and he lay face downward in front of me for several hours, until just before dawn he was able to stand up with the rest of us . . . I now felt for the first time after the lifeboats left us aboard ship that I had some chance of escape from the horrible fate of drowning in the icy waters of the middle Atlantic . . . The only time of any stress whatever was during the swim, just described, under water, at the moment when I gained my second wind which brought me to the surface gasping somewhat, but full of vigour. I was all the time on the lookout for the next danger that was to be overcome. I kept my presence of mind and courage throughout it all . . .

All my companions in shipwreck who made their escape with me on top of the bottomside-up Engelhardt boat, must recall the anxious moment after the limit was reached when 'about 30 men had clambered out of the water on to the boat'. The weight of each additional body submerged our life craft more and more beneath the surface. There were men swimming in the water all about us. One more clambering aboard would have swamped our already crowded craft. The situation was a desperate one, and was only saved by the refusal of the crew, especially those at the stern of the boat, to take aboard another passenger . . .

. . . The men with the paddles, forward and aft, so steered the boat as to avoid contact with the unfortunate swimmers pointed out struggling in the water. I heard the constant explanation made as we passed men swimming in the wreckage, 'Hold on to what you have, old boy; one more of you aboard would sink us all.' In no instance, I am happy to say, did I hear any word of rebuke uttered by a swimmer because of refusal to grant assistance. There was no case of cruel violence. But there was one transcendent piece of heroism that will remain fixed in my memory as the most sublime and coolest exhibition of courage and cheerful resignation to fate and fearlessness of death. This was when a reluctant refusal of assistance met with the ringing response in the deep manly voice of a powerful man, who, in his extremity, replied: 'All right, boys; good luck and God bless you' . . .

It was shortly after we had emerged from the horrible scene of men swimming in the water that I was glad to notice the presence among us on the upturned boat of the same officer with whom all my work that night and all my experience was connected in helping to load and lower the boats on the *Titanic*'s boat deck and Deck 'A'. I identified him at once by his voice and his appearance, but his name was not learned until I met him again later in my cabin on board the *Carpathia* – Charles

H. Lightoller. For what he did on the ship that night whereby six or more boatloads of women and children were saved and discipline maintained aboard ship, as well as on the Engelhardt upturned boat, he is entitled to honour and the thanks of his own countrymen and of us Americans as well. As soon as he was recognized, the loquacious member of the crew astern, already referred to, volunteered in our behalf and called out to him 'We will all obey what the officer orders.' The result was at once noticeable. The presence of a leader among us was now felt, and lent us purpose and courage. The excitement at the stern was demonstrated by the frequent suggestion of, 'Now boys, all together'; and then in unison we shouted, 'Boat ahoy! Boat ahoy!' This was kept up for some time until it was seen to be a mere waste of strength. So it seemed to me, and I decided to husband mine and make provision for what the future, or the morrow, might require. After a while Lightoller, myself and others managed with success to discourage these continuous shouts regarded as a vain hope of attracting attention.

When the presence of the Marconi boy at the stern was made known, Lightoller called out, from his position in the bow, questions which all of us heard, as to the names of the steamships with which he had been in communication for assistance. We on the boat recall the names mentioned by Bride – the *Baltic*, *Olympic* and *Carpathia*. It was then that the *Carpathia*'s name was heard by us for the first time, and it was to catch sight of this sturdy little Cunarder that we strained our eyes in the direction whence she finally appeared.

Some time before dawn a call came from the stern of the boat, 'There is a steamer coming behind us.' At the same time a warning cry was given that we should not all look back at once lest the equilibrium of our precarious craft might be disturbed. Lightoller took in the situation and called out, 'All you men stand steady and I will be the one to look astern.' He looked, but there was no responsive chord that tickled our ears with hope.

. . . Finally dawn appeared and there on the port side of our upset boat where we had been looking with anxious eyes, glory be to God, we saw the steamer *Carpathia* about four or five miles away, with other *Titanic* lifeboats rowing towards her. But on our starboard side, much to our surprise, for we had seen no lights on that quarter, were four of the *Titanic*'s lifeboats strung together in line . . .

Meantime, the water had grown rougher, and, as previously described, was washing over the keel and we had to make shift to preserve the equilibrium. Right glad were all of us on our upturned boat when in that awful hour the break of day brought this glorious sight to our eyes. Lightoller put his whistle to his cold lips and blew a shrill blast, attracting the attention of the boats about half a mile away. 'Come over and take us off,' he cried. 'Aye, aye, sir,' was the ready response as two of the boats cast off from the others and rowed directly towards us. Just before the bows of the two boats reached us, Lightoller ordered us not to scramble, but each to take his turn, so that the transfer might be made in safety. When my turn came, in order not to endanger the lives of the others, or plunge them into the sea, I went carefully, hands first, into the rescuing lifeboat. Lightoller remained to the last, lifting a lifeless body into the boat beside me. I worked over the body for some time, rubbing the temples and the wrists . . . Lightoller was uncertain as to which one he was of two men he had in mind; but we both know that it was not the body of Phillips, the senior Marconi operator.

4

Cities in Shock

'Where is the *Titanic?*'
Captain Rostron of *Carpathia* to Officer Boxhall

Through wireless telegraphy and the daily newspapers that fed from the recent technology, the Titanic *disaster established among far-flung cities an immediate, frequent and intense interconnection. Readers of the* New York Times *were apprised as early as the afternoon of Monday, 15 April that* Titanic *had sunk, thanks to an inspired inference by Carr Van Anda, the newspaper's editor, that a wounded liner with a powerful wireless that did not communicate over the course of hours was probably gone.*

In New York City, concern became agitation on Monday evening when fears were confirmed; by the next morning the vicinity of the White Star Line offices was in tumult. The mass anxiety was repeated in London on the Wednesday. One reporter observed that the 'poor and rich alike condoled with each other in the common anxiety'. The democracy of anxiety, later of death, loss and grief, became one of the ideas throughout the Titanic *tragedy from which many people appeared to derive comfort.*

The coverage of the loss of Titanic *by the* New York Times *has been called 'a classic of American journalism', and the tragedy was in many ways a field day for newspapers everywhere. But in the first days of the disaster, not every newspaper showed the regard for confirmation that the* New York Times *showed. Readers could be treated to a farrago of information and misinformation; the* Titanic *tragedy is a case-study in information dynamics.*

The truth when it emerged shocked millions, many of them in the cities of New York, London, Southampton and Belfast, where interest in the ship and its passengers was most deeply vested. But concern was intense in other cities too. *The arrival of* Carpathia *in New York with the survivors at once broke the tension of fearful anticipation and renewed the shock of the news.*

Meanwhile, daily newspaper bulletins from Wall Street registered, as on a seismograph, the economic strength of the shock waves, and reminded readers that economic life goes on.

Ministers of the cloth were versed in calamity, and come the Sunday after the sinking, they were ready with their sermons, some delivered in the blistering tones of retribution. Services on 21 April were devoted to the Titanic *disaster in hundreds of churches across the English-speaking world, including New York, Washington, London, Ottawa, Toronto, Melbourne, Cape Town, Liverpool, Southampton, Glasgow and Belfast. Themes included the heroism displayed by individuals, the male gender and the Anglo-Saxon race; the revelation in the calamity of the Power of the Cross; and the greatness of God and the littleness of mankind.*

Other less admiring or reassuring notes were struck. Titanic *and her sister ships had already been attacked for being 'degenerate in size, foolish in enjoyment, sybaritic in luxury, and criminal in speed'. The Bishop of Winchester preached that the disaster was a monumental warning against human pride and a lesson against our confident belief in machinery.*

This lead story informed readers that '1,500 Perish on Liner Titanic'.
Everyone awaited the mute Carpathia *with, as it proved, 705 survivors
on board. The well-written article, of which this is a brief excerpt, pays
passing tribute to H. R. Hertz's work on frequency that helped make
wireless telegraphy possible.*

The Marvellous Hertzian Waves

(*San Francisco Examiner*, 16 April 1912)

After the first desperate calls of the *Titanic* for help had been
sent flying through space and brought vessels for hundreds of miles
around speeding to the scene, what seems to have been an impenetrable
wall of silence was raised between New York and the ocean.

The giant liner, so far as last night's advices appear, went to its fate
without so much as a whisper of what must have been the scenes of
terrible tragedy enacted on its decks.

In the lack of even a line from a survivor imagination pauses before
even trying to conjecture what passed as the inevitable became known
and it was seen that of the more than 2,000 human lives with which the
steamship was freighted there could be hope of saving, as it appears,
far less than a half.

Other than the news that 866 persons, largely women and children,
had been rescued from the liner's boats by the Cunarder *Carpathia*,
several hours passed without a word as to the fate of the rest of those
on board at the time of the fateful crash . . .

Early last night there was hope that any moment might bring cheer.
But anxiety deepened and many friends and relatives of those who
sailed on the *Titanic* began to despair as hours passed and the night
grew old without word from either of the Allan liners, the *Parisian* or
the *Virginian*, believed to be, with the exception of the *Carpathia*, the
vessels nearest the *Titanic*'s ocean burial place.

As the *Titanic* sank before 3 o'clock in the morning and it was not
hoped that the *Virginian* could reach the scene before 10 o'clock the
next morning at the earliest, the *Parisian* was said to be some distance
farther away.

It was feared even by the White Star officials, trying their best to calculate accurately, that they would not have reached the scene in time to be of service.

As mute evidence of the disaster that overwhelmed the *Titanic* on its maiden trip is the comment of the captain of the *Carpathia* in a wireless message received tonight:

'We found only a sea covered with wreckage and debris.'

The *Carpathia*'s captain also said he had picked up the survivors in the boats and had sheltered them on board. They will be landed at either New York or Boston some time on Thursday.

The *Carpathia* also sent the tidings that the *Titanic* had gone to the bottom at 2.20 o'clock on Monday morning.

A hundred vessels of all descriptions are making for the scene of the disaster at top speed in the faint hope that some of the survivors may yet be saved. But it seems a forlorn hope . . .

At every wireless station on the Atlantic Coast from New York to Cape Race, wireless operators are bending over their wireless instruments feeling for the marvellous Hertzian waves that will bring further details of the catastrophe.

The stations, which are faithfully recording every piece of information that comes from the deep, hear nothing.

Extra men are on duty, spurred on by hundreds of telegrams from all parts of the world for some intelligence of those on board.

In the afternoon and as far into the night as midnight, tiny bits of news filtered in over the wonderful mechanicism, but after that there was silence.

In this city all the steamship offices remained open all night. Crowds thronged the White Star offices in lower Broadway clamouring for some information of the *Titanic*. To all there was the same reply:

'Nothing more has been heard.'

The dawn of Tuesday after the sinking saw New Yorkers' anxious attention fasten on the offices of the White Star Line. Vincent Astor inherited $87,000,000. Though it was rumoured that Benjamin Guggenheim, the smelting millionaire, had stayed in Paris with his French mistress, he nevertheless became a legend because he and his valet donned evening dress, the millionaire announcing: 'We've dressed in our best and are prepared to go down like gentlemen.'

The Siege of Bowling Green

(*New York Times*, 17 April 1912)

From early dawn yesterday until early this morning the local offices of the White Star Line in Bowling Green were besieged by relatives and friends of persons known to have been on the ill-fated *Titanic*. It was an orderly but pathetic crowd of men and women, and there was not a moment when a tear-stained face was not scanning anxiously the printed lists of known survivors that were posted on the bulletin boards.

Besides the hundreds who called the White Star Line received hundreds of telegrams from all parts of the United States and Canada, one of the enquiries being from a White House attaché, who, in the name of the President, asked if there was any definite news of the fate of Major Archibald Butt, USA, President Taft's military aide and intimate friend. There was little hope in the answer that was quickly sent back to the White House. It was the same message that sent women weeping from the offices and made strong men turn pale:

'There is no mention of the name in the list of the rescued so far received from the *Carpathia*.'

There were many cablegrams received from relatives and friends of *Titanic* passengers living in distant lands, who harboured the forlorn hope that may be there was good news in New York that had not yet reached them. As for telephone calls, both long distance and local, there was not a second of the day when the wires were not busy. Telephone operators and clerks answered the calls and gave what comfort there was to be derived from the fact that among the names yet to be received from the *Carpathia* might appear that of the father, mother, brother, sister or friend enquired about.

P. A. S. Franklin, Vice President and General Manager of the International Mercantile Marine, was early in his office. Mr Franklin was in great distress. His admission that he no longer had any hope that other survivors had been picked up by the Allan liners, *Parisian* and *Virginian*, was pathetic.

Bright and early yesterday morning the steamship officials prepared for the ordeal they knew was coming. Monday night the lesser officials and clerks who answered enquiries concerning the *Titanic*'s passengers were always careful to follow the definite information they had about the *Carpathia*'s rescue with expressions of hope that equally good news was expected from the *Virginian* and the *Parisian*. Yesterday they did not refer to the Allan liners, but tried to instill hope with the suggestion that perhaps those about whom enquiries were made were among the fortunate whose names have not yet been reported by the Captain of the *Carpathia*.

Vincent Astor, son of Col. John Jacob Astor, who is believed to have gone down with the *Titanic*, was among the earliest to make enquiries. The young man was grief-stricken, for he was a chum as well as a son of John Jacob. He was told that his stepmother, who was Miss Madeleine Force, was known to be among the saved, but that the worst was feared concerning the fate of his father, whose name was missing from the slender list that had been wirelessed from the *Carpathia*.

Young Mr Astor had remained up all night, hoping against hope for some reassuring word. He went to the Associated Press, and scanned its late reports. He also visited the Marconi Company's offices early in the morning. He was almost hysterical from grief, and one of the operators said he cried out that he would give all the money that could be asked for if the operator would only tell him that he had news of his father's safety. The operator was unable to give this assurance. He then tried to get in touch by wireless with the *Carpathia*, but it was not until the partial list received by the line was bulletined that he learned of the rescue of Mrs Astor, news that carried with it a reasonable confirmation of his fears that his father had gone down with the ship.

By 8 o'clock yesterday morning the White Star offices were crowded from booking rail to booking rail, while outside on the opposite side of Broadway and filling Bowling Green Park was another crowd, in which could be seen many a tear-stained face. The crowd increased in size so rapidly that the four policemen detailed to duty in front of the steamship offices asked for reinforcements. Two mounted policemen were then ordered to duty in front of the office, while half a dozen others were sent from the Old Slip Station to duty in the park space, on which the office fronts.

Within the two big main offices of the International Mercantile Marine men and women, some of the latter with eyes red from weeping, were banked in between the long booking desks, each anxiously waiting a chance to enquire for some dear one who had been a passenger on the *Titanic*. Every now and then a woman would reach the rail, and, bending over, ask the clerk if the person of whom she sought news was safe.

Sometimes a grief stricken cry followed the giving of the information. On one or two occasions, when the news was good, it was a hysterical joyous expression of relief. This was true not only of the women enquirers, but also of some of the men.

Of the latter one of the first to appear at the office of the company was Edward Frauenthal, of 783 Lexington Avenue, who had two brothers on the *Titanic*, Dr Hyman and J. C. Frauenthal, the latter a lawyer. Both are reported saved. When he was told that his brothers' names appeared on the *Carpathia*'s list of survivors Mr Frauenthal was so overcome that he hardly could walk to the telephone to send the good news to his home. In a voice that was scarcely audible to those near him he called his home number. When Mrs Frauenthal answered he broke down and sobbed.

'I tell you they are saved!' he cried in a hoarse voice. 'Yes! yes! they are safe! Do you hear what I say?'

The telephone receiver fell from his hand and Mr Frauenthal sank to the floor, completely overcome by the good news. Helped to his feet, he turned to the reporters.

'Young men,' he said in a broken voice, 'pardon me, but I could not help it. My nerves are all unstrung' . . .

Many enquiries were made at the office during the day about Benjamin Guggenheim, but no hopeful reply could be given as Mr Guggenheim's name was not included in any of the lists of survivors received.

About 10 o'clock, just when the crowd in the office was largest, Mrs Benjamin Guggenheim arrived, accompanied by her brother and sister-in-law, Mr and Mrs De Witt F. Seligman. Mrs Guggenheim gave every evidence of great mental agitation. Although she bore up bravely, it was apparent that the terrible suspense was threatening a complete breakdown.

Like all the others who were there Mrs Guggenheim carefully went over the lists supplied by the company and questioned several of the clerks. Then when she found that there was no message of hope for her she sank down on a bench. She talked freely with the newspaper men, seeking from them every bit of information she could obtain about the disaster.

'If so many were lost then the White Star Line did not have enough boats,' declared Mrs Guggenheim passionately. 'There should have been more boats.'

Then she suddenly drew back in her seat and sat for some minutes staring quietly ahead of her at the line of weeping women and broken men who were passing by, but giving no indication that she saw them at all. After nearly an hour had elapsed she demanded an interview with Mr Franklin and was shown to his office. He could only tell her that no reports had been received of her husband, and then Mrs Guggenheim left the building, going to the St Regis Hotel. Mr Franklin promised that any news would be telephoned to her immediately upon its receipt at his office.

*Victorian Southampton was the child of the steam era and its rail link
to London guaranteed its growth. White Star moved its express service
to Southampton in 1907, and many crew followed it and took residence
in the southern port. One teacher said to her elementary school class:
'Stand up any child who has a relative on the* Titanic' *– and the whole
class stood up.*

A Town of Mourning

(*Daily Sketch*, 17, 19 April 1912)

Southampton is a town of mourning. Ninety per cent of the
crew of the *Titanic* were born or had residences in the port and its
neighbourhood, and there is scarcely a house but is apprehensive for
the safety of a relative or friend.

In the absence of definite news the White Star officials here are still
hopeful, but the optimism is not shared by the townsfolk. The Mayor
(Councillor H. Bowyer), a lieutenant in the R.N.R., has caused the blue
ensign on the Town Hall to be placed at half-mast. Elsewhere on the
public buildings and churches and at the quays flags are similarly flying.

Several shopkeepers have put up shutters, and there are many private
houses in which blinds are drawn. The suspense is almost more wearing
than the actual knowledge of death would be.

Down at the docks before dawn this morning a crowd waited at the
White Star offices, which have been open since 2 a.m., and the numbers
have been steadily increased throughout the day. Women with babies
in their arms, their cheeks pale and drawn and their eyes red with
weeping, have stood for hours reading and re-reading those vague
messages of the disaster which the company had posted up . . .

The Mayor received me at the Town Hall and stated that, unable
longer to doubt that a disaster had overtaken a portion of the crew at
least, he was opening a national relief fund for the relatives.

'I have written to the Lord Mayor of London today,' he said, 'and
shall visit him personally tomorrow. I have suspended the meeting of
the Harbour Board, of which I am the chairman, *sine die*. Southampton
has been plunged into grief and the sympathy of the country, of the
whole world in fact, will go out to the town.'

The Mayor inclines to the view that of the 700 passengers and crew reported saved only two per cent would be members of the crew. That crew was the cream of the profession. Most of the men were members of the British Seafarers' Union, which is a new organization started in October last. Mr T. Lewis, the President, told me that a few of the stewards came from Liverpool by process of promotion. The *Titanic* had absorbed the most capable officers of the White Star line.

One prominent officer is said to have been on the *Oceana*, which was sunk off Eastbourne recently. Not a few of the seamen and firemen joined because their vessels were detained in port by lack of coal. It is recalled as a bad omen that when leaving Southampton on Wednesday the *Titanic* nearly fouled the *New York*, which the suction caused to break her cable.

There are men in the town congratulating themselves that by fortuitous circumstances they did not sail in her. Six firemen who should have been on board by noon on Wednesday were a few minutes late, and were summarily dismissed in accordance with regulations. Another fireman left the *Titanic* when she reached Queenstown.

THOMAS C. SHOTWELL
Wall Street Report

(*San Francisco Examiner*, 17 April 1912)

The loss of life on the *Titanic* came as a shock to the financial district. Almost every banker of importance lost one or more friends in the disaster, and there was a feeling of depression of which the bear traders were quick to take advantage.

The money loss is not worth considering as a market influence. It is not likely, either, that there will be any speedy sales for the estates of the drowned men. Some confusion may result for a few days in the foreign exchange market, but as a market influence the *Titanic* may be dismissed.

Belfast's human loss did not compare with Southampton's, though the deaths of Tommy Andrews and his Harland & Wolff's engineering staff on board were felt keenly. The blow to Ulster pride was perhaps greater than the sense of human loss.

Belfast and the Disaster

(*Belfast News-Letter*, 17 April 1912)

It is no exaggeration to say that the details of the loss of the *Titanic*, as published in our columns yesterday, created a profound impression in Belfast, and the disaster was the main topic of conversation throughout the day. Indeed it cast quite a gloom over the city, and on every side, and amongst all classes of the community, one heard expressions of deep regret and genuine sympathy for those who have suffered through the sinking of the huge vessel. There were few, if any, of the citizens who did not take a keen personal interest in the *Titanic* by reason of the fact that, like all the vessels of the White Star fleet, she was built at Queen's Island.

The feeling of pride and admiration which she excited was heightened by the thought that she represented the very latest achievement in the mercantile shipbuilding world, embodying in herself the most recent improvements and ideas both in the matter of construction and equipment. It was only a fortnight yesterday since, after long months expended on her building and fitting out, during which time she was a constant theme of discussion both in conversation and the press, she left her birthplace to enter on the maiden voyage which has ended in such dire disaster; and it seems scarcely possible to believe that, after an all too brief career, she now lies at the bottom of the Atlantic Ocean.

The conflicting nature of the earlier messages received regarding the vessel's collision with the iceberg led people to hope that although she had suffered very severe damage the passengers had all been saved. Unfortunately, however, the reports published in our columns yesterday morning indicated all too clearly that there had been great loss of life, and that the disaster had been converted into an appalling catastrophe. No language can describe the pity and horror of such a tragedy nor express all that one feels in its contemplation. When the *Titanic* left

Belfast everyone predicted a great future for her. There was no vessel afloat on which so much money had been spent, so much human ingenuity exercised, so much care taken to secure the comfort and safety of the passengers. So elaborate were the precautions which had been adopted to guard against accident that it was thought to be practically impossible for her to sink.

But all the hopes which were centred in her when she was launched in the presence of thousands of cheering spectators, who were proud of her because she was the product of one of our local shipbuilding yards and because she marked the beginning of a new era in naval architecture, have been violently shattered – shattered in a manner which has brought grief into hundreds of homes.

Wall Street Report

(Daily Telegraph, 19 April 1912)

The feeling of depression increases in financial circles as the *Carpathia*, bearing the *Titanic*'s survivors, crawls to port beneath a shroud of fog. Even professional speculators are so appalled by the disaster that they remain in a state of stupor, and allow prices to drift aimlessly. The market is at half-mast, and will doubtless remain so until there is a rift in the gloom.

In the circumstances, prices show remarkable firmness. There has been a steady absorption of securities on decline for the last three days, but good support has been afforded, especially by the Morgan interests.

There have been recoveries in many issues today, and New York Central stock made a new high record for the present movement.

International Mercantile Marines declined only slightly. The Common on small transactions broke 5⅛ to 4⅞, and Preferred 21½ to 20¼. The absurd report that the worst phase of the disaster was held back on Monday to allow insiders to raid Marine stocks was disproved by facts. Fewer than 10,000 shares of each class of stock were traded in during the first three days of the week, and only 8,000 shares were borrowed in loan, indicating that the short interest had been trivial.

The *Titanic* catastrophe called the attention of the public to the utility of wireless telegraphy to such an extent as further to augment the speculative craze for Marconi stocks. American Marconis, which several months ago were going a-begging at $2 a share, advanced today on the kerb from $170 a share to $220. Conservative brokers regard this as an absurd price in view of the company's earning potentialities under the best conditions. At a meeting today the stockholders voted an increase of capital to $1,662,500.

One of those who met S S Carpathia when she docked in New York on Thursday 18 April was Henry Arthur Jones (1851–1929), a popular English playwright of the time; he wrote comedies and also plays of social theme, such as the double standard of behaviour expected of men and women, a theme that the Titanic *shipwreck evoked. The survivors here seem like dramatis personae.*

HENRY ARTHUR JONES
A Transcendent Calamity

(*Daily Telegraph*, 20 April 1912)

The long, gaunt, iron shed where the Cunard passengers land was not very crowded at eight o'clock last evening, an hour before the *Carpathia* was due to arrive. There was little evidence of the intense excitement and interest that had possessed New York for the past three days. To prevent an unmanageable crush it had been widely and wisely reported in the newspapers that the *Carpathia* would not dock until midnight, or possibly on the following morning. In about half an hour, however, the bare spaces began to fill, until there was a crowd of possibly the same dimensions as would await the homecoming of an ordinary steamer.

Outwardly there was little sign that anything unusual had brought them there last evening. There was a subdued ordinariness about the manner, dress and movements of the gathering crowd. Now and then, however, touching and significant figures could be seen threading their way through the unpicturesque groups – a few Salvation Army uniforms, a short procession of nurses with their red-crossed arms, an ambulance corps with stretchers, and two or three white-suited surgeons. For in the past day or two, in the growing excitement, and in the absence of any authentic news of the last hours of those on the sinking ship, and of the survivors in this terrible suspense, the wildest rumours gained credence of fearful scenes, of panic, of injuries, of widely spread pneumonia and of dementia amongst those who had been rescued.

To meet all possible exigencies of this kind a group of New York's leading citizenesses had given themselves up to organize a splendid and ample scheme of relief. Amongst those who had come on this errand of mercy was the beautiful and graceful figure whom English and

American playgoers will always affectionately remember as Eleanor Robson. All through the evening she was the busiest amongst those who were attending to the distracted and suffering survivors.

Very soon the onlookers saw the dark ship slowly creeping up the dark river to the dock, scarcely visible except for her long rows of lighted portholes. And behind those portholes? The bright flashes of photographers on the river played about her every few moments like ominous lightning darts. The always slow and tedious business of docking seemed interminably prolonged. A strictly guarded gateway had been fixed up to forbid all entrance to the ship except to those who could show their claim to admittance on board. Inside the shed the large and hushed crowd gathered into two long lines, allowing a narrow passage between them for the survivors of the *Titanic* to pass through. Again the time of waiting seemed indescribable. Then, at last, they began to reach land, those who had been so sorely buffeted at sea.

They came slowly down the gangway and through the guarded gate, assuming to us for the moment the importance of historical figures. Had they not for the last three days filled our imaginations like those who had been present and had escaped from some great battle in the past? Every figure, every face seemed to be remarkable, while it was passing. One face had a startled, frightened look, a look that seemed as if it would always be there. Another had a set and staring gaze. Another showed an angry rebellious desperation. This one was dazed; the next one seemed as though it had upon it some shadow of the dread event.

A woman came hurrying through, refusing to be comforted by her supporting friends, wildly calling, 'Where's my husband; where's my husband; where's my husband?' She passed on down the long line, her friends trying in vain to console her. A huddled and muffled figure came moaning by in a nurse's arms.

Then came a stalwart, healthy man, who apparently had suffered comparatively little. He gave a handshake and a cheery salutation to a friend in the crowd: 'All right, Harry?' the friend enquired. 'All right,' was the reply, with an undertone of deep thankfulness. Another woman came down, giving hurried and anxious glances on all sides. She uttered a great cry of joy, burst from her friends, and fell into the arms of a man who rushed up the line to meet her. They kissed each other again and again, and uttered extravagant, delighted cries as they staggered together down the line in each other's arms, quite unconcerned and unconscious of those around.

Four or five of the rescued crew, with the White Star plainly showing on their blue jerseys, came slowly and seriously through the lines and passed out. Another woman was brought off shrieking with hysteria, and could not be quieted. She was taken to a side place and gradually, after a long while, grew calmer and was led away.

Here there might be heard snatches of eager talk among survivors and their friends. 'Don't tell her anything about her father, for she doesn't know; we must keep it from her for a time.' A tearful, excited woman came up impatiently to an official leading a silent friend, whose face had the look of heavy settled despair. From their dress and manner they evidently belonged to the best social class in New York. 'She wants to go on board and search for her husband.'

Then came the ominous enquiry: 'Is his name on the published list of those saved?'

'No, but she must go and see. She doesn't know whether he is alive or dead. She must go and see whether he is there.'

The official coldly refused. A tender, protecting man was comforting a sobbing woman. 'Come right along home now; perhaps he may be saved after all. You can't tell,' he said.

A little poorly-clad, under-sized, consumptive steerage passenger, with a ghastly white face, bright eyes, and cheek bones almost protruding through his skin, was eagerly questioned how he came to be saved. 'Well, I was one of the lucky ones,' he said. 'I was asleep when it happened, and I went up on deck, and happened to be near one of the boats, and I didn't know whether to go on or stay where I was. I thought I'd better hang on to the ship. Then I thought I'd risk it, and jumped on. I was one of the lucky ones.'

A pitifully tender sight was one of the last ones. Five or six babies, whose mothers had been drowned, were brought out one after another in the arms of the ship's porters and carried to the waiting-rooms. They were from one to three years old. They had just been wakened from their sleep. One or two of them were crying; one or two were looking out with blank baby wonder on the new world they were being brought into. They, too, had found land after strange rockings in a dangerous cradle.

We turn away from these heart-breaking scenes. Deep calleth unto deep; the deep that swallowed the *Titanic* called forth an answering deep of compassion and heroism. Inspiring stories are told of the calmness and bravery of passengers, officers and the captain, a splendid sailor of our best breed. Captain Smith will always be gratefully remembered and regretted by those who have crossed the Atlantic in his care.

Another comforting remembrance is of the ready and boundless charity and eagerness to help which the city of New York has shown during the last days, and is continuing to show to the sufferers. Most fortifying of all is the thought that there is no great evil or disaster but has some issue of good. It was the cholera visitation in England that brought about our almost perfect system of English sanitation, and thereby saved a hundred times as many lives as the cholera had destroyed. It is only in transcendent calamity, in war, in famine, in pestilence, in tempests that shake and rend a State – it is only in these transcendent calamities that the heart of man can show itself possessed of a yet more transcendent courage, and in face of them all can steadily keep its undaunted way.

*Titanic's junior wireless operator dictated his story to a New York Times
reporter in the wireless room of SS Carpathia a few minutes after the
rescue ship docked. The accuracy of the transcript has been questioned:
for 'secretary' we should read 'secondary', and the American expressions
'through sleeping', 'back of' and 'I guess' are not Bride's words. But his
account rooted three Titanic legends: the tenacity of Jack Phillips, the
incident of the thieving stoker and the resoluteness of the band. Nothing
was known of Bride's whereabouts after 1913 until a private investigator
in 1987 discovered that he had died in Glasgow in 1956, having concealed
his past even from his new family.*

HAROLD BRIDE
This Kind of a Time

(*New York Times*, 19 April 1912)

To begin at the beginning, I joined the *Titanic* at Belfast. I
was born at Nunhead, England, twenty-two years ago, and joined the
Marconi forces last July. I first worked on the *Hoverford*, and then on
the *Lusitania*. I joined the *Titanic* at Belfast.

I didn't have much to do aboard the *Titanic* except to relieve [John
George] Phillips from midnight until some time in the morning, when
he should be through sleeping. On the night of the accident I was not
sending, but was asleep. I was due to be up and relieve Phillips earlier
than usual. And that reminds me – if it hadn't been for a lucky thing,
we never could have sent any call for help.

The lucky thing was that the wireless broke down early enough for
us to fix it before the accident. We noticed something wrong on Sunday,
and Phillips and I worked seven hours to find it. We found a 'secretary'
burned out, at last, and repaired it just a few hours before the iceberg
was struck.

Phillips said to me as he took the night shift, 'You turn in, boy, and
get some sleep, and go up as soon as you can and give me a chance.
I'm all done for with this work of making repairs.'

There were three rooms in the wireless cabin. One was a sleeping
room, one a dynamo room, and one an operating room. I took off my
clothes and went to sleep in bed. Then I was conscious of waking up

and hearing Phillips sending to Cape Race. I read what he was sending. It was traffic matter.

I remembered how tired he was, and I got out of bed without my clothes on to relieve him. I didn't even feel the shock. I hardly knew it had happened after the Captain had come to us. There was no jolt whatever.

I was standing by Phillips telling him to go to bed when the Captain put his head in the cabin.

'We've struck an iceberg,' the Captain said, 'and I'm having an inspection made to tell what it has done for us. You better get ready to send out a call for assistance. But don't send it until I tell you.'

The Captain went away and in ten minutes, I should estimate the time, he came back. We could hear a terrible confusion outside, but there was not the least thing to indicate that there was any trouble. The wireless was working perfectly.

'Send the call for assistance,' ordered the Captain, barely putting his head in the door.

'What call should I send?' Phillips asked.

'The regulation international call for help. Just that.'

Then the Captain was gone. Phillips began to send 'C.Q.D.' He flashed away at it and we joked while he did so. All of us made light of the disaster.

We joked that way while he flashed signals for about five minutes. Then the Captain came back.

'What are you sending?' he asked.

'C.Q.D.,' Phillips replied.

The humour of the situation appealed to me. I cut in with a little remark that made us all laugh, including the Captain.

'Send "S.O.S.",' I said. 'It's the new call, and it may be your last chance to send it.'

Phillips with a laugh changed the signal to 'S.O.S.' The Captain told us we had been struck amidships, or just back of amidships. It was ten minutes, Phillips told me, after he had noticed the iceberg that the slight jolt that was the collision's only signal to us occurred. We thought we were a good distance away.

We said lots of funny things to each other in the next few minutes. We picked up first the steamship *Frankfurd* [*sic*]. We gave her our position and said we had struck an iceberg and needed assistance. The *Frankfurd* operator went away to tell his Captain.

He came back, and we told him we were sinking by the head. By that time we could observe a distinct list forward.

The *Carpathia* answered our signal. We told her our position and said we were sinking by the head. The operator went to tell the Captain, and in five minutes returned and told us that the Captain of the *Carpathia* was putting about and heading for us.

Our Captain had left us at this time and Phillips told me to run and tell him what the *Carpathia* had answered. I did so, and I went through an awful mass of people to his cabin. The decks were full of scrambling men and women. I saw no fighting, but I heard tell of it.

I came back and heard Phillips giving the *Carpathia* fuller directions. Phillips told me to put on my clothes. Until that moment I forgot that I was not dressed.

I went to my cabin and dressed. I brought an overcoat to Phillips. It was very cold. I slipped the overcoat upon him while he worked.

Every few minutes Phillips would send me to the Captain with little messages. They were merely telling how the *Carpathia* was coming our way and gave her speed.

I noticed as I came back from one trip that they were putting off women and children in lifeboats. I noticed that the list forward was increasing.

Phillips told me the wireless was growing weaker. The Captain came and told us our engine rooms were taking water and that the dynamos might not last much longer. We sent that word to the *Carpathia*.

I went out on deck and looked around. The water was pretty close up to the boat deck. There was a great scramble aft, and how poor Phillips worked through it I don't know.

He was a brave man. I learned to love him that night, and I suddenly felt for him a great reverence to see him standing there sticking to his work while everybody else was raging about. I will never live to forget the work of Phillips for the last awful fifteen minutes.

I thought it was about time to look about and see if there was anything detached that would float. I remembered that every member of the crew had a special lifebelt and ought to know where it was. I remembered mine under my bunk. I went and got it. Then I thought how cold the water was.

I remembered I had some boots, and I put those on, and an extra jacket and I put that on. I saw Phillips standing out there still sending away, giving the *Carpathia* details of just how we were doing.

We picked up the *Olympic* and told her we were sinking by the head and were about all down. As Phillips was sending the message I strapped his lifebelt to his back. I had already put on his overcoat.

I wondered if I could get him into his boots. He suggested with a sort of laugh that I look out and see if all the people were off in the boats, or if any boats were left, or how things were.

I saw a collapsible boat near a funnel and went over to it. Twelve men were trying to boost it down to the boat deck. They were having an awful time. It was the last boat left. I looked at it longingly a few minutes. Then I gave them a hand, and over she went. They all started to scramble in on the boat deck, and I walked back to Phillips. I said the last raft had gone.

Then came the Captain's voice: 'Men you have done your full duty. You can do no more. Abandon your cabin. Now it's every man for himself. You look out for yourselves, I release you. That's the way of it at this kind of a time. Every man for himself.'

I looked out. The boat deck was awash. Phillips clung on sending and sending. He clung on for about ten minutes, or maybe fifteen minutes, after the Captain had released him. The water was then coming into our cabin.

While he worked something happened I hate to tell about. I was back in my room getting Phillips's money for him, and as I looked out the door I saw a stoker, or somebody from below decks, leaning over Phillips from behind. He was too busy to notice what the man was doing. The man was slipping the lifebelt off Phillips's back.

He was a big man, too. As you can see, I am very small. I don't know what it was I got hold of. I remembered in a flash the way Phillips had clung on – how I had to fix that lifebelt in place because he was too busy to do it.

I knew that man from below decks had his own lifebelt and should have known where to get it.

I suddenly felt a passion not to let that man die a decent sailor's death. I wished he might have stretched rope or walked a plank. I did my duty. I hope I finished him. I don't know. We left him on the cabin floor of the wireless room, and he was not moving.

From aft came the tunes of the band. It was a ragtime tune, I don't know what. Then there was 'Autumn'. Phillips ran aft, and that was the last I ever saw of him alive.

I went to the place I had seen the collapsible boat on the boat deck, and to my surprise I saw the boat and the men still trying to push it off. I guess there wasn't a sailor in the crowd. They couldn't do it. I went up to them and was just lending a hand when a large wave came awash of the deck.

The big wave carried the boat off. I had hold of an oarlock, and I went off with it. The next I knew I was in the boat.

But that was not all. I was in the boat, and the boat was upside down, and I was under it. And I remember realizing that I was wet through, and that whatever happened I must not breathe, for I was under water.

I knew I had to fight for it, and I did. How I got out from under the boat I do not know, but I felt a breath of air at last.

There were men all around me – hundreds of them. The sea was dotted with them, all depending on their lifebelts. I felt I simply had to get away from the ship. She was a beautiful sight then.

Smoke and sparks were rushing out of her funnel. There must have been an explosion, but we heard none. We only saw the big stream of sparks. The ship was gradually turning on her nose – just like a duck does that goes down for a dive. I had only one thing on my mind – to get away from the suction. The band was still playing. I guess all of the band went down.

They were playing 'Autumn' then. I swam with all my might. I suppose I was 150 feet away when the *Titanic* on her nose, with her after-quarter sticking straight up in the air, began to settle – slowly.

When at last the waves washed over her rudder there wasn't the least bit of suction I could feel. She must have kept going just so slowly as she had been.

I forgot to mention that, besides the *Olympic* and *Carpathia*, we spoke [to] some German boat, I don't know which, and told them how we were. We also spoke to the *Baltic*. I remembered those things as I began to figure what ships would be coming towards us.

I felt, after a little while, like sinking. I was very cold. I saw a boat of some kind near me and put all my strength into an effort to swim to it. It was hard work. I was all done when a hand reached out from the boat and pulled me aboard. It was our same collapsible. The same crowd was on it.

There was just room for me to roll on the edge. I lay there, not caring what happened. Somebody sat on my legs. They were wedged in between slats and were being wrenched. I had not the heart left to ask the man to move. It was a terrible sight all around – men swimming and sinking.

I lay where I was, letting the man wrench my feet out of shape. Others came near. Nobody gave them a hand. The bottom-up boat already had more men than it would hold and it was sinking.

At first the larger waves splashed over my clothing. Then they began to splash over my head, and I had to breathe when I could.

As we floated around on our capsized boat, and I kept straining my eyes for a ship's lights, somebody said, 'Don't the rest of you think we ought to pray?' The man who made the suggestion asked what the religion of the others was. Each man called out his religion. One was a Catholic, one a Methodist, one a Presbyterian.

It was decided the most appropriate prayer for all was the Lord's Prayer. We spoke it over in chorus with the man who first suggested that we pray as the leader.

Some splendid people saved us. They had a right-side-up boat, and it was full to its capacity. Yet they came to us and loaded us all into it. I saw some lights off in the distance and knew a steamship was coming to our aid.

I didn't care what happened. I just lay and gasped when I could and felt the pain in my feet. At last the *Carpathia* was alongside and the people were being taken up a rope ladder. Our boat drew near and one by one the men were taken off of it.

One man was dead. I passed him and went to the ladder, although my feet pained terribly. The dead man was Phillips. He had died on the raft from exposure and cold, I guess. He had been all in from work before the wreck came. He stood his ground until the crisis had passed, and then he had collapsed, I guess.

But I hardly thought that then. I didn't think much of anything. I tried the rope ladder. My feet pained terribly, but I got to the top and felt hands reaching out to me. The next I knew a woman was leaning over me in a cabin, and I felt her hand waving back my hair and rubbing my face.

I felt somebody at my feet and felt the warmth of a jolt of liquor. Somebody got me under the arms. Then I was hustled down below to the hospital. That was early in the day, I guess. I lay in the hospital until near night, and they told me the *Carpathia*'s wireless man was getting 'queer', and would I help.

After that I never was out of the wireless room, so I don't know what happened among the passengers. I saw nothing of Mrs Astor or any of them. I just worked wireless. The splutter never died down. I knew it soothed the hurt and felt like a tie to the world of friends and home.

How could I, then, take news queries? Sometimes I let a newspaper ask a question and get a long string of stuff asking for full particulars about everything. Whenever I started to take such a message I thought of the poor people waiting for their messages to go – hoping for answers to them.

I shut off the enquirers, and sent my personal messages. And I feel I did the white thing.

If the *Chester* [U.S. navy ship] had had a decent operator I could have worked with him longer, but he got terribly on my nerves with his insufferable incompetence. I was still sending my personal messages when Mr Marconi and the *Times* reporter arrived to ask that I prepare this statement.

There were, maybe, 100 left. I would like to send them all, because I could rest easier if I knew all those messages had gone to the friends waiting for them. But an ambulance man is waiting with a stretcher, and I guess I have got to go with him. I hope my legs get better soon.

The way the band kept playing was a noble thing. I heard it first while still we were working wireless, when there was a ragtime tune for us, and the last I saw of the band, when I was floating out in the sea with my lifebelt on, it was still on deck playing 'Autumn'. How they ever did it I cannot imagine.

That and the way Phillips kept sending after the Captain told him his life was his own, and to look out for himself, are two things that stand out in my mind over all the rest.

THOMAS C. SHOTWELL
Wall Street Report

(*San Francisco Examiner*, 19 April 1912)

Such was the depression of mind caused by further realization of the
Titanic disaster that nothing of importance was attempted in the stock
market today. The opening was strong with new high records in New
York Central, Bethlehem Steel, Beet Sugar and Wabash 4 per cent
bonds. Steel rose a point and all issues showed material advances over
the closing of the previous day. The trading was light and prices gradually
worked an average of nearly a point lower from sheer inertia. There
was no further attempt to raid the market, for the big people are in the
humour to punish severely any person who might attempt to make
money out of the great calamity.

*Brown's numbers have been amended to 190 bodies aboard the home-
bound* Mackay-Bennett *(with 116 consigned to the deeps). Brown,
though, captures the merely human episode (however poignant) in a
yearly narrative of impressive grandeur.*

RICHARD BROWN
The Search for the Dead

(*Voyage of the Iceberg*, 1983)

The search for the dead begins before *Carpathia* ties up in New
York. The White Star Line charters a cable ship, *Mackay-Bennett*, and
she sails from Halifax early on 18 April. She carries a minister and a
mortician among her crew, and a macabre cargo of coffins, shrouds,
ice, embalming fluid and scrap-iron for weighting burials at sea. The
search is slow because the weather is still very bad. The storm which
blew up after *Titanic* sank has scattered the bobbing corpses eastward
in a line fifty miles long. The grinding floes have crushed them into
anonymity, and the mortician has a difficult time trying to identify so
many battered faces. He recognizes John Jacob Astor only by the papers
in his wallet, and brings him home for burial, but most of the anonymous
bodies are buried at sea. The ship's doctor does some autopsies, and
he finds that none of them have water in the lungs. He believes they
all died peacefully, shocked instantly into death by the sudden cold of
the water. But he has not yet heard about the awful howling after *Titanic*
went down.

Minia, another cable ship, takes over the search at the end of April
and *Mackay-Bennett*, her store of ice and coffins exhausted, heads back
to Halifax. She has 219 bodies on board, and she has buried a hundred
more at sea. Other ships take over the search but there is little left to
find. Everyone who died in *Titanic* is either buried with her, two miles
down, or drifts on until the tapes of their life-jackets rot and let them
sink at last. For many years afterwards the Western Ocean mail steamships steer well clear of 41°46' N, 50°14' W, where *Titanic* lies, for fear
of meeting the bodies or their ghosts. But it is not long before the war
at sea makes bodies in life-jackets common enough in the North Atlantic.

The Iceberg vanishes before *Mackay-Bennett* comes home, as completely as if it had never existed. Most of the bergs from Greenland are caught up by the Gulf Stream long before they reach the Tail of the Bank, and drift northeast until they melt away. But in 1912 the eddies of the Stream take many of the bergs south instead, on unusual courses toward Bermuda and the Azores. The Iceberg goes no farther south than 38° N, 300 miles north of Bermuda, and then it is nothing.

There is a very sharp line between the Labrador Current and the Gulf Stream. It is the boundary between the cold, grey world of ice and seabirds, and the warm blue one of flying fish and sargassum weed. A thin bank of mist lies along it, like a magic curtain. The sea on the other side is suddenly 5°C warmer, in a matter of yards, and the Iceberg's days are numbered. Soon it is no more than a lump of ice no bigger than a table, scarcely strong enough to scratch a whaleboat.

The ice is clear as glass, and it glows a brilliant blue in the Sargasso water.

On 30 April the first shearwaters of the spring are coming up from the South Atlantic. They fly past in endless lines, tacking and gliding across the westerly winds, hungry for squid and capelin on the Grand Banks. One of them stalls, turns and circles around a greyish patch in the blue water. There is a soft fizz and crackle as the last of the air which was trapped 3,000 years ago on the Greenland Ice Cap breaks free from the sargassum weed. But there is nothing to eat and the shearwater turns north again.

On 30 April Captain Gardner brings *Mackay-Bennett* slowly into Halifax harbour. Every flag is at half-mast, and the naval band on the pier plays the 'Dead March from Saul'. The civic dignitaries reverently remove their hats as the endless line of coffins comes ashore. The black-draped hearses clop slowly up the hill to the armouries, where the bodies are to be laid out for identification. There are few people to speak for the bodies of the emigrants, who find their Promised Land in a common grave, as anonymous as if they had been buried at sea.

On 30 April spring in Jakobshavn Ice Fiord is slowly bringing the arctic world back to life. It is light again, and the snow buntings sing, the ptarmigan cackle, the foxes bark and the dovekies stream north along the coast. The glacier creeps down from the Ice Cap, sixty-five feet every day, and its tongue pushes out into the fiord. The tides work under it, up and down, and it breaks off at last in a crash of spray, with a roar that echoes off the mountains. Another iceberg is launched. It rocks itself slowly into stillness, but it does not quite stop. Slowly, very slowly, the current takes hold of it, and it drifts down the fiord to Baffin Bay.

THOMAS C. SHOTWELL
Wall Street Report

(*San Francisco Examiner*, 20 April 1912)

The *Titanic* horror reached a climax in the stock market today. Business dwindled to about 400,000 shares and the number of active issues was materially reduced. Prices, however, held firm. There was activity in spots and this activity caused advances. Bethlehem Steel and Western Union were conspicuous.

Adverse influences were ignored. Among these were the Mexican situation, the bombardment of the Dardanelles, the ultimatum of the locomotive engineers and further advance of the grain market. The Mississippi river flood grows worse. The wheat traders insist that this flood is a destructive influence and they are advancing the price of grain as a result. The cotton market has not been moved on flood news. In 1908, as well as in earlier years, cotton was planted as late as June 1 and made a big crop on land that was under flood in May. The big operators look on the flood as the biggest of all arguments for big crops and higher prices for securities this year.

There has been nothing the matter with the stock market the last few days but the depression growing out of the *Titanic* disaster. That influence promises to wear away by the middle of next week.

There were many memorial and fund-raising Titanic *concerts; the French actress Sarah Bernhardt crossed the Channel to take part in a Covent Garden theatrical benefit matinée. The biggest single event was perhaps that held in memory of the ship's bandsmen in the Royal Albert Hall on Empire Day (24 May); the largest orchestra ever assembled was conducted by Sir Henry Wood and Sir Edward Elgar; the audience of 10,000 sang 'Nearer My God to Thee'. There were other avenues of emotional display, as this report in rather strained prose tells us. The congregation was 5,000 strong.*

St Paul's Cathedral, Friday 19 April

(*The Deathless Story of the* Titanic, 1912)

The pity of all people was poured out in another way – in prayer and solemn memorial services for those who were lost. Most solemn and most beautiful was the great memorial service held in St Paul's Cathedral on Friday the 19th of April.

Out of the sunlit streets, gay with the beauty of life, there came into the dim twilight, and into the great hush, of St Paul's Cathedral a vast crowd of men and women, moved by an emotion as poignant as unshed tears.

These people of life came to think of death. They came to express their pity for a great human tragedy, which for a little while, in its awfulness, has made our brotherhood close its ranks like little children who cling together in fear and grief. These people of all classes, of spiritual belief and unbelief, came out of the streets of London to pray for those who have passed through the waters of death, and for those who have been left behind to weep. Seldom has any service in St Paul's spoken so directly to the hearts of the people who listened, and answered with tears.

Outside, the newspaper placards were telling in grim, black letters, the awful tale of the *Titanic* after the homecoming of the rescue-ship. Out of the long silence there had come the first tidings of how brave men died, and of how love and chivalry shone above the black terror of it all. It was with these messages speaking to them that the great crowds streamed towards the steps of St Paul's and surged into its nave.

The great doors were closed an hour before the service. The cathedral was full, and many were left outside. It was a vast, black multitude, upon which shafts of light poured down from the high windows. But here and there those glancing rays fell upon coloured ribbons and the flowers in women's hats, even red ties worn by men whose hearts were in mourning. What did it matter how people came dressed?

These people of rank and wealth, these City clerks and shopkeepers, and slum-dwellers had come together into the quiet sanctuary, not in any formal spirit, but in a comradeship of grief, greater than the small conventions of life. Their hearts were unclothed.

A military band picked from the best musicians of the Household troops was grouped below the choir-stalls, and as the hour of the service drew near they played sacred music which came in waves of sound between the pillars and rose in tremulous melody to the high dome. It was music full of sadness, so plaintive sometimes that it seemed like tears of pity falling upon the bowed heads of the people.

After the intoning of the Lesson there was a great silence for a little while. Then suddenly there was a vague, soft noise. It was as though great birds were fluttering their wings outside the windows of the Cathedral. The noise increased. It was the sound of a mighty wind. Louder and louder it grew as the ruffle was played on the massed drums, until the vast Cathedral was filled with a tempest of prodigious sound as though all the winds of heaven were rushing over the heads of the people, as though the sea were rising in fury. Then came the boom of great guns, the echo of tremendous thunder, and great crashes as though the sky were rent.

That music of the drums was magnificent and awe-inspiring. It was the story of the *Titanic* in her last agony. Through the dim light between the pillars one saw that mighty ship struck by a mortal blow. One saw her stagger and reel above the waters. One heard the dreadful voice of Nature pronouncing her doom. One heard the groans of her people, the last great noise as she sank into the depths and then the gradual stilling of the engulfing waters, and at last – the quietude of death that reigned over the scene of dreadful tragedy.

Now, as when soldiers and heroes go to their graves, the Dead March in 'Saul' was played, and again the drums thundered, as though great guns were being fired in the last salute to men who have found victory in death, and there rose that music, sad as death itself, pitiful as the cry of broken hearts, solemn, tragic, yet in the end triumphant as any music that may be heard by the ears of men.

There were many people weeping while that tune of death was played. There were soldiers and sailors in St Paul's who have heard it played for dead comrades, and they, too, stood erect, with tears streaming down their cheeks, not ashamed of tears. It may be said in all sincerity that the hearts of all these people were stirred to their uttermost depths by thoughts deeper than may be put into words, by a human pity touched by the divine spirit of compassion.

Dr Charles Parkhurst preached this sermon in Madison Square Presby-
terian Church, New York on 21 April. It anticipates some of the prurient
imagery in Thomas Hardy's famous poem, 'The Convergence of the
Twain'. Parkhurst is having none of the notion that heroism somehow
redeemed commerce, materialism and arrogance.

CHARLES H. PARKHURST
This Sunken Palace of the Sea

(*Literary Digest*, 4 May 1912)

Different temperaments have, of course, seized upon different
aspects of this unparalleled tragedy. Each of you has your own line of
contemplation. I am going to tell you mine, and I am going to cut as
close to the line of truth and to the nerve of the sensitive heart as I
know how; for if this event is treated as it ought to be, it is going to
produce some searchings of heart that will modify to a degree the
attitude of the general mind toward certain vital questions of individual
and public life.

The picture which presents itself before my eyes is that of the glassy,
glaring eyes of the victims, staring meaninglessly at the gilded furnishings
of this sunken palace of the sea; dead helplessness wrapt in priceless
luxury; jewels valued in seven figures becoming the strange playthings
of the queer creatures that sport in the dark depths. Everything for
existence, nothing for life. Grand men, charming women, beautiful
babies, all becoming horrible in the midst of the glittering splendour
of a $10,000,000 casket!

And there was no need of it. It is just so much sacrifice laid upon the
accurst altar of the dollar. The boat had no business to be running in
that lane. They knew that the ice was there. They dared it. They would
dare it now were it not for the public. It is cheaper to run by the
short route. There is more money in it for the stockholders. The
multimillionaires want more money. They want as much as they can
get of it. The coal is now saved. It is starting a little mine at the bottom
of the ocean between Sable Island and Cape Race.

It is a lesson all around to the effect that commercialism, when pushed
beyond a certain pace, breaks down and results in stringency and poverty;

and that action, when crowded, produces reaction that wipes out the results of action . . .

We can conceive no severer punishment for those steamship men – the one who is here now with the others – than to be compelled to read and reread the harrowing details of those two hours from midnight to 2 a.m. on the morning of the sinking of the ship. We will not be angry with them. Rather will we pity them, for if their hearts have not been hardened to the consistency of the metal in which they deal, the perusal of the ghastly record, the contemplation of the vivid drama of men leaping to their death, bidding long good-byes to those loved ones, and all to the accompaniment of the infernal music of the orchestra, ought to give them a foretaste of the tortures of the damned.

Yes, we pity them, for unless their hearts are clean gone and burnt to a crisp, these days are to them days of remorse, of gnawing of the soul. Their guilt is not momentary. It is driven home with a gold hammer, which will beat them into sensibility. Had Providence held back the tragedy the moral lesson only would have been delayed.

The two sore spots which really run into one another and which constitute the disease that is gnawing into our civilization are love of money and passion for luxury. Those two combined are what sunk the *Titanic* and sent 1,500 souls prematurely to their final account.

5
A Knot of Puzzles

The Court is passing to the knot of puzzles in which the whole tragedy
still seems hopelessly tangled.   *Daily Sketch*

The knot to which the Daily Sketch *referred had already intrigued and
exasperated newspaper editors and readers before, during and after the
U.S. Senate Hearings in April and May. The wreck has played host to
puzzles from 1912 to the present, and is still regarded as harbouring
'secrets' she is keeping from us.*

The questions most pressingly asked at the time were these: Was
Titanic *speeding through ice-fields and if so, why, since she had received
ice-warnings? Why was the iceberg not seen in time? Why did this ship
not have sufficient lifeboats to accommodate all her passengers? Why
were many lifeboats unfilled? Why didn't lifeboats return to the wreckage
to look for passengers in the sea? Why were a disproportionate number
of the lost from steerage? Were third-class passengers prevented from
reaching the boat deck? Of those on board, on whose shoulders should
guilt settle: Captain Smith? President Ismay? the officers and crew?
How far are the owners, White Star and IMM, responsible? And
speaking of responsibility: How far away was SS* Californian, *and did
she see or ignore* Titanic's *pleas for help?*

*Behind these were larger questions: Have ships become too large to
be structurally strong or navigationally safe? Have we become obsessed
with speed at the expense of safety? What practical steps can be taken
as soon as possible to prevent another such disaster? And smaller, but
still provocative, questions: How come Ismay survived, but hundreds of
passengers did not? Did the ship break in two before she sank? How
chivalrous in their comportment were first-class men? What became of
Captain Smith?*

The arrival of SS Carpathia *in New York after its obstinately silent approach tied another knot of puzzles that particularly exercised the American Enquiry since they concerned social issues of moment. The British, for their part, and to the irritation of the Commission chairman, were more interested in the small number of survivors in a lifeboat in which Sir Cosmo and Lady Duff Gordon were passengers: Was there a nasty reversal of* noblesse oblige *at work? Indecent (rather than ordinary) inequities of social class were to the British what trusts and denial of information were to the Americans.*

Two official enquiries and innumerable newspaper and magazine articles, and indeed books, all within the year, showed that answers to these questions were not readily forthcoming. This did not prevent some observers, including famous English writers, from holding and expressing very firm opinions, particularly on the question of heroism and the overnight legends of Titanic. *Occasionally, such firm opinions stepped on toes on the other side of the Atlantic at a time when Britain and the United States were jostling for supremacy on the world stage if not the high seas – the rivalry there was between Britain and Germany.*

Thomas Scanlan, the lawyer representing the National Sailors' and Firemen's Union, interrogated Lightoller on the issue of speed (wishing to establish negligence at the levels of officers and owners). Lightoller recalled: 'I am never likely to forget that long-drawn out battle of wits . . . Pull devil, pull baker, till it looked as if they would pretty well succeed in pulling my hide off completely, each seemed to want his bit.' Despite the finding of the British Commission that excessive speed was the greatest contributory factor to the disaster, Lightoller was unscathed.

Banging On? Charles Lightoller's British Testimony

(*British Commission of Enquiry into the Loss of the S.S.* Titanic, May–June 1912)

14359. *Mr Scanlan.* Can you tell us at what speed the *Titanic* was going when you left the bridge at 10 o'clock? – About 21½ knots.

14360. What was the indication from which you make that calculation? – I judge from what I remember of the revolutions. I think, as far as I remember, the revolutions were 75, and I think that will give an average speed of about 21½.

14361. The speed was taken down, I understand, in the log? – Yes, that would be kept in the scrap log.

14362. I do not suggest that you wanted to make a record passage on this occasion, but had not you all in mind the desirability of making a very good first trip, from the speed point of view? – No, I am afraid not, because we know that in the White Star, particularly the first voyages – in fact you may say pretty well for the first twelve months – the ship never attains her full speed.

14363. Were not you on this occasion taking as much speed as you could get out of the *Titanic*? – Oh, no, not at all; I am under the impression she was under a very reduced speed compared with what she was capable of doing.

14364. What maximum speed do you think you could have attained? – Well, just as a matter of hearsay, or rather, what we estimated roughly, for instance myself, I judged that the ship would eventually do about 24 knots.

14365. Did you say yesterday that you were going at as high a speed as you could in view of the coal you had on board? – Did I say so yesterday?

14366. Yes? – I was not on the stand yesterday.

The Solicitor-General: Yes, you were.

14367. *Mr Scanlan.* You were being examined yesterday? – Oh, yes; I beg your pardon. Not only with regard to shortage of coal, but I understand several boilers were off.

14368. Do you know any reason for those boilers being off? – Merely that there was no wish for the ship to travel at any great speed.

14369. There was no reason, I take it, why you should not go fast; but, in view of the abnormal conditions and of the fact that you were nearing ice at ten o'clock, was there not a very obvious reason for going slower? – Well, I can only quote you my experience throughout the last 24 years, that I have been crossing the Atlantic most of the time, that I have never seen the speed reduced.

14370. You were asked by my Lord this forenoon how an unfortunate accident like this could have been prevented in what you describe as abnormal circumstances? – Yes.

14371. Is it not quite clear that the most obvious way to avoid it is by slackening speed? – Not necessarily the most obvious.

14372. Well, is it one way? – It is one way. Naturally, if you stop the ship you will not collide with anything.

14373. There was no reason why you might not slacken speed on this voyage, you were not running to any scheduled time? – No . . .

14412. Am I to understand, even with the knowledge you have had through coming through this *Titanic* disaster, at the present moment, if you were placed in the same circumstances, you would still bang on at 21½ knots an hour? – I do not say I should bang on at all; I do not approve of the term banging on.

14413. I mean drive ahead? – That looks like carelessness you know; it looks as if we would recklessly bang on and slap her into it regardless of anything. Undoubtedly we should not do that.

14414. What I want to suggest to you is that it was recklessness, utter recklessness, in view of the conditions which you have described as abnormal, and in view of the knowledge you had from various sources that ice was in your immediate vicinity, to proceed at 21½ knots? – Then all I can say is that recklessness applies to practically every commander and every ship crossing the Atlantic Ocean.

14415. I am not disputing that with you, but can you describe it yourself as other than recklessness? – Yes.

14416. Is it careful navigation in your view? – It is ordinary navigation, which embodies careful navigation . . .

14425. What I want to suggest is that the conditions having been so dangerous, those in charge of the vessel were negligent in proceeding at that rate of speed? – No.

"UNSINKABLE"

Dozens of North American cartoonists greeted the tragedy with anger, cynicism or (as here) wryness.

The Titanic *disaster blighted untold lives, and Frederick Fleet was a notable casualty. He began life handicapped anyway, an orphan in a Dr Barnardo's Home, hoisting himself up from deck boy to* Titanic *lookout. After the tragedy, he spent twenty-four years at sea, became on retirement a newspaper seller on the street in Southampton and in 1965 hanged himself after his wife's death: a life, it seems, poisoned by one night's astounding event. At both enquiries he was an awkward customer, very touchy: 'Is there any more likes to have a go at me?' he asked the British Commission. His dialogue with Senator Smith (the soul of patience) at the American Inquiry resembles a scene in a Harold Pinter play, humorous, repetitive and pointless all at the same time.*

A Sharp Lookout for Small Ice: Frederick Fleet's American Testimony

(Titanic *Disaster: Hearings before a Subcommittee of the Committee on Commerce, United States Senate*, April–May 1912)

SENATOR SMITH. I want to get on the record the place where you were stationed in the performance of your duty.

MR FLEET. I was on the lookout.

SENATOR SMITH. On the lookout?

MR FLEET. At the time of the collision.

SENATOR SMITH. In the crow's nest?

MR FLEET. Yes.

SENATOR SMITH. At the time of the collision?

MR FLEET. Yes, sir.

SENATOR SMITH. Can you tell how high above the boat deck that is?

MR FLEET. I have no idea.

SENATOR SMITH. Can you tell how high above the crow's nest the masthead is?

MR FLEET. No, sir.

SENATOR SMITH. Do you know how far you were above the bridge?

MR FLEET. I am no hand at guessing.

SENATOR SMITH. I do not want you to guess; but, if you know, I would like to have you tell.

MR FLEET. I have no idea.

SENATOR FLETCHER. You hardly mean that; you have some idea?

MR FLEET. No; I do not.

SENATOR FLETCHER. You know whether it was a thousand feet or two hundred?

SENATOR SMITH. Was there any other officer or employee stationed at a higher point on the *Titanic* than you were?

MR FLEET. No, sir.

SENATOR SMITH. You were the lookout?

MR FLEET. Yes, sir.

SENATOR SMITH. Where are the eyes of the ship?

MR FLEET. The eyes of the ship?

SENATOR SMITH. The ship's eyes?

MR FLEET. Forward.

SENATOR SMITH. At the extreme bow?

MR FLEET. Yes, sir.

SENATOR SMITH. And on the same level as the boat deck or below it?

MR FLEET. Below it.

SENATOR SMITH. How far below it?

MR FLEET. I do not know, sir.

SENATOR SMITH. Mr Fleet, can you tell who was on the forward part of the *Titanic* Sunday night when you took your position in the crow's nest?

MR FLEET. There was nobody.

SENATOR SMITH. Nobody?

MR FLEET. No, sir.

SENATOR SMITH. Who was on the bridge?

MR FLEET. When I went up to relieve the others?

SENATOR SMITH. Yes.

MR FLEET. Mr Murdock [*sic*].

SENATOR SMITH. Officer Murdock?

MR FLEET. First officer.

SENATOR SMITH. Who else?

MR FLEET. I think it was the third officer.

SENATOR SMITH. What was his name?

MR FLEET. The man that was here, Pitman.

SENATOR SMITH. Mr Pitman, the man who just left the stand?

MR FLEET. I do not know the officers on the bridge.

SENATOR SMITH. You do not recall any more of them?

MR FLEET. No; I do not know whether he was there or not.

SENATOR SMITH. I do not want any confusion if I can help it. I want to get this down right. Was the captain on the bridge?

MR FLEET. I do not know, sir.

SENATOR SMITH. You did not see him?

MR FLEET. No, sir.

SENATOR SMITH. What time did you take your watch Sunday night?

MR FLEET. Ten o'clock.

SENATOR NEWLANDS. Whom did you relieve?

MR FLEET. Symons and Jewell.

SENATOR SMITH. Who was with you on the watch?

MR FLEET. Lee.

SENATOR SMITH. What, if anything, did Symons and Jewell, or either one, say to you when you relieved them of the watch?

MR FLEET. They told us to keep a sharp lookout for small ice.

SENATOR SMITH. What did you say to them?

MR FLEET. I said 'All right'.

SENATOR SMITH. What did Lee say?

MR FLEET. He said the same.

SENATOR SMITH. And you took your position in the crow's nest?

MR FLEET. Yes, sir.

SENATOR SMITH. Did you keep a sharp lookout for ice?

MR FLEET. Yes, sir.

SENATOR SMITH. Tell what you did?

MR FLEET. Well, I reported an iceberg right ahead, a black mass.

SENATOR SMITH. When did you report that?

MR FLEET. I could not tell you the time.

SENATOR SMITH. About what time?

MR FLEET. Just after seven bells.

SENATOR SMITH. How long after you had taken your place in the crow's nest?

MR FLEET. The watch was nearly over. I had done the best part of the watch up in the nest.

SENATOR SMITH. How long a watch did you have?

MR FLEET. Two hours; but the time was going to be put back – that watch.

SENATOR SMITH. The time was to be set back?

MR FLEET. Yes, sir.

SENATOR SMITH. Did that alter your time?

MR FLEET. We were to get about 2 hours and 20 minutes.

SENATOR SMITH. How long before the collision or accident did you report ice ahead?

MR FLEET. I have no idea.

SENATOR SMITH. About how long?

MR FLEET. I could not say, at the rate she was going.

SENATOR SMITH. How fast was she going?

MR FLEET. I have no idea.

SENATOR SMITH. Would you be willing to say that you reported the presence of this iceberg an hour before the collision?

MR FLEET. No, sir.

SENATOR SMITH. Forty-five minutes?

MR FLEET. No, sir.

SENATOR SMITH. A half hour before?

MR FLEET. No, sir.

SENATOR SMITH. Fifteen minutes before?

MR FLEET. No, sir.

SENATOR SMITH. Ten minutes before?

MR FLEET. No, sir.

SENATOR SMITH. How far away was this black mass when you first saw it?

MR FLEET. I have no idea, sir.

SENATOR SMITH. Can you not give us some idea? Did it impress you as serious?

MR FLEET. I reported it as soon as ever I seen it.

SENATOR SMITH. I want a complete record of it, you know. Give me, as nearly as you can, how far away it was when you saw it. You are accustomed to judging distances, are you not, from the crow's nest? You are there to look ahead and sight objects, are you not?

MR FLEET. We are only up there to report anything we see.

SENATOR SMITH. But you are expected to see and report anything in the path of the ship, are you not?

MR FLEET. Anything we see – a ship, or anything.

SENATOR SMITH. Anything you see?

MR FLEET. Yes; anything we see.

SENATOR SMITH. Whether it be a field of ice, a 'growler', or an iceberg, or any other substance?

MR FLEET. Yes, sir.

SENATOR SMITH. Have you trained yourself so that you can see objects as you approach them with fair accuracy?

MR FLEET. I do not know what you mean, sir.

SENATOR SMITH. If there had been a black object ahead of this ship, or a white one, a mile away, or 5 miles away, 50 feet above the water or 150 feet above the water, would you have been able to see it, from your experience as a seaman?

MR FLEET. Yes, sir.

SENATOR SMITH. When you see these things in the path of the ship, you report them?

MR FLEET. Yes, sir.

SENATOR SMITH. What did you report when you saw this black mass Sunday night?

MR FLEET. I reported an iceberg right ahead.

SENATOR SMITH. To whom did you report that?

MR FLEET. I struck three bells first. Then I went straight to the telephone and rang them up on the bridge.

SENATOR SMITH. You struck three bells and went to the telephone and rang them up on the bridge?

MR FLEET. Yes.

SENATOR SMITH. Did you get anyone on the bridge?

MR FLEET. I got an answer straight away – what did I see, or 'What did you see?'

SENATOR SMITH. Did the person who was talking to you tell you who he was?

MR FLEET. No. He just asked me what did I see. I told him an iceberg right ahead.

SENATOR SMITH. What did he say then?

MR FLEET. He said: 'Thank you.'

SENATOR SMITH. Do you know to whom you were talking?

MR FLEET. No; I do not know who it was.

SENATOR SMITH. What was the object in sending the three bells?

MR FLEET. That denotes an iceberg right ahead.

SENATOR SMITH. It denotes danger?

MR FLEET. No; it just tells them on the bridge that there is something about.

SENATOR SMITH. You took both precautions; you gave the three bells, and then you went and telephoned to the bridge?

MR FLEET. Yes, sir.

SENATOR SMITH. Where did you have to go to telephone?

MR FLEET. The telephone is in the nest.

SENATOR SMITH. The telephone is right in the crow's nest?

MR FLEET. Yes.

SENATOR SMITH. You turned and communicated with the bridge from the nest?

MR FLEET. Yes, sir.

SENATOR SMITH. Did you get a prompt response?

MR FLEET. I did.

SENATOR SMITH. And you made the statement that you have indicated?

MR FLEET. Yes.

SENATOR SMITH. Then what did you do?

MR FLEET. After I rang them up?

SENATOR SMITH. Yes, sir.

MR FLEET. I kept staring ahead again.

SENATOR SMITH. You remained in the crow's nest?

MR FLEET. I remained in the crow's nest until I got relief.

SENATOR SMITH. And Lee remained in the nest?

MR FLEET. Yes.

SENATOR SMITH. How long did you stay there?

MR FLEET. About a quarter of an hour to 20 minutes after.

SENATOR SMITH. After what?

MR FLEET. After the accident.

SENATOR SMITH. And then did you leave this place?

MR FLEET. We got relieved by the other two men.

SENATOR SMITH. The other two men came?

MR FLEET. Yes.

SENATOR SMITH. Did they go up?

MR FLEET. They came up in the nest.

SENATOR SMITH. And you got down?

MR FLEET. We got down; yes.

SENATOR SMITH. Can you not indicate, in any way, the length of time that elapsed between the time that you first gave this information by telephone and by bell to the bridge officer and the time the boat struck the iceberg?

MR FLEET. I could not tell you, sir.

SENATOR SMITH. You cannot say?

MR FLEET. No, sir.

SENATOR SMITH. You cannot say whether it was five minutes or an hour?

MR FLEET. I could not say, sir.

SENATOR SMITH. I wish you would tell the committee whether you apprehended danger when you sounded these signals and telephoned; whether you thought there was danger?

MR FLEET. No; no, sir. That is all we have to do up in the nest; to ring the bell, and if there is any danger ring them up on the telephone.

SENATOR SMITH. The fact that you did ring them up on the telephone indicated that you thought there was danger?

MR FLEET. Yes, sir.

SENATOR SMITH. You thought there was danger?

MR FLEET. Well, it was so close to us. That is why I rang them up.

SENATOR SMITH. How large an object was this when you first saw it?

MR FLEET. It was not very large when I first saw it.

SENATOR SMITH. How large was it?

MR FLEET. I have no idea of distances or spaces.

SENATOR SMITH. Was it the size of an ordinary house? Was it as large as this room appears to be?

MR FLEET. No; no. It did not appear very large at all.

SENATOR SMITH. Was it as large as the table at which I am sitting?

MR FLEET. It would be as large as those two tables put together, when I saw it at first.

SENATOR SMITH. When you first saw it, it appeared about as large as these two tables put together?

MR FLEET. Yes, sir.

SENATOR SMITH. Did it appear to get larger after you first saw it?

MR FLEET. Yes; it kept getting larger as we were getting nearer it.

SENATOR SMITH. As it was coming toward you and you were going toward it?

MR FLEET. Yes.

SENATOR SMITH. How large did it get to be, finally, when it struck the ship?

MR FLEET. When we were alongside, it was a little bit higher than the forecastle head.

SENATOR SMITH. The forecastle head is how high above the water line?

MR FLEET. Fifty feet, I should say.

SENATOR SMITH. About 50 feet?

MR FLEET. Yes.

SENATOR SMITH. So that this black mass, when it finally struck the boat, turned out to be about 50 feet above the water?

MR FLEET. About 50 or 60.

SENATOR SMITH. Fifty or sixty feet above the water?

MR FLEET. Yes.

SENATOR SMITH. And when you first saw it it looked no larger than these two tables?

MR FLEET. No, sir.

SENATOR SMITH. Do you know whether the ship was stopped after you gave that telephone signal?

MR FLEET. No, no; she did not stop at all. She did not stop until she passed the iceberg.

SENATOR SMITH. She did not stop until she passed the iceberg?

MR FLEET. No, sir.

SENATOR SMITH. Do you know whether her engines were reversed?

MR FLEET. Well, she started to go to port while I was at the telephone.

SENATOR SMITH. She started to go to port?

MR FLEET. Yes; the wheel was put to starboard.

SENATOR SMITH. How do you know that?

MR FLEET. My mate saw it and told me. He told me he could see the bow coming around.

SENATOR SMITH. They swung the ship's bow away from the object?

MR FLEET. Yes; because we were making straight for it.

SENATOR SMITH. But you saw the course altered? And the iceberg struck the ship at what point?

MR FLEET. On the starboard bow, just before the foremast.

SENATOR SMITH. How far would that be from the bow's end?

MR FLEET. From the stem?

SENATOR SMITH. From the stem.

MR FLEET. About 20 feet.

SENATOR SMITH. About 20 feet back from the stem?

MR FLEET. From the stem to where she hit.

SENATOR SMITH. When she struck this obstacle, or this black mass, was there much of a jar to the ship?

MR FLEET. No, sir.

SENATOR SMITH. Was there any?

MR FLEET. Just a slight grinding noise.

SENATOR SMITH. Not sufficient to disturb you in your position in the crow's nest?

MR FLEET. No, sir.

SENATOR SMITH. Did it alarm you seriously when it struck?

MR FLEET. No, sir; I thought it was a narrow shave.

SENATOR SMITH. You thought it was a narrow shave?

MR FLEET. Yes, sir.

SENATOR SMITH. Did any of this ice break on to the decks?

MR FLEET. Yes; some on the forecastle light and some on the weather deck.

SENATOR SMITH. How much?

MR FLEET. Not much; only where she rubbed up against it.

SENATOR SMITH. Did Lee and you talk over this black object that you saw?

MR FLEET. Only up in the nest.

SENATOR SMITH. What did you say about it? What did he say about it to you or what did you say about it to him?

MR FLEET. Before I reported, I said, 'There is ice ahead,' and then I put my hand over to the bell and rang it three times, and then I went to the phone.

SENATOR SMITH. What did he say?

MR FLEET. He said nothing much. He just started looking. He was looking ahead while I was at the phone and he seen the ship go to port.

SENATOR SMITH. Did Lee survive this wreck, or was he drowned?

MR FLEET. He is one that survived it.

SENATOR SMITH. You cannot recollect just what he said to you when she struck?

MR FLEET. No, sir.

SENATOR SMITH. Nor when you first sighted this black mass?

MR FLEET. No, sir.

SENATOR SMITH. Who sighted the black mass first; you or Lee?

MR FLEET. I did. I say I did, but I think he was just as soon as me.

Fifth Officer Lowe herded lifeboats together and took command of the flotilla, and in the morning headed for the rescuing Carpathia. Senator Smith implies that Lowe showed a reluctance to return to the scene and save as many survivors as his boat could accommodate. Testimony was mixed on the question. Archibald Gracie was of the opinion that Lowe's conduct as an officer was exemplary. Able Seaman Scarrott's narrative of their entrance among the bodies complements Lowe's dispassionate replies to Senator Smith; Scarrott concludes, having earlier recalled the terrible cries of those in the water: 'As we left that awful scene we gave way to tears. It was enough to break the stoutest heart.'

The Return of Boat 14: Harold Lowe's American Testimony

(*U.S. Senate Hearings*, 1912)

SENATOR SMITH. You say there were how many people in your boat?

MR LOWE. Fifty-eight, sir.

SENATOR SMITH. And that was when you left the davits?

MR LOWE. That was when I left the davits.

SENATOR SMITH. How many people got into that boat after it reached the water, or at any other deck?

MR LOWE. None, sir. You see, I chased all of my passengers out of my boat and emptied her into four other boats that I had. I herded five boats all together.

SENATOR SMITH. Yes; what were they?

MR LOWE. I was in No. 14. Then I had 10, I had 12, and I had another collapsible, and one other boat the number of which I do not know. I herded them together and roped them – made them all tie up – and of course I had to wait until the yells and shrieks had subsided – for the people to thin out – and then I deemed it safe for me to go amongst the wreckage. So I transferred all my passengers – somewhere about 53 passengers – from my boat, and I equally distributed them between my other four boats. Then I asked for volunteers to go with me to the wreck, and it was at this time that I found this Italian. He came aft, and he had a shawl over his head and I suppose he had skirts. Anyhow, I pulled this shawl off his face and saw he was a man. He was in a great hurry to get into the other boat, and I caught hold of him and pitched him in.

SENATOR SMITH. Pitched him in?

MR LOWE. Yes; because he was not worthy of being handled better.

SENATOR SMITH. You pitched him in among the women?

MR LOWE. No, sir; in the fore part of the lifeboat in which I transferred my passengers.

SENATOR SMITH. Did you use some pretty emphatic language when you did that?

MR LOWE. No, sir; I did not say a word to him.

SENATOR SMITH. Just picked him up and pitched him into this other lifeboat?

MR LOWE. Yes. Then I went off and I rowed off to the wreckage and around the wreckage and I picked up four people.

SENATOR SMITH. Dead or alive?

MR LOWE. Four alive.

SENATOR SMITH. Who were they?

MR LOWE. I do not know.

SENATOR SMITH. Have you ever found out?

MR LOWE. I do not know who these three live persons were; they never came near me afterwards, either to say this, that, or the other. But one died, and that was a Mr Hoyt of New York, and it took all the boat's crew to pull this gentleman into the boat, because he was an enormous man, and I suppose he had been soaked fairly well with water, and when we picked him up he was bleeding from the mouth and from the nose. So we did get him on board and I propped him up at the stern of the boat, and we let go his collar, took his collar off and loosened his shirt so as to give him every chance to breathe; but, unfortunately, he died. I suppose he was too far gone when we picked him up. But the other three survived. I then left the wreck. I went right around and, strange to say, I did not see a single female body, not one, around the wreckage.

SENATOR SMITH. Did you have a light in your boat?

MR LOWE. No, sir. I left my crowd in boats somewhere, I should say, about between half past 3 and 4 in the morning, and after I had been around it was just breaking day, and I am quite satisfied that I had a real good look around, and that there was nothing left . . .

SENATOR SMITH. I want to take you back a moment. Before you

transferred the 53 people from your lifeboat, No. 14, to other life-boats, including this Italian in woman's attire, you say you lay off a bit. Where; how far from the *Titanic*?

MR LOWE. I lay off from the *Titanic*, as near as I could roughly estimate, about 150 yards, because I wanted to be close enough in order to pick up anybody that came by.

SENATOR SMITH. I understand; but you said you lay off a bit to wait until it quieted down.

MR LOWE. Yes.

SENATOR SMITH. Until what quieted down?

MR LOWE. Until the drowning people had thinned out.

SENATOR SMITH. You lay off a bit until the drowning people had quieted down?

MR LOWE. Yes.

SENATOR SMITH. Then you went to the scene of the wreck?

MR LOWE. Yes.

SENATOR SMITH. Had their cries quieted down before you started?

MR LOWE. Yes; they had subsided a good deal. It would not have been wise or safe for me to have gone there before, because the whole lot of us would have been swamped and then nobody would have been saved.

SENATOR SMITH. But your boat had, according to your own admission, a water capacity of 65 people?

MR LOWE. Yes; but then what are you going to do with a boat of 65 where 1,600 people are drowning?

SENATOR SMITH. You could have saved 15.

MR LOWE. You could not do it, sir.

SENATOR SMITH. At least, you made no attempt to do it?

MR LOWE. I made the attempt, sir, as soon as any man could do so, and I am not scared of saying it. I did not hang back or anything else.

SENATOR SMITH. I am not saying you hung back. I am just saying that you said you lay by until it had quieted down.

MR LOWE. You had to do so. It was absolutely not safe. You could not do otherwise, because you would have hundreds of people around your boat, and the boat would go down just like that [indicating].

SENATOR SMITH. About how long did you lay by?

MR LOWE. I should say an hour and a half; somewhere under two hours.

SENATOR SMITH. On your oars?

MR LOWE. No; we did not. We unshipped our oars, and I made the five boats fast together and we hung on like that.

SENATOR SMITH. Did you see the *Titanic* sink?

MR LOWE. I did, sir.

SENATOR SMITH. How long after you left her side in the lifeboat did she sink?

MR LOWE. I suppose about half an hour. No – yes; somewhere about half an hour.

SENATOR SMITH. Then you laid an hour after she sank?

MR LOWE. An hour after she sank.

SENATOR SMITH. Before going to the scene of the wreck?

MR LOWE. Before going to the scene of the wreck.

SENATOR SMITH. You were about 150 yards off?

MR LOWE. I was just on the margin. If anybody had struggled out of the mass, I was there to pick them up; but it was useless for me to go into the mass.

SENATOR SMITH. You mean for anybody?

MR LOWE. It would have been suicide.

SENATOR SMITH. Do you mean that if anybody had applied to you for permission to get aboard, you would have accorded them the right?

MR LOWE. I would have taken anybody and everybody; that is, because we could have handled them there. We could never have handled them in the mass.

Both enquiries took place against a background of violent labour disputes in both countries. Many Americans, socialist or no, fastened on the possible class discrimination aboard a British ship. And for the committed left, the ship herself could be seen as a product of an exploitative capitalism. H. G. Wells saw in Ismay and the capitalist system at work during the sinking 'the abandonment of every noble pretension'. Appeal to Reason was a socialist magazine from Girard, Kansas. (There was, of course, no golf course on Titanic *and only one swimming pool.)*

A Capitalist Disaster

(*Appeal to Reason* (Kansas), 4 May 1912)

When the *Titanic*, the greatest ocean liner ever launched, went down to the bottom on her maiden trip, she carried sixteen hundred human beings down with her. The *Titanic* illustrated in herself and in her destruction within three days after she put to sea the greed and rapacity and contempt for human life which under capitalism inspired and presided over her creation.

There are a thousand reasons why this horror upon the high sea should never have occurred; why it was absolutely inexcusable and indefensible: why it was courted and inevitable, and why, in fact, it will prove in the lapse of time to have been a blessing to humanity.

Had there not been an inexperienced boy twenty years of age in charge of the wireless mechanism the passengers would all have been saved; better still, if there had been a lookout glass in the hands of the man on the bridge, which the niggardly policy of the company regarded as a useless expense, the fatal berg would have been located in time and the horrible disaster averted.

The White Star Line had millions for the wanton and wicked luxury of the pampered millionaires, but not a dollar for a lookout glass.

Had there been the requisite number of lifeboats aboard, not a passenger need[ed] to have been lost. These and scores of other reasons might be given for our declaring that the sixteen hundred deaths on the *Titanic* were *sixteen hundred deliberate, cold-blooded murders*, chargeable to the owners and managers of the White Star Line.

The *Titanic* was to make *a record* that was to bring a harvest of gold

– *a record for profit*, for greasy lucre – and it made a record, but a different one than its owners calculated on.

The *Titanic* rushed headlong to her terrible fate – *in pursuit of profit*.

So much space had to be given to the private promenades, golf links, swimming pools for the plutocrats aboard that there was no space left for lifeboats when the crash came. Could misdirected ingenuity, perverted taste and mental and moral insanity go farther?

Had the *Titanic* been a mudscow with the same number of useful working-men on board and it had gone down while engaged in some useful social work the whole country would not have gasped with horror, nor would all the capitalist papers have given pages for weeks to reciting the terrible details.

We have been told a thousand times and with as many variations of the bravery of the rich and prominent men aboard, but very little has been heard about the bravery of *the men and women in the steerage*. We have not time for detail. But suppose we give just a moment's thought to the fifty bell boys, proletarian lads, who went down after having been shut in under command of a captain so they would not interfere with the escape of the rich first-class passengers.

The valet of Mrs John Jacob Astor delivered to her in the lifeboat her costly furs and then humbly bowed himself back to the boat and *went down to the bottom*.

With two exceptions the heroes in the hold, the stokers and the men who do the work that moves every boat on every sea, and without whom not another boat would ever move an inch, went down without the ghost of a chance to escape and no one has heard of a single one of them shrinking from his tragic fate.

The steerage passengers, penned in like cattle, were long held back in the passageway with loaded revolvers pointed at them, and it was only when the rich passengers had been given all the favoured opportunities to make sure of their escape that the women and children of the steerage were shown any consideration.

The one fine thing for which we give full credit to the men on the *Titanic, both rich and poor*, was that they observed the sea rule, 'Women and Children First'. For that we thank and honour them all without respect to station.

But would it not be a good thing to make this the rule of life instead of its extremely rare exception when a calamity enforces it?

Why not organize society on the basis of women and children first?

There are a thousand lessons to this monstrous marine disaster. We have time and space for but one or two. First, as long as profit is supreme its shocking penalties will be enforced upon men. Second, life is life, and when we come down to it the rich man's life is not worth a particle more than the life of a pauper.

John Jacob Astor went down with the stokers in the hold. In the flash of an instant they were on a level. Death equalized them, established their kinship, made them brothers. In life capitalism separated them as widely as the poles but at the supreme moment and in the presence of the infinite they were united and *stood on one common basis of equality in the democracy of death* . . .

As if to enforce its supreme lessons by providential command Ismay was saved with the women and children.

Ismay, the managing director, worth one hundred million dollars and drawing an annual salary from the White Star Line of one hundred and seventy-five thousand dollars per year!

Ismay is the epitome of capitalism as revealed in the *Titanic* disaster. Old ocean would not receive him and he is spurned of men. And so it will soon be with the system which produced him and of which he has furnished us its most striking incarnation.

The Titanic *disaster is a capitalist disaster. The evidence is overwhelming. Had the* Titanic *been constructed under social supervision and been socially owned and in social service, instead of being privately owned and launched and operated for private profit this appalling disaster would never have blackened the annals of humanity.*

Just as the *Titanic* went down in wreck and disaster so will capitalism which she so tragically typified also go down, but it is to be hoped that when the crisis comes there may be life boats enough to carry humanity safely into the Socialist Republic.

*Tillett was a leading trade unionist and anti-capitalist. Board of Trade
officials noted on the file cover of this letter that it was not to be answered.*

BEN TILLETT
The Vicious Class Antagonism

(Letter to the British Board of Trade, 18 April 1912)

RESOLVED.

The Executive of the Dock, Wharf, Riverside & General
Workers' Union hereby offers its sincere condolences to the
bereaved relatives of the Third Class passengers of the S/S *Titanic*,
whose tragic sinking we deplore. We also send our sincere regret
to the relatives of the Crew, who were drowned. We also offer
our strongest protest against the wanton and callous disregard of
human life and the vicious class antagonism shown in the practical
forbidding of the saving of the lives of the third-class passengers.
The refusal to permit other than the first-class passengers to be
saved by the boats, is in our opinion a disgrace to our common
civilization.

We therefore call upon the Government and the Board of Trade
to insist on the provision of adequate life-saving appliances in boats,
rafts and belts, which shall not only provide means of safety to the
passengers, but to the whole members of the ship's staff.

We express our regret that in order to save time and cost, at
the risk of life, shorter and quicker routes were insisted on, in
spite of the knowledge of the presence of ice.

We trust the saving of so many first-class passengers' lives will
not deaden the solicitude of the Government for the lives of those
who belong to the wage earning classes, and call upon the members
of the Labour Party to force upon the Government the necessity
of proper protection to the lives of all mariners and all passengers,
irrespective of class or grade.

Signed for the Executive,
BEN TILLETT.

Lost and Saved Statistics by Class, Sex and Age

(*U.S. Senate Hearings*, 1912)

	On board			Saved			Lost			
	Women and children	Men	Total	Women and children	Men	Total	Women and children	Men	Total	Per cent saved
Passengers:										
First class..............	156	173	329	145	54	199	11	119	130	60
Second class...........	128	157	285	104	15	119	24	142	166	42
Third class	224	486	710	105	69	174	119	417	536	25
Total passengers.	508	816	1,324	354	138	492	154	678	832	....
Crew	23	876	899	20	194	214	3	682	685	24
Total....................	531	1,692	2,223	374	332	706	157	1,360	1,517	32

Alden Smith after his enquiry privately concluded that aft steerage passengers got no physical warning of the danger until the ship tilted and was doomed; a third-class passenger from Sweden blamed in part the passive Catholicism of many steerage migrants who prayed and despaired; Charles Joughin, Chief Baker (who survived by swigging down whisky and stepping off the ship as though off a bus, and paddling around for an hour and a half before being rescued) testified that there was no discrimination practised between first-, second- and third-class women during evacuation. Lord Mersey concluded this in his Report of the British Enquiry, *though he called not a single steerage survivor. Butler's analysis is persuasive.*

DANIEL ALLEN BUTLER
Terra Incognita

('Unsinkable': The Full Story of RMS Titanic, 1998)

At half past midnight the word came down to third class to send the women and children up to the boat deck. Steward [John Edward] Hart, who had realized early on that the third-class passengers had almost no chance of negotiating the passageways and corridors that were usually inaccessible to steerage if left to themselves, began to organize his charges into little groups. Around 12.50 he set off for the boat deck, leading a score of women, some with children in tow. Other stewards continued to organize and reassure the rest of the third-class passengers. It wasn't an easy trip: the design of the ship, because of those outdated American immigration laws that required third class physically separated from the other classes of passengers, allowed no direct route from the third-class berthing areas to the boat deck, and access to what routes there were was very limited. That was why Hart had to lead his group up the stairs to the third-class Lounge on C deck, across the after well deck, past the second-class Library, into first class, along a stretch of corridor that led past the surgeon's office and the private dining saloon for the first-class' servants, and finally out to the grand staircase, which carried them up to the boat deck.

Once on deck Hart led his charges to boat 8, where as quickly as he got them in, several jumped right back out and ran inside where it was warm. Exasperated, Hart gave up after a few minutes and began the long trip back to third class.

It was well after 1.00 a.m. when he got back to E deck and prepared to set out with his second group. This time many of the married women refused to go without their husbands, while several of the men, some rather forcefully, demanded to go along. But Hart had his orders – women and children only – and after firmly reinforcing the order, he set off, reaching the boat deck around 1.15. This time he led his group to boat 15, but was stopped by First Officer Murdoch when he started back down for steerage again. Overriding Hart's protests, Murdoch ordered him to go with boat 15 when it was ready to be lowered.

Hart's efforts underscored the fact that, despite later accusations to the contrary, there really was no deliberate policy of discrimination against third class. What there was, and what may have been all the more insidious by being purely unintentional, was that simply no policy or procedure for looking after the third-class passengers existed. Instead, they were left to shift for themselves, not because they were being purposely ignored, but rather because they had simply been overlooked.

Future generations would have a hard time understanding how this could be, preferring instead to attribute it to the innate snobbery of the Edwardian society, but the truth was far less malign and much more tragic. Somewhere in the chain of command communications had broken down, and as had happened so many times before on this night, when Captain [Edward J.] Smith had given no specific instructions, Chief Officer [H. T.] Wilde seemed incapable of initiating any actions himself. The other officers were already thoroughly occupied and had little time to spare for wondering about what or who the captain and the chief officer may have overlooked. That discrimination was never intended by the White Star Line lay in the fact that none of the women and children from steerage who reached the boat deck were prevented from getting into the lifeboats. The problem was that so few made it there.

Nevertheless, a lot of them tried. Singly and in small groups, some steerage passengers began to make their way to the upper deck. A few of the barriers that closed off third class from the rest of the ship were down, and some of the steerage passengers began to work their way into the ship, unsure of where they were going, but certain that if they kept climbing, eventually they would reach the boat deck.

But most of the barriers were still up, confining third class to the forward and after well decks, where there were no boats. At this point, two components of the geography of the ship defeated the efforts of many of the third-class passengers to reach the boat deck. The first was in the design of the *Titanic*: there were only a handful of exits from the third-class areas that gave access to the upper decks – seven to be exact; all of them, be they doors, gates or hatchways, by law were required to be kept locked. The second was the interior layout of the ship: the complex route that Steward Hart followed when leading his group of women passengers up to the boats was actually the most direct route to the boat deck, but for the third-class passengers, it was a venture into *terra incognita*, abounding with dead ends and circuitous passages.

A sense of the growing danger they were in communicated itself to some of the steerage passengers and they started finding ways up to the boat deck. Soon a thin but steady stream of third-class passengers could be seen crawling up on to a cargo crane in the after well deck, inching across the boom to a railing on B deck, then clambering over the railing and on up to the boat deck.

Some of them got lost and wandered into the second-class promenade on B deck, which turned out to be an apparent dead end. The only way out was an emergency ladder, meant for the crew's use only, that passed very near the first-class *à la carte* restaurant. The restaurant, which was still brightly lit, could be seen through the French doors, with table after table already set with gleaming china, sparkling crystal and freshly polished silver in preparation for the morning's breakfast. Anna Sjoblom, one of those who got lost, would always remember how the sight had taken her breath away – she had never seen anything like it growing up in Finland.

Two decks below them, another group of young women from steerage found their way barred by a locked gate, this one guarded by a seaman. The three young colleens – Kate Murphy, Kate Mullins and Kathy Gilnagh – frantically pleaded with the man, who refused to allow them to pass through (regulations were regulations, after all). Suddenly a big, tough-looking Irishman from the girls' home county, Jim Farrell, the piper, came up the corridor. He took one look at the girls, at the gate and at the seaman, then bellowed 'Good God, man! Open the gate and let the girls through!' Thoroughly intimidated, the sailor meekly complied, then ran off.

A larger group was clamouring at another guarded gate barring the way to the upper decks, this one down on E deck by the second-class staircase. As Daniel Buckley approached the barrier, the man ahead of him was roughly shoved back by the seaman standing before the gate. Howling in fury the man charged forward again. The seaman promptly ducked through the gate, locked it behind him, and fled. The passenger broke the lock, then took off in pursuit of the offending seaman, shouting that he would chuck the sailor into the sea if he caught him. Buckley and dozens of others rushed through the open gate and hurried up the stairs.

Yet they were only a handful – there were still hundreds of steerage passengers walking about aimlessly in the after well deck or at the foot of the staircase on E deck. Also left behind on E deck were most of the second- and third-class kitchen staff, along with chefs and waiters from the *à la carte* restaurant. The majority of them were French and Italian, and, owing to a longstanding British animosity toward France and Italy, were objects of suspicion in 1912. No one knows who, if anyone, actually gave the order, or why it was given, but about an hour after the collision they were shepherded into their quarters by members of the deck crew, locked in and promptly forgotten.

Many of those steerage passengers left behind returned to their cabins; others turned to prayer: around 1.30 Gus Cohen passed through the third-class dining saloon and saw a large number of them gathered there, many with rosaries in their hands, 'huddled together, weeping, jumping up and down as they cried to their "Madonna" to save them'. August Wennerstrom, also a third-class passenger, later observed bitterly:

> Hundreds were in a circle with a preacher in the middle, praying, crying, asking God and Mary to help them. They lay there, still crying, till the water was over their heads. They just prayed and yelled, never lifting a hand to help themselves. They had lost their own willpower and expected God to do all their work for them.

Clearly not all of the barriers for third class were of the physical kind. It is a difficult concept to grasp from the late-twentieth-century perspective of an egalitarian, socially mobile society, but it was an undeniable reality that in the first decade of this century feudal society was far from dead. The rigid class structure that had shaped, driven and defined Europe for more than a thousand years still exerted an overwhelming influence on the lives of almost everyone born into it, dictating every aspect of life: an individual's vocabulary, diet, education, clothing, housing, profession, even choice of friends were to greater or lesser degrees prescribed or proscribed by their position in society.

And nowhere was that rigidity more prevalent than in the working class. Sons and daughters followed the life paths of their fathers and mothers, each generation putting its successor on the treadmill. Centuries of being the source of an endless supply of labour led to an ingrained mindset among the majority of working men and women whereby they expected to be told where to go, what to do and when to do it – initiative was never expected of them. Leaving behind the strictures of their working-class origins was equally unthinkable: though Great Britain's recently formed Labour party had as its proclaimed goal the amelioration of the worst physical conditions of the working-man's lot, it was not yet ready to articulate the idea of creating a society that would overcome all the poor conditions of the working-man's life.

This is not to say that the working class viewed itself as oppressed, ready to spring to the barricades in defiance of the patriciate. The working men and women of the early twentieth century – the steel and textile mill workers, chimney sweeps, tanners, coachmen, dustmen, butlers and maids – were no more ready to rebel than the serfs from whom they had descended. They were good at what they did and proud of it. A contemporary American, Richard Harding Davis, wrote in *Our English Cousins*:

> In America we hate uniforms because they have been twisted into meaning badges of servitude; our housemaids will not wear caps, nor will our coachmen shave their moustaches. This tends to make every class of citizen more or less alike. But in London you can always tell a 'bus driver from the driver of a four-wheeler, whether he is on his box or not. The Englishman recognizes that if he is in a certain social grade he is likely to remain there, and so, instead of trying to dress like someone else who is in a class to which he will never reach, he 'makes up' for the part in life he is meant to play, and the 'bus driver buys a high white hat, and the barmaid is content to wear a turned-down collar and turned-back cuffs, and a private coachman would as soon think of wearing a false nose as wearing a moustache. He accepts his position and is proud of it, and the butcher's boy sits up in his cart just as smartly, and squares his elbows and straightens his legs and balances his whip with just as much pride, as any driver of a mail-cart in the Park.

Third class then may have been descriptive of these people's level of accommodation on a transatlantic liner, but not of the way they viewed themselves. There was nothing fatalistic or resigned in their wilful acceptance of their station and of the consequences of that acceptance: they were behaving according to beliefs and values handed down to them by their parents, their grandparents and their great-grandparents. And if, as far as August Wennerstrom was concerned, they showed little or no inclination to take matters into their own hands, it was because they believed until it was too late that the people in charge, the officers and crew, knew what they were doing. When that belief finally proved false, there would [be] no time for anything but prayer.

Many survivors of Titanic *remembered seeing lights of a ship that had
failed to come to their assistance. Stanley Lord, captain of the Leyland
steamer* Californian, *denied that the mystery ship was his. Ernest Gill,
assistant engineer ('second donkeyman'), contradicted Lord's version in
a sworn affidavit printed in the* Boston American *(and for which Gill
was paid). Smith questioned Gill after reading the affidavit into the
record; Smith later described Lord's conduct as 'reprehensible'. The
Lordites and anti-Lordites have waged a strenuous debate that was
not stilled even by a British Ministry of Transport formal reappraisal
between 1990 and 1992.*

The Donkeyman's Affidavit: Ernest Gill's Testimony

(*U.S. Senate Hearings*, 1912)

. . . SENATOR SMITH. I want to read to you the following
statement and ask you whether it is true:

I, the undersigned, Ernest Gill, being employed as second donkeyman
on the steamer *Californian*, Capt. Lloyd [*sic*], give the following statement of the incidents of the night of Sunday, April 14:

I am 29 years of age; native of Yorkshire; single. I was making my
first voyage on the *Californian*.

On the night of April 14 I was on duty from 8 p.m. until 12 in the
engine room. At 11.50 I came on deck. The stars were shining brightly.
It was very clear and I could see for a long distance. The ship's engines
had been stopped since 10.30, and she was drifting amid floe ice. I
looked over the rail on the starboard side and saw the lights of a very
large steamer about 10 miles away. I could see her broadside lights. I
watched her for fully a minute. They could not have helped but see her
from the bridge and lookout.

It was now 12 o'clock and I went to my cabin. I woke my mate,
William Thomas. He heard the ice crunching alongside the ship and
asked, 'Are we in the ice?' I replied, 'Yes, but it must be clear off to the
starboard, for I saw a big vessel going along full speed. She looked as
if she might be a big German.'

I turned in, but could not sleep. In half an hour I turned out, thinking to smoke a cigarette. Because of the cargo I could not smoke 'tween decks, so I went on deck again.

I had been on deck about 10 minutes when I saw a white rocket about 10 miles away on the starboard side. I thought it must be a shooting star. In seven or eight minutes I saw distinctly a second rocket in the same place, and I said to myself, 'That must be a vessel in distress.'

It was not my business to notify the bridge or the lookouts; but they could not have helped but see them.

I turned in immediately after, supposing that the ship would pay attention to the rockets.

I knew no more until I was awakened at 6.40 by the chief engineer, who said, 'Turn out to render assistance. The *Titanic* has gone down.'

I exclaimed and leaped from my bunk. I went on deck and found the vessel under way and proceeding full speed. She was clear of the field ice, but there were plenty of bergs about.

I went down on watch and heard the second and fourth engineers in conversations. Mr J. O. Evans is the second and Mr Wooten is the fourth. The second was telling the fourth that the third officer had reported rockets had gone up in his watch. I knew then that it must have been the *Titanic* I had seen.

The second engineer added that the captain had been notified by the apprentice officer, whose name, I think, is [James] Gibson, of the rockets. The skipper had told him to Morse to the vessel in distress. Mr [Herbert] Stone, the second navigating officer, was on the bridge at the time, said Mr Evans.

I overheard Mr Evans say that more lights had been shown and more rockets went up. Then, according to Mr Evans, Mr Gibson went to the captain again and reported more rockets. The skipper told him to continue to Morse until he got a reply. No reply was received.

The next remark I heard the second pass was, 'Why in the devil they didn't wake the wireless man up?' The entire crew of the steamer have been talking among themselves about the disregard of the rockets. I personally urged several to join me in protesting against the conduct of the captain, but they refused, because they feared to lose their jobs.

A day or two before the ship reached port the skipper called the quartermaster, who was on duty at the time the rockets were discharged, into his cabin. They were in conversation about three-quarters of an hour. The quartermaster declared that he did not see the rockets.

I am quite sure that the *Californian* was less than 20 miles from the *Titanic*, which the officers report to have been our position. I could not have seen her if she had been more than 10 miles distant, and I saw her very plainly.

I have no ill will toward the captain or any officer of the ship, and I am losing a profitable berth by making this statement. I am actuated by the desire that no captain who refuses or neglects to give aid to a vessel in distress should be able to hush up the men.

ERNEST GILL

Sworn and subscribed to before me

this 24th day of April 1912

SAMUEL PUTNAM, *Notary Public*

I will ask you, witness, whether this statement is true?

MR GILL. Yes, sir; that is correct.

Marcus re-creates with typically stylish succinctness events on board Californian *while* Titanic *foundered. Company signals were registered, were usually coloured, and were lower reaching than distress signals with which, it was thought, they must not be confusable.*

GEOFFREY MARCUS
'The Middle Watch'

(*The Maiden Voyage*, 1969)

... Though on the night of the 14th dozens of spark transmissions in diverse keys had filled the ether, from the ship's station which lay nearest of them all to the stricken liner there came not a whisper. This was MWL, the 6,000-ton Leyland liner *Californian*, whose name, together with that of the *Carpathia*, will always be linked with the *Titanic* disaster.

Earlier that night the *Californian*, bound from London to Boston, on a course of S. 89 W. true, had run into an immense mass of field ice which stretched as far as could then be seen to north and to south. At 10.20 p.m. she reversed her engines and stopped, and there remained until 6 o'clock on the following morning. At about 11 o'clock a steamer's light was seen approaching from the eastward. The O.O.W. [Officer on Watch], Charles Victor Groves, the Third Officer, went to the chart-room and told the Master, Captain Stanley Lord, that a passenger steamer was approaching.

'Call her up on the Morse lamp,' said the Master, 'and see if you can get any answer.'

Returning to the bridge, Groves pushed in the electric plug and worked away with the signal-lamp; but without success.

The Master went along to the wireless cabin and asked the operator, Cyril Evans, a young man fresh from the training school, whether he had had any ships. Evans said he had had the *Titanic*. He judged by the strength of the signals she was within one hundred miles of the *Californian* in the afternoon. He could hear the other ship working a long time before he actually got into communication with MGY. The Master said, 'Better advise him we are surrounded by ice and stopped.' The operator switched on his transmitter and called up MGY. '*Say, old man,*' he began conversationally, '*we are surrounded by ice and stopped.*' MGY's reply thereupon 'came in with a bang'. '*Shut up, shut up, I am busy; I am working Cape Race, you are jamming me*' . . .

Half an hour afterwards Evans still had the telephones on his head and heard MGY still working MCE; this time the former was transmitting passengers' telegrams. At 11.35 p.m. Evans decided to turn in. He put down the headphones, took off his clothes and climbed into his bunk . . .

At about this time the Third Officer, watching the steamer in the distance, saw her lights apparently go out. He remembered that it was then 11.40 because 'one bell was struck to call the middle watch'. When the Master later joined him on the bridge, the other vessel had stopped. Groves believed that 'she had starboarded to avoid some ice'.

'That does not look like a passenger steamer,' observed Captain Lord.

'It is, sir. When she stopped her lights seemed to go out, and I suppose they have been put out for the night.'

After he had been relieved Groves, at about 12.15 a.m., left the bridge. On his way to bed he went into the Marconi cabin and switched on the electric light. Evans and he were on friendly terms, and he would very often drop in for a chat. Wireless interested him, and he had learnt to read slow Morse. Groves now asked Evans what ships he had had, and if there were any news. The latter, still half asleep, told him drowsily that he had had the *Titanic* – 'You know, the new boat on its maiden voyage. I got it this afternoon.' Groves picked up the telephones and put them on his head, as he had often done before. He heard nothing at all, for the receiver was 'dead'. The clockwork which activated the magnetic detector had first to be wound up; Groves did not know about this and Evans was too sleepy to tell him. The result was, Groves presently put down the headphones, switched off the light and left the room, while Evans fell asleep again.

Herbert Stone, the Second Officer, had relieved Groves at midnight. On his way up to the bridge he saw the Master, who told him that the ship was stopped and surrounded by ice; and he pointed to a steamer in the distance, showing one mast-head light and a red side-light. Lord asked him to let him know if the bearing of the steamer altered or if she came any closer to them; adding, that the Third Officer had called her up on the Morse lamp and received no reply.

On the bridge that watch with the Second Officer was a young apprentice called [James] Gibson. The latter, looking at the other steamer through his glasses, could make out a mast-head light, her red light and a 'glare of white lights on her after deck'. He tried, but to no effect, to get into communication with the other ship with the Morse lamp. Later in the watch he had to leave the bridge for about half an hour to do something to the patent log.

While he was gone Stone, pacing up and down the bridge, thought he saw a white flash in the sky immediately above the distant steamer. Lifting the glasses to his eyes, he saw four more white flashes, which 'had the appearance of white rockets bursting in the sky', as they flung out a cascade of white stars. The rockets went up at intervals of three or four minutes. At about 1.15 a.m. Stone reported by voice pipe to the Master that he had just seen five white rockets from the direction of the steamer. Lord asked him if they were 'Company's signals'. Stone replied that he did not know, but they appeared to him to be white rockets; and he added that he had called up the other ship on the Morse lamp. The Master thereupon told him to 'go on Morseing', and when he had any information to send the apprentice down to him with it. On Gibson's return to the bridge Stone told him what had been going on and asked him to call up the other ship on the Morse lamp. Gibson accordingly sent the calling-up signal, but again without success. He called her up for about three minutes, and had just got the glasses on her when he saw her fire three more rockets. His companion saw these rockets with his naked eye. At about 1.20 a.m. Stone remarked that she was steaming away towards the south-west. Slowly the minutes passed. The Second Officer and young Gibson continued to watch the distant steamer, looking at her from time to time with their glasses. 'Look at her now,' Stone said to the apprentice, 'she looks very queer out of the water, her lights look queer.' Gibson gazed through the glasses. He, too, thought there was something wrong about the position of her lights. What it was he could not exactly say, but it appeared to him as if she had a heavy list to starboard. 'She looks rather to have a big side out of the water' (i.e. her port light seemed to be higher out of the water than before); and the officer agreed. Stone went on to observe significantly that, 'a ship is not going to fire rockets at sea for nothing'.

At 2 a.m., about twenty minutes after the eighth and last rocket had been fired, Stone told Gibson to go down to the Master, 'and be sure and wake him up', and tell him that altogether they had seen eight of these white lights like rockets in the direction of this other steamer; that this steamer was disappearing in the south-west, that they had called her up repeatedly on the Morse lamp and that they had received no answer. Gibson went below and knocked on the chart-room door, then went inside and delivered the message. The Master, referring to the 'white lights like rockets', asked him if he were sure there were no colours in them, red or green. Were they all white? Gibson assured him that they were all white. Captain Lord then asked him the time. The youngster replied that it was five past two by the wheel-house clock. As he closed the door, Gibson heard the Master say something he did not quite catch. He returned to the bridge and reported to the O.O.W.

The officer and the apprentice continued to keep the ship under observation until she disappeared. How it appeared to them, Stone later declared, was 'a gradual disappearing of all her lights, which would be perfectly natural with a ship steaming away from us'. At about 2.40 a.m. the O.O.W. again called up the Master by voice pipe and told him that the ship from the direction of which they had seen the rockets coming had disappeared, bearing S.W. ½ W. The Master again asked him if he were certain there was no colour in the lights; and Stone again assured him they were all white, 'just white'.

When the Chief Officer relieved the Second at 4 a.m., the latter told him about the strange steamer which had puzzled them so sorely in the middle watch, how at one o'clock he had seen some white rockets, and 'the moment the ship started firing them she started to steam away'. The Chief Officer presently called the Master and informed him that Stone had told him he had seen rockets in the middle watch. 'Yes, I know,' said the Master, 'he has been telling me.'

The Chief Officer hurried along to the wireless cabin and roused the sleeping operator. As Evans awoke with a start, Stewart began, 'Wireless, there is a ship that has been firing rockets in the night. Will you come in and see if you can find out what is wrong – what is the matter?' Evans pulled on his trousers and took up the headphones. There was no one working, so he switched on his transmitter and sent out the general call. The *Mount Temple* quickly answered him. '*Do you know the* Titanic *has struck an iceberg, and she is sinking.*'

Stung by what they saw as American violation of British jurisdiction and anti-British sentiment in American newspapers, British commentators attempted to discredit the Senate Hearings by belittling its chairman. But 'Smithisms' were fewer than his British enemies imagined; 'Do you know what an iceberg is composed of?' he notoriously asked Officer Lowe. 'Ice, I suppose, sir.' Although it hardly mattered, it transpired that icebergs can have earth and rock embedded in them. The 'extravagant rhetoric' in his Report, *of which British newspapers complained, was, when he wrote of Captain Smith, an impressive way of condemning in sorrow rather than anger.*

ALDEN SMITH
The Mystery of Indifference

(*Report of the Committee on Commerce United States Senate*, Report No. 806, 1912)

Capt. Smith knew the sea and his clear eye and steady hand had often guided his ship through dangerous paths. For forty years storms sought in vain to vex him or menace his craft. But once before in all his honourable career was his pride humbled or his vessel maimed. Each new advancing type of ship built by his company was handed over to him as a reward for faithful services and as an evidence of confidence in his skill. Strong of limb, intent of purpose, pure in character, dauntless as a sailor should be, he walked the deck of this majestic structure as master of her keel.

Titanic though she was, his indifference to danger was one of the direct and contributing causes of this unnecessary tragedy, while his own willingness to die was the expiating evidence of his fitness to live. Those of us who knew him well – not in anger, but in sorrow – file one specific charge against him: Overconfidence and neglect to heed the oft-repeated warnings of his friends. But in his horrible dismay, when his brain was afire with honest retribution, we can still see, in his manly bearing and his tender solicitude for the safety of women and little children, some traces of his lofty spirit when dark clouds lowered all about him and angry elements stripped him of his command. His devotion to his craft, even 'as it writhed and twisted and struggled' for mastery over its foe, calmed the fears of many of the stricken multitude who hung upon his words, lending dignity to a parting scene as inspiring as it is beautiful to remember.

The mystery of his indifference to danger, when other and less pretentious vessels doubled their lookout or stopped their engines, finds no reasonable hypothesis in conjecture or speculation; science in shipbuilding was supposed to have attained perfection and to have spoken her last word; mastery of the ocean had at last been achieved; but overconfidence seems to have dulled the faculties usually so alert. With the atmosphere literally charged with warning signals and wireless messages registering their last appeal, the stokers in the engine room fed their fires with fresh fuel, registering in that dangerous place her fastest speed.

Americans were worried about the anti-democratic concentration of power in trusts and monopolies, and also (by analogy) about the possible anti-democratic control of information. In their desire for an exclusive story from the wireless operators on Carpathia *(including Harold Bride), had the* New York Times *engaged in a compact with the Marconi Company that threatened the right of citizens to know details of the disaster? Frederick M. Sammis, General Engineer of the Marconi Wireless Telegraph Co. of America, came under Smith's scrutiny: the American ability to seek truth and achieve drama in such hearings is impressive.*

Marketing Disaster: The Marconi–*New York Times* Affair

(*U.S. Senate Hearings*, 1912)

SENATOR SMITH. I will come right to the point and ask you whether the following message, which was intercepted by the chief wireless operator, J. R. Simpson, chief electrician United States Navy, is familiar to you:

> *To Marconi officer, Carpathia and Titanic:* 8.30 P.M.
> Arranged for your exclusive story for dollars in four figures. Mr Marconi agreeing. Say nothing until you see me. Where are you now?
> J. M. [*sic*] SAMMIS, *Opr. C.*

MR SAMMIS. I only know about that exact message from what I have read in the newspapers.

If you will allow me, I will describe this unpleasant business, because it is unpleasant, as it has brought upon me a country-wide publicity that I little desire, and has pointed the finger of scorn at me by my neighbours, simply because in their estimation, either intentionally or otherwise, the date and time of these messages, when they were first published, at any rate, were not disclosed. In the second place because it has not been stated, I believe, thus far, that at 8.30 the ship was either across the end of her pier or nearly so.

I sat in my office at 8.10 on that night and was told by the operating department that the ship had passed the Narrows, and the

Seagate Station itself is at the Narrows, New York Harbor.

It is not my desire to throw on to anybody else any responsibility for the sense of this message. Mr Marconi did agree that the boys, when they got ashore, should be allowed to sell the report of their personal experiences, which numerous other people on board the ship did. In these days, when corporations are counted as not caring very much about their employees or what happens to them, or what they get, it seemed to me that the men who had been responsible mainly and chiefly for saving 700 lives ought in some way to be recognized substantially.

It was not I who originated this scheme or this arrangement at all. The arrangement was made, however, and the information was telephoned to Seagate Station, which I say is at the Narrows, New York, to explain to these boys. In telephoning that I told them, 'I know the boys are exhausted, but give them this news; maybe it will spur them on and make them feel better.' I remember definitely telling them that.

SENATOR SMITH. With whom were you talking at that time?

MR SAMMIS. To Mr Davidson, the man temporarily in charge of Seagate Station. He is not regularly in our employ, but was sent there because he was an expert operator and one of the best men we have ever had. But he was not regularly under our control. He was sent there, and we made use of his services, and he handled the wireless entirely. I have a statement from him, and he made an affidavit, that messages about which so much noise has been made were of his own construction, and that he realizes, as we all do, that they were not gems of English literature, but they were, on the spur of the moment, instructions to the men, carrying out and explaining to them the arrangements which had been made.

SENATOR SMITH. We are not passing upon the literary character of these productions.

MR SAMMIS. I do not think I ought to be—

SENATOR SMITH (interposing). And the work of digging into the story you are telling has not been entirely pleasant to me. But these messages were picked up and transmitted to me by the Secretary of the Navy, and they bear your signature, and I would like to know whether or not you are responsible for that injunction of secrecy to the operators of the *Carpathia*?

MR SAMMIS. There was no injunction of secrecy whatsoever,

except with respect to their actions after they got ashore.

SENATOR SMITH. I will read one. 'Seagate to *Carpathia*, 8.12.' Do you know what time the *Carpathia* passed quarantine?

MR SAMMIS. I was told that night that she passed the Battery at 8.10. I have not verified that. She was certainly very close, however.

SENATOR SMITH. As a matter of fact, she did not land until 9.30?

MR SAMMIS. You mean the passengers did not land?

SENATOR SMITH. No; I mean the boat was not made fast to the Cunard Dock until 9.30. Am I right, Mr Franklin?

MR FRANKLIN. Yes.

MR SAMMIS. I should say that half an hour, or 45 minutes, possibly, would be consumed in coming from the Battery up to the pier, in the slow way they usually go.

SENATOR SMITH. Here is a telegram which was intercepted by the Navy Department.

MR SAMMIS. May I interrupt to say that the one you have already quoted is quite evidently erroneously copied. The initial, you may note, is not correct. The words after the signature have absolutely no meaning to me. I say those are self-evident facts to anybody. I did not know what these messages contained until I read them in the paper.

SENATOR SMITH. I will proceed:

Seagate to Carpathia: 8.12 P.M.
  Say, old man, Marconi Co. taking good care of you. Keep your mouth shut and hold your story. It is fixed for you so you will get big money. Do your best to clear.

Do you know anything about that message?

MR SAMMIS. Only what I have already stated. I read it in the paper.

SENATOR SMITH. And you disavow all responsibility for it?

MR SAMMIS. No; I do not. I telephoned the information to Seagate – I have already stated that – that such an arrangement had been made with reference to the boys' stories after they got ashore. It is quite evident that in the vernacular of the wireless men the last few words which you have just quoted were sent in response to my injunction that perhaps this would spruce the boys up a little bit, and make them feel happy, and they would clear their traffic. That is what is meant by the sentence: 'Do your best to clear.' In other words, 'Get your messages off, all you have, hurriedly.'

SENATOR SMITH. He could not have been at the dock at that time, or that could have been sent to him personally.

MR SAMMIS. I understand that the man was found telegraphing after he was tied up to the pier, absolutely unconscious of the fact that he had arrived there.

SENATOR SMITH. Which operator?

MR SAMMIS. Mr McBride [*sic*].

SENATOR SMITH. But Cottam, the regular operator of the *Carpathia*, left the ship immediately when she arrived, did he not?

MR SAMMIS. I understand so; yes.

SENATOR SMITH. Did he do that in obedience to your request to meet you at the Strand Hotel?

MR SAMMIS. He probably did; yes.

SENATOR SMITH. Why did you want him to meet you?

MR SAMMIS. Simply so that he could get in touch with the *New York Times* reporter, with whom the arrangement had been made, and give him the story.

SENATOR SMITH. Then we may presume the arrangement he made with the *Times* and carried out was with your consent?

MR SAMMIS. With the consent of the company, Mr Marconi and Mr Bottomley, as well. I simply passed along the arrangement which had been made.

SENATOR SMITH. But with your consent?

MR SAMMIS. Yes. I had not very much to say. He did not need my consent.

SENATOR SMITH. With your concurrence?

MR SAMMIS. With my approval; yes, sir. My unofficial approval.

SENATOR SMITH. Did he meet you at the Strand Hotel, or was he to meet you?

MR SAMMIS. No.

SENATOR SMITH. Were you there?

MR SAMMIS. I was at the Strand Hotel; yes. That was the headquarters of the *New York Times*.

SENATOR SMITH. Five hundred and two West Fourteenth Street?

MR SAMMIS. Yes, sir.

SENATOR SMITH. Whom did you go there to meet – Mr Cottam?

MR SAMMIS. I went there to meet the operators; yes.

SENATOR SMITH. To meet Mr Cottam?

MR SAMMIS. Not Mr Cottam any more than Mr Bride, particularly, but to meet both of them.

SENATOR SMITH. Did you go to the side of the *Carpathia* at all when she docked?

MR SAMMIS. Yes.

SENATOR SMITH. At what time?

MR SAMMIS. I have not the least idea. It took me 45 minutes to get across the street. At the time I got to the *Carpathia* I lost all sense of time. I should say, roughly, it might have been a couple of hours after she had docked.

SENATOR SMITH. Did you find Mr Bride there?

MR SAMMIS. Yes.

SENATOR SMITH. But had you seen Mr Cottam in the meantime?

MR SAMMIS. No.

SENATOR SMITH. Did you go to the Cunard Dock with Mr Marconi?

MR SAMMIS. Yes.

SENATOR SMITH. Was that the first time he had been there that evening?

MR SAMMIS. I assume so.

SENATOR SMITH. Was he with you at the Strand Hotel?

MR SAMMIS. No.

SENATOR SMITH. Was anybody with you?

MR SAMMIS. You could not be in the Strand Hotel that night without having somebody with you. There were *Times* men and all the other newspaper men.

SENATOR SMITH. Yes; but who went with you to the Strand Hotel?

MR SAMMIS. Nobody.

SENATOR SMITH. Who left the Strand Hotel with you?

MR SAMMIS. One of the *Times* men; I have forgotten his name.

SENATOR SMITH. How much was Mr Cottam, the operator on the *Carpathia*, to get for that story?

MR SAMMIS. The *Times* agreed to pay $1,000 for the two stories. I do not know how they were going to divide it; I did not interest myself in it.

SENATOR SMITH. For his and Cottam's story of the loss of the *Titanic*?

MR SAMMIS. Yes.

SENATOR SMITH. With whom was that arrangement made?

MR SAMMIS. With the *New York Times*.

SENATOR SMITH. I know; but who made it on behalf of these boys?

MR SAMMIS. You mean what representative of the *Times*?

SENATOR SMITH. No; who made the arrangement on behalf of the company?

MR SAMMIS. Well, everybody had something to do with it. I had something to do with it; Mr Bottomley had something to do with it; it was a general conversation carried on by the *New York Times* office and our office and Mr Bottomley's house.

SENATOR SMITH. Was the contract on the part of the operators completed? Did they give their stories?

MR SAMMIS. I think they did.

SENATOR SMITH. Both to the same paper?

MR SAMMIS. I think so.

SENATOR SMITH. Did they receive their money?

MR SAMMIS. I understand they did, and more besides.

SENATOR SMITH. How much more?

MR SAMMIS. I understood they got $250 more apiece than was promised them.

SENATOR SMITH. That is, they got $750 apiece?

MR SAMMIS. That is my rough recollection; I did not see the money or handle it, and do not wish to. That is hearsay.

SENATOR SMITH. In order that we may clear this up as we go along, were you to have any part in this yourself?

MR SAMMIS. Absolutely none.

SENATOR SMITH. And you have had no part in it?

MR SAMMIS. No.

SENATOR SMITH. Mr Cottam says he has not yet received his money.

MR SAMMIS. Perhaps that is Mr Cottam's fault. Perhaps he has not been accessible.

SENATOR SMITH. Is the money being held for him by anybody, to your knowledge?

MR SAMMIS. I presume, if anybody were holding it, it would be the *Times*.

SENATOR SMITH. Nobody else?

MR SAMMIS. I understood Mr Cottam had received his money.

SENATOR SMITH. He had not when he was on the stand a day or two ago.

MR SAMMIS. I understand that he has since.

SENATOR SMITH. Were these payments made through yourself or any other officer of the Marconi Co.?

MR SAMMIS. I have already stated that I did not see the money, did not expect to, and did not wish to.

SENATOR SMITH. Do you mean that you did not see a cheque or an envelope containing the money?

MR SAMMIS. I have not taken part in the transaction one iota, one way or the other.

SENATOR SMITH. Let us clear this up as we go along. I think it is a most distasteful matter to you, as it is to the committee, and I think to the public.

MR SAMMIS. I have not done anything I am ashamed of, and if I can clear my record, that the newspapers have impugned, I want to do it, and I am sure you want to help me.

SENATOR SMITH. Have you done anything in this matter, about which we have just been speaking, that you are very proud of?

MR SAMMIS. I have not done anything I am ashamed of.

SENATOR SMITH. I did not ask you that. I want to know whether you are proud of it?

MR SAMMIS. Yes; I am proud of the fact that, being an employer of labour, and being the superior of poorly paid men, or mediumly paid men – men who do not see very much of this world's goods – I will do them a good turn honestly if I can, and that I consider I have done. I know of no law that can forbid a man selling his personal experience, after he comes ashore, and we have no rule by which we could prevent them from doing it.

SENATOR SMITH. Then am I to understand from what you say that, so far as your opinion goes, this practice to which I am calling attention will be continued?

MR SAMMIS. I should consider it very dangerous indeed – and I had intended to bring it to your attention – to forbid them, by some hard and fast rule, which you have indicated, along that line, because the result would be that you would obtain the very results you now have. It would seem only reasonable that if no recognition whatsoever, in standing or financially, should be made of the efforts of those men to get the news off the ships, they would not stir themselves very much to do it. I believe it could be regulated. I believe an error was made. I believe it would have been better to have sent this news to the Associated Press and let them settle with the boys, if they liked. The news then would have had more general distribution, and there would not have been any sore toes.

SENATOR SMITH. I have not seen any sore toes, and I do not know of anybody who is complaining of any, myself. But do you not think it would have been better to communicate this intelligence to your office, in answer to the numerous inquiries made by Mr Marconi, from the time of the accident until the arrival of the *Carpathia*, and then disseminate it to the public, that they might be relieved of the anxiety under which they were suffering?

MR SAMMIS. With all due deference to the question, my judgement would not be that that was the best course to pursue, for this reason, that the international telegraph convention has already placed itself on record as putting news dispatches last in the list; ship service telegrams first, paid passenger telegrams second and then press messages.

SENATOR SMITH. How general is this custom of receiving and accepting money for exclusive stories of sea disasters?

MR SAMMIS. I should say it was quite general. I perused the copies of messages from the shore stations. I saw messages from practically every paper in New York City asking practically everybody, from the captain down to the survivors, for exclusive stories. Whether they got them or not I am unable to say, except that I did see in the *New York World*, on the day after the *Carpathia* arrived, that they had published an exclusive story two hours and a half before the *New York Times* had theirs on the street.

SENATOR SMITH. The committee are not very much concerned with that.

MR SAMMIS. It demonstrated that there were not exclusive stories.

SENATOR SMITH. If this custom about which we are talking, and which was followed by Binns, the operator in the *Republic* disaster—

MR SAMMIS. But Binns sent his wireless messages from the ship.

SENATOR SMITH. All right; I do not care where they came from. (Continuing.) If this custom, which was followed by Binns, and which you say is quite general among wireless operators—

MR SAMMIS (interrupting). No; pardon me, I did not say quite general among wireless operators: I said it was quite general on the part of papers to endeavour to secure exclusive stories.

SENATOR SMITH. Is it a recognized standard of ethics among operators?

MR SAMMIS. No; absolutely not.

SENATOR SMITH. Injunctions of secrecy, such as these messages indicate, and the hope of private reward, such as you say is often the case—

MR SAMMIS. I do not remember of having made such a statement—

SENATOR SMITH. Well, such as you do not regard—

MR SAMMIS. As dishonourable?

SENATOR SMITH. As dishonourable. I will ask the stenographer to read the beginning of my question.

The stenographer read as follows:

> Injunctions of secrecy, such as these messages indicate, and the hope of private reward, such as you say is often the case—

SENATOR SMITH (continuing). Might cut some figure in the ability of the public, and even owners of the ship, and the people vitally affected, to obtain the news, might they not, if the custom be recognized among operators?

MR SAMMIS. I should say absolutely they would have nothing to do with it. At such times, and at all times, our operator on the ship has his messages censored by the captain. It is a part of our contract that the captain shall censor messages. The operators are there on board in the same manner that any other officer is on board, and they hold the position of junior officer. The captain would have nothing whatever to do, and would have had nothing to do in this case, except file the message, tell the man to send it, and it would have gone to whomever it was addressed, and at any time, had it been filed. The matter has been thrown over on to Mr Bride and Mr Cottam, who did the best they knew how. They followed their rules blindly and were worked up. The responsibility, I must say, if there is responsibility existing, was on the part of the captain, if he realized that the people were waiting for news; and if he did not realize it, why should our men have realized it? He should have filed a brief account, and the captain had such a message requesting such an account from the White Star Line.

SENATOR SMITH. You heard Mr Marconi say a few minutes ago that he did not regard it as a desirable practice and that he thought it ought not to obtain.

MR SAMMIS. Yes, sir.

SENATOR SMITH. And you disagree with him?

MR SAMMIS. Not altogether. I would say that you would have to be very careful what rules you might make or you would defeat the purpose of the rule. I think that is self-evident.

The writer Joseph Conrad wrote in a letter of 22 April that 'this Titanic *business has disturbed me'. It disturbed him enough to engage it in print in the* Budget *and the* English Review *(twice). To begin with, he smarted as an 'effete' European at what he saw as the inelegant meddling of the U.S. Senate. ('Yamsi' was Bruce Ismay's code name for telegrams he wished to receive or send as private business.)*

JOSEPH CONRAD
These Bumble-like Proceedings

('Some Reflexions, Seamanlike and Otherwise, on the Loss of the *Titanic*', *English Review*, May 1912)

In what light one is to look at the action of the American Senate is more difficult to say. From a certain point of view the sight of the august senators of a great Power rushing to New York and beginning to bully and badger the luckless 'Yamsi' – on the very quay-side so to speak – seems to furnish the Shakespearian touch of the comic to the real tragedy of the fatuous drowning of all these people who to the last moment put their trust in mere bigness, in the reckless affirmations of commercial men and mere technicians and in the irresponsible paragraphs of the newspapers booming these ships! Yes, a grim touch of comedy. One asks oneself what these men are after, with this very provincial display of authority. I beg my friends in the United States pardon for calling these zealous senators men. I don't wish to be disrespectful. They may be of the stature of demi-gods for all I know, but at that great distance from the shores of effete Europe and in the presence of so many guileless dead, their size seems diminished from this side. What are they after? What is there for them to find out? We know what had happened. The ship scraped her side against a piece of ice, and sank after floating for two hours and a half, taking a lot of people down with her. What more can they find out from the unfair badgering of the unhappy 'Yamsi', or the ruffianly abuse of the same.

'Yamsi', I should explain, is a mere code address, and I use it here symbolically. I have seen commerce pretty close. I know what it is worth, and I have no particular regard for commercial magnates, but one must protest against these Bumble-like proceedings. Is it indignation at the loss of so many lives which is at work here? Well, the American railroads kill very many people during one single year, I dare say. Then why don't these dignitaries come down on the presidents of their own railroads, of which one can't say whether they are mere means of transportation or a sort of gambling game for the use of American plutocrats. Is it only an ardent and, upon the whole, praiseworthy desire for information? But the reports of the enquiry tell us that the august senators, though raising a lot of questions testifying to the complete innocence and even blankness of their minds, are unable to understand what the second officer is saying to them. We are so informed by the press from the other side. Even such a simple expression as that one of the look-out men was stationed in the 'eyes of the ship' was too much for the senators of the land of graphic expression. What it must have been in the more recondite matters I won't even try to think, because I have no mind for smiles just now. They were greatly exercised about the sound of explosions heard when half the ship was under water already. Was there one? Were there two? They seemed to be smelling a rat there! Has not some charitable soul told them (what even schoolboys who read sea stories know) that when a ship sinks from a leak like this, a deck or two is always blown up; and that when a steamship goes down by the head, the boilers may, and often do break adrift with a sound which resembles the sound of an explosion? And they may, indeed, explode, for all I know. In the only case I have seen of a steamship sinking there was such a sound, but I didn't dive down after her to investigate. She was not of 45,000 tons and declared unsinkable, but the sight was impressive enough. I shall never forget the muffled, mysterious detonation, the sudden agitation of the sea round the slowly raised stern, and to this day I have in my eye the propeller, seen perfectly still in its frame against a clear evening sky.

But perhaps the second officer has explained to them by this time this and a few other little facts. Though why an officer of the British merchant service should answer the questions of any king, emperor, autocrat or senator of any foreign power (as to an event in which a British ship alone was concerned, and which did not even take place in the territorial waters of that power) passes my understanding.

*Chesterton gazed at the American enquiry with a cooler eye. He knew
the cross-criticisms between Americans and Britons were caused by the
cross-currents of British–American power, with the tide turning in
America's favour. (Lord Mersey had been a member of the Jameson
Raid committee of investigation that cleared the government of the
accusation that it had been involved in a Cecil Rhodes-inspired conspiracy to instigate a rising against President Kruger of the Transvaal.)*

G. K. CHESTERTON
Cross-Criticisms: England and America

(*Illustrated London News*, 4 May 1912)

Amerika is one with us in that it is founded on the Christian
order and drawn from the European fountains; that is, it is akin to us
as are France and Germany and Russia. It is not any more akin to us
than they are. It is quite certain that we and they are not now of the
same race; it is more and more doubtful whether we can even be said
to speak the same language . . .

For the truth is, that so far from England and America being alike,
they are very nearly opposite. Exactly the qualities which one lacks the
other exaggerates. Precisely those particular passions which America
carries into vices, England cannot be induced to begin to practise as
virtues. The divergence is rapidly becoming as dark and awful as an
abyss over this particular question of the responsibility for the great
Atlantic shipwreck. Of course, both nations join in the mere mortal
emotion, the purification of pity and terror; but then all nations would
join in that. But the two nations entangled in actual responsibility are
entangled yet more in an increasing misunderstanding; because their
faults are opposite faults; and the easiest thing to forgive in one country
is the hardest thing to forgive in the other.

It is perfectly true, as English papers are saying, that some American
papers are what we should call both vulgar and vindictive; that they set
the pack in full cry upon a particular man; that they are impatient of
delay and eager for savage decisions; and that the flags under which
they march are often the rags of a reckless and unscrupulous journalism.
All this is true; but if these be the American faults, it is all the more

necessary to emphasize the opposite English faults. Our national evil is exactly the other way: it is to hush everything up; it is to damp everything down; it is to leave every great affair unfinished, to leave every enormous question unanswered. It is essential to realize, therefore, that the accusations on both sides may be real. The educated Englishman tends to say to the Americans, 'I know you and your popular persecutions. You will hunt poor Mr Ismay from court to court, as if he were the only man that was saved – just as you hunted poor old Gorki from hotel to hotel, as if he were the only man not living with his wife.' But it is essential to remember that the educated American can say a similar thing on the other side. He will say, 'I know you and your gentlemanly privacies and hypocrisies. You will shirk this inquiry into the *Titanic* tragedy, just as you shirked the inquiry into the Jameson Raid. You will ignore plain questions and suppress existing telegrams to save the face of some rich man, just as you did it to save the face of the African millionaires. We are not so careful of millionaires. We are hounding on the pack, and we think a pack of dogs, even if it is a pack of mongrels, is not so bad a thing for dealing with wolves – or foxes.'

Now, it is important to insist that each of these cross-criticisms is unjust. It is perfectly true, perilously true, that English courts and committees tend to hush things up. It is not true that the English motive is a mere snobbish fear and nothing else. There is in the English dilatoriness and inconclusiveness something more than this mean motive which, for the rest, certainly exists in some of us. There is also something of sportsmanship, something of the generosity of the gentleman, something that makes 'sneaking' at school almost illogically impossible. It is a feeling peculiar to certain classes of people, but it is not a feeling of mere class pride or class terror; it is a good feeling. In so far as Americans would put it down to common calculated servility, Americans would be wrong. Well, we shall be even more frightfully wrong if we make the American outcry and inquisition a mere example of scare-line journalism and sensational demagogy. If there is an element of real clemency in our desire to conceal things, there is an element of real and righteous indignation in their desire to reveal them. I confess that in a case like this I am in sympathy with that element.

Thus, for instance, I see all the English papers are sneering at Senator Smith for not knowing certain facts about shipping. Now, I can quite understand a contrary feeling in this affair. I can understand people thinking that it does not much matter whether Senator Smith knows the facts; what matters is, whether he is really trying to find them out. It is not a complete answer to say that we could have appointed a president who knew much more about shipping. We might have appointed one in his place who knew far too much about shipping. He might have known far too much to let anyone tell the truth about it. The Americans affect me altogether as foreigners; but I know enough about foreigners to know that foreigners can correct and complete a nation. This American excitement is a thing that hardly exists in England at all. It is a thing called Public Opinion. It is impatient, inquisitive, often ferocious; but I assure you, it has its uses. Do not despise it.

The New York book collector John Quinn defended the U.S. Senate
Inquiry in a letter to Conrad, and Conrad opened his second essay for
the English Review *with an acknowledgement of his friend's criticism.*
Conrad was on firmer ground with the structural recommendations in
his second essay, during which he remarked that 'for the hazards of her
existence I should think [Titanic] *about as strong as a Huntley and*
Palmer biscuit tin'. His earlier condemnation of 'the new seamanship'
was equally to the point. He disdained the 'ineffable hotel exquisites' for
whom a ship like Titanic, *'a sort of marine Ritz', was built.*

JOSEPH CONRAD
The New Seamanship

('Some Reflexions')

The only authority [an officer of the British merchant service] is bound to answer is the Board of Trade. But with what face the Board of Trade, which, having made the regulations for 10,000 ton ships, put its dear old bald head under its wing for ten years, took it out only to shelve an important report, and with a dreary murmur, 'Unsinkable', put it back again, in the hope of not being disturbed for another ten years, with what face it will be putting questions to that man who has done his duty, as to the facts of this disaster and as to his professional conduct in it – well, I don't know! I have the greatest respect for our established authorities. I am a disciplined man, and I have a natural indulgence for the weaknesses of human institutions; but I will own that at times I have regretted their – how shall I say it? – their imponderability. A Board of Trade – what is it? A Board of ... I believe the Speaker of the Irish Parliament is one of the members of it. A ghost. Less than that; as yet a mere memory. An office with adequate and no doubt comfortable furniture and a lot of perfectly irresponsible gentlemen who exist packed in its equable atmosphere softly, as if in a lot of cotton wool, and with no care in the world; for there can be no care without personal responsibility – such, for instance, as the seamen have – those seamen from whose mouths this irresponsible institution can take away the bread – as a disciplinary measure. Yes – it's all that. And what more? The name of a politician – a party man! Less than nothing; a mere void without as much as a shadow of responsibility cast into it from that light in which move the masses of men who work, who deal in things and face the realities – not the words – of this life.

Years ago I remember overhearing two genuine shellbacks of the old type commenting on a ship's officer, who, if not exactly incompetent, did not commend himself to their severe judgement of accomplished sailor-men. Said one, resuming and concluding the discussion in a funnily judicial tone:

'The Board of Trade must have been drunk when they gave him his certificate.'

I confess that this notion of the Board of Trade as an entity having a brain which could be overcome by the fumes of strong liquor charmed me exceedingly. For then it would have been unlike the limited companies of which some exasperated wit has once said that they had no souls to be saved and no bodies to be kicked, and thus were free in this world and the next from all the effective sanctions of conscientious conduct. But, unfortunately, the picturesque pronouncement overheard by me was only a characteristic sally of an annoyed sailor. The Board of Trade is composed of bloodless departments. It has no limbs and no physiognomy, or else at the forthcoming enquiry it might have paid to the victims of the *Titanic* disaster the small tribute of a blush. I ask myself whether the Marine Department of the Board of Trade did really believe, when they decided to shelve the report on equipment for a time, that a ship of 45,000 tons, that *any* ship, could be made practically indestructible by means of watertight bulkheads? It seems incredible to anybody who had ever reflected upon the properties of material, such as wood or steel. You can't, let builders say what they like, make a ship of such dimensions as strong proportionately as a much smaller one. The shocks our old whalers had to stand amongst the heavy floes in Baffin's Bay were perfectly staggering, notwithstanding the most skilful handling, and yet they lasted for years. The *Titanic*, if one may believe the last reports, has only scraped against a piece of ice which, I suspect, was not an enormously bulky and comparatively easily seen berg, but the low edge of a floe – and sank. Leisurely enough, God knows – and here the advantage of bulkheads comes in – for time is a great friend, a good helper – though in this lamentable case these bulkheads served only to prolong the agony of the passengers who could not be saved. But she sank, causing, apart from the sorrow and the pity of the loss of so many lives, a sort of surprised consternation that such a thing should have happened at all. Why? You build a 45,000 tons hotel of thin steel plates to secure the patronage of, say, a couple of thousand rich people (for if it had been for the emigrant trade alone, there would have been no such exaggeration of mere size), you decorate it in the style of the Pharaohs or in the Louis Quinze style – I don't know which – and to please the aforesaid fatuous handful of individuals, who have more money than they know what to do with, and to the applause of two continents, you launch that mass with two thousand people on board at twenty-one knots across the sea – a perfect exhibition of the modern blind trust in mere material and appliances. And then this happens. General uproar. The blind trust in material and appliances has received a terrible shock. I will say nothing of the credulity which accepts any statement which specialists, technicians and office-people are pleased to make, whether for purposes of gain or glory. You stand there astonished and hurt in your profoundest sensibilities. But what else under the circumstances could you expect?

For my part I could much sooner believe in an unsinkable ship of 3,000 tons than in one of 40,000 tons. It is one of those things that stand to reason. You can't increase the thickness of scantling and plates indefinitely. And the mere weight of this bigness is an added disadvantage. In reading the reports, the first reflection which occurs to one is that, if that luckless ship had been a couple of hundred feet shorter, she would have probably gone clear of the danger. But then, perhaps, she could not have had a swimming bath and a French café. That, of course, is a serious consideration. I am well aware that those responsible for her short and fatal existence ask us in desolate accents to believe that if she had hit end on she would have survived. Which, by a sort of coy implication, seems to mean that it was all the fault of the officer of the watch (he is dead now) for trying to avoid the obstacle. We shall have presently, in deference to commercial and industrial interests, a new kind of seamanship. A very new and 'progressive' kind. If you see anything in the way, by no means try to avoid it; smash at it full tilt. And then – and then only you shall see the triumph of material, of clever contrivances, of the whole box of engineering tricks in fact, and cover with glory a commercial concern of the most unmitigated sort, a great Trust, and a great shipbuilding yard, justly famed for the super-excellence of its material and workmanship. Unsinkable! See? I told you she was unsinkable, if only handled in accordance with the new seamanship. Everything's in that. And, doubtless, the Board of Trade, if properly approached, would consent to give the needed instructions to its examiners of Masters and Mates. Behold the examination-room of the future. Enter to the grizzled examiner a young man of modest aspect: 'Are you well up in modern seamanship?' 'I hope so, sir.' 'H'm, let's see. You are at night on the bridge in charge of a 150,000 tons ship, with a motor track, organ-loft, etc., etc., with a full cargo of passengers, a full crew of 1,500 café waiters, two sailors and a boy, three collapsible boats as per Board of Trade regulations, and going at your three-quarter speed of, say, about forty knots. You perceive suddenly right ahead, and close to, something that looks like a large ice-floe. What would you do?' 'Put the helm amidships.' 'Very well. Why?' 'In order to hit end on.' 'On what grounds should you endeavour to hit end on?' 'Because we are taught by our builders and masters that the heavier the smash, the smaller the damage, and because the requirements of material should be attended to.'

And so on and so on. The new seamanship: when in doubt try to ram fairly – whatever's before you. Very simple. If only the *Titanic* had rammed that piece of ice (which was *not* a monstrous berg) fairly, every puffing paragraph would have been vindicated in the eyes of the credulous public which pays. But would it have been? Well, I doubt it. I am well aware that in the eighties the steamship *Arizona*, one of the 'greyhounds of the ocean' in the jargon of that day, did run bows on against a very unmistakable iceberg, and managed to get into port on her collision bulkhead. But the *Arizona* was not, if I remember rightly, 5,000 tons register, let alone 45,000, and she was not going at twenty knots per hour. I can't be perfectly certain at this distance of time, but her sea-speed could not have been more than fourteen at the outside. Both these facts made for safety. And, even if she had been engined to go twenty knots, there would not have been behind that speed the enormous mass, so difficult to check in its impetus, the terrific weight of which is bound to do damage to itself or others at the slightest contact.

6
Hymns and Heroism

Any fate was titanic.
    E. M. Forster, *Howards End*

*The vindictiveness with which American newspapers uttered Ismay's
name – J. Brute Ismay in some quarters – is one of the familiar epilogues
of the* Titanic *drama. The anger that can succeed or inform grief, or the
affected anger of public spokesmen, requires a target, and Ismay, a man
never popular with the press, was the most reasonable candidate. The
effective owner of the ship had left in a lifeboat (knowing there were
insufficient lifeboats on board) while helpless hundreds had drowned.
As Ben Hecht scathingly put it: 'To hold your place in the ghastly face/
Of death on the sea at night/ Is a seaman's job, but to flee with the mob/
Is an owner's noble right'.*

*The U.S. enquiry wanted to know if Ismay had interfered in the
navigation of the ship by deciding its high speed; whether he bore any
responsibility for any equipment inadequacies of the ship that would
endanger life; under what circumstances he had left the foundering
vessel; whether he had planned to escape American jurisdiction with
his surviving officers and crew once* S S Carpathia *reached New York.*

*Alden Smith's Report did not condemn Ismay directly; it merely
remarked that 'the presence of Mr Ismay and Mr Andrews stimulated
the ship to greater speed'. The question of Ismay's moral shirking Smith
courteously put aside. Ismay was cheered by well-wishers on his arrival
back in Liverpool (he had become a conduit for mutual British–American
resentment) and escaped vilification by the British press. But there was
still the British Commission of Enquiry to come.*

*Ismay was designated by many to play coward amid the other
undoubted male heroes of the tragedy. It seems stories of heroism, with
episodes of discipline and self-sacrifice, were necessary. The heroism,*

like the disaster itself, was in some senses waiting to happen. It is probably the case that Sir Arthur Conan Doyle was more receptive to the idea of heroism than George Bernard Shaw, with whom he got into a scrap. Only implacable sceptics such as Shaw and Conrad dared question the musicians' part in the tragedy, even if only to translate their conduct into naïve courage. They were assumed to be heroic in their passive suffering (like the soldiers of the War soon to happen). They shared the fate of steerage passengers, yet unlike them the band was eloquent; indeed, they became the voice of those left on board when the lifeboats had gone, a voice soon to give way to the hideous chorus of the abandoned in the sea.

Identification of the tune that was last played on board became of disproportionate importance, suggesting again that the satisfaction of some deep longing was at stake. Most wanted it to have been a hymn, for hymns were a profound mode of expression, personal and national, in Victorian Britain and beyond, especially in times of crisis. Hymns, as D. H. Lawrence knew, worked at a level below criticism and analysis, the same level upon which Titanic and her fate work even upon sceptical and sophisticated minds guiltily aware of the sentimentalism into which the tragedy has often been degraded, and disdainful of the commercialism into which the ship has been sunk.

If Americans with their Titanic enquiry created drama inadvertently,
the British through the eyes of their newspapers sought it in theirs as
Society Drama. Among witnesses, physical appearance and wardrobe
were seen as telling, and the perspective of social rank rarely absent.
Herbert Asquith was Prime Minister at the time, David Lloyd George
his successor in that office.

The White Star Chief

(*Daily Sketch*, 5 June 1912)

All eyes were focused on the witness-stand at the Scottish Hall
when, a little after noon yesterday, Mr Bruce Ismay, the head of the
White Star Line, made his first appearance as a witness before the
Titanic Commission.

The attendance of spectators was small in comparison with the crowds
that had filled the hall during the many dramatic hours before the
Whitsuntide holidays intervened.

Had there been any general expectation of seeing so prominent a
survivor of the Atlantic tragedy as Mr Ismay, the courtroom would
doubtless have been packed with an eager throng. But no one guessed
that so quickly after resuming the business of the enquiry the Commission would come to grips with points of absorbing interest. Only a
few privileged visitors had any notion of the evidence that the day might
bring forth.

Among those present was Mrs Lloyd George who, with her young
daughter, early took a seat in one of the reserved rows just behind counsel
and, wearing a large mauve-plumed hat, followed the proceedings with
attentive interest. So did Mrs Asquith, who has been a frequent visitor
to the enquiry.

Ladies, in fact, again formed the largest half of the spectators present
when Lord Mersey took his seat with all five assessors beside him. Large
and much-feathered hats provided a showy array of millinery, though
with the considerateness of the really well-bred matinée girl many of
the fair onlookers promptly removed their hats.

Several witnesses of minor importance preceded Mr Bruce Ismay in
the box, but it was the advent of the White Star's chief that visibly

quickened the interest of all in Court. Fashionably-dressed dames levelled lorgnettes and opera glasses at the simple green-carpeted dais close beside the big model of the *Titanic*.

They saw a quietly-dressed, rather youthful man of unassuming mien step up to take the oath. Speaking in a low, well-modulated voice that carried well in this hall of vocal difficulties, Mr Ismay proceeded to tell his own story in a series of crisp, direct answers to the Attorney-General's steady fire of questions.

No one looking at Bruce Ismay as he stood at the witness-table, now folding his arms before him, now clasping his hands behind his back or occasionally slipping his left hand into his trousers-pocket with quite a boyish air, would have pictured this man as the head of one of the wealthiest and most powerful shipping corporations in the world. He looks and speaks so unlike the commonly accepted type of commercial monarchs as could well be conceived. A cultured cosmopolitan, if you like, but not a strong ruler of strong men.

Ismay's British inquisitors considered his departure from the ship more seriously than did their American counterparts, tangled as it was with British concerns with rank and class. He was roughly handled, in spite of Lord Mersey's attempt to shield him or, perhaps, to thwart Clement Edwards, M.P., Counsel for the Dock Workers' Union, and Thomas Scanlan. It is hard not to detect in Mersey's impatience with these counsel a class distaste. Had Ismay not jumped into the lifeboat, Mersey said in his Report, 'he would merely have added one more life, namely his own, to the number of those lost'.

Mr Ismay's Duty

(British Commission of Enquiry)

18848 [Clement Edwards]. You were one of those, as the managing director, responsible for determining the number of boats? – Yes, in conjunction with the shipbuilders.

18849. When you got into the boat you thought that the *Titanic* was sinking? – I did.

18850. Did you know that there were some hundreds of people on that ship? – Yes.

18851. Who must go down with her? – Yes, I did.

18852. Has it occurred to you that, except perhaps apart from the captain, you, as the responsible managing director, deciding the number of boats, owed your life to every other person on that ship? – It has not.

The Commissioner [Lord Mersey]: I do not think that is a question to put to him; that is an observation which you may make when you come to make your speech. It is not a question for him.

Mr Edwards: I thought the witness ought to have an opportunity of answering before I attempted to make the observation.

The Commissioner: You will make that observation, if you think it worth while, when the time comes.

18853. (Mr Edwards – To the witness). According to your statement you got into the boat last of all? – I did.

18854. So that if a witness says that you, in fact, got into the boat earlier and helped the women and children in, that would not be true? – It would not.

18855. I suppose you know that it has been given in evidence here by [Edward] Brown? – Yes.

The Commissioner: What evidence?

18856. (Mr Edwards). The evidence of Brown was that Mr Ismay got into this particular boat some time earlier. On page 223, at Question 10520, the question was: 'Was Mr Bruce Ismay taking any part in connection with that boat? – (A.) Yes, he was calling out for the women and children first. He helped to get them into that boat, and he went into it himself to receive the women and children.' That is not true? – No, it is not.

18857. Now, it has been given in evidence here that you took an actual part in giving directions for the women and children to be placed in the boats. Is that true? – I did, and I helped as far as I could.

18858. If you had taken this active part in the direction up to a certain point, why did you not continue and send to other decks to see if there were passengers available, for this last boat? – I was standing by the boat; I helped everybody into the boat that was there, and as the boat was being lowered away I got in.

18859. That does not answer the question. You had been taking a responsible part, according to the evidence and according to your own admission, in directing the filling of the boats? – No, I had not; I had been helping to put the women and children into the boats as they came forward.

18860. I am afraid we are a little at cross purposes. Is it not the fact that you were calling out 'Women and children first'? and helping them in? – Yes, it is.

18861. Is it not the fact that you were giving directions as to the women and children getting in? – I was helping the women and children in.

18862. Please answer my question. Is it not the fact that you were giving directions in helping them? – I was calling for the women and children to come in.

18863. What I am putting to you is this, that if you could take an active part at that stage, why did you not continue the active part and give instructions, or go yourself to other decks, or round the other side of the deck, to see if there were other people who might find a place in your boat? – I presumed that there were people down below who were sending the people up.

18864. But you knew there were hundreds who had not come up.

That is your answer, that you presumed that there were people down below sending them up? – Yes.

18865. And does it follow from that that you presumed that everybody was coming up who wanted to come up? – I knew that everybody could not be up.

18866. Then I do not quite see the point of the answer? – Everybody that was on the deck got into that boat.

The Commissioner: Your point, Mr Edwards, as I understand is this: That, having regard to his position, it was his duty to remain upon that ship until she went to the bottom. That is your point?

Mr Edwards: Yes, and inasmuch . . .

The Commissioner: That is your point? . . .

18867. (Mr Edwards). Frankly, that is so; I do not flinch from it a little bit. But I want to get it from this witness, inasmuch as he took upon himself to give certain directions at a certain time, why he did not discharge the responsibility even after that, having regard to the other persons or passengers? – There were no more passengers to get into that boat. The boat was actually being lowered away.

18868. That is your answer? – Yes.

Ismay released this statement during the American hearings in order to defend himself against what he regarded as defamation in the U.S. press. He denied requesting high speed of Captain Smith. E. E. Carter was actually William E. Carter, 'polo player and clubman', returning from Europe with a new English motor-car; his wife subsequently divorced him, and it was soon after revealed that she believed he saved himself and left her and their children to their own devices.

Statement Issued by J. Bruce Ismay on 21 April 1912

(Cable sent to *The Times*)

... It has been stated that Captain Smith and I were having a dinner party in one of the saloons from 7.30 to 10.30 Sunday night and that at the time of the collision Captain Smith was sitting with me in the saloon.

Both of these statements are absolutely false. I did not dine with the captain nor did I see him during the evening of April 14th. The doctor dined with me in the restaurant at 7.30, and I went direct to my stateroom and went to bed at about 10.30. I was asleep when the collision occurred. I felt a jar, went into the passage way without dressing, met a steward, asked him what was the matter and he said he did not know. I returned to my room. I felt the ship slow down, put on an overcoat over my pyjamas and went up to the bridge. I asked Captain Smith what was the matter and he said we had struck ice. I asked him whether he thought it serious and he said he did. On returning to my room, I met the chief engineer and asked him whether he thought the damage serious and he said he thought it was.

I then returned to my room and put on a suit of clothes. I had been in my overcoat and pyjamas up to this time. I then went back to the boat deck and heard Captain Smith give the order to clear the boats. I helped in this work for nearly two hours as far as I can judge. I worked at the starboard boats helping women and children into the boats and lowering them over the side. I did nothing with regards to the boats on the portside. By that time every wooden lifeboat on the starboard side had been lowered away and I found that they were engaged in getting out the forward collapsible boat on the starboard side. I assisted in this work and all the women who were on this deck were helped into the boat. They were I think third-class passengers. As the boat was going over the side, Mr Carter, a passenger, and myself got into it. At that time there was not a woman on the boat deck nor any passengers of any class, so far as we could see or hear the boat had between 35 and 40 in it, I should think, most of them women. The rest were perhaps four or five men, and it was afterwards discovered that there were four Chinamen concealed under the thwarts in the bottom of the boat. The distance that the boat had to be lowered into the water was, I imagine, about 20 feet. Mr Carter and I did not get into the boat until after they had begun to lower away. When the boat reached the water I helped to row it, pushing the oar from me. This is the explanation of the fact that my back was to the sinking steamer. The boat would have accommodated certainly six or more passengers in addition if there had been any on the boat deck to go. These facts can be substantiated by Mr E. E. Carter of Philadelphia, who got in at the time that I did and was rowing the boat with me. I hope I need not say that neither Mr Carter or myself would for any moment have thought of getting into the boat if there had been any women to go in it, nor should I have done so if I had thought that by remaining on the ship I could have been of the slightest further assistance.

It is impossible for me to answer every false statement, rumour, or invention that has appeared in the newspapers. I am prepared to answer any questions that may be asked by the committee of the Senate or any other responsible person. I shall therefore make no further statement of this kind except to explain the messages which I sent from the *Carpathia*. These messages have been completely misunderstood. An inference has been drawn from them that I was anxious to avoid the Senate committee's enquiry which it was intended to hold in New York. As a matter of fact when despatching these messages I had not the slightest idea that any enquiry was contemplated and I had no information regarding it until the arrival of the *Carpathia* at the Cunard dock in New York on Thursday night when I was informed by Senators Smith and Newlands of the appointment of the special committee to hold the enquiry. The only purpose I had in sending these messages was to express my desire to have the crews returned to their homes in

England for their own benefit at the earliest possible moment, and I also was naturally anxious to return to my family, but left the matter of my return entirely to our representatives in New York.

I deeply regret that I am compelled to make my personal statement when my whole thought is on the horror of the disaster. In building the *Titanic* it was the hope of my associates and myself that we had built a vessel which could not be destroyed by the perils of the sea or dangers of navigation. The event has proved the futility of that hope. The present legal requirements have proved inadequate. They must be changed, but whether they are changed or not this awful experience has taught the steamship owners of the world that too much reliance has been placed on watertight compartments and on wireless telegraphy, and they must equip every vessel with lifeboats and rafts sufficient to provide for every soul on board, and sufficient men to handle them.

The retired President of IMM spent much of his later life at The Lodge, Costelloe, Co. Galway, Ireland. The Irish poet Derek Mahon has always been drawn to the abandoned, disused or deserted, and Bruce Ismay duly takes his place as a figure in Mahon's landscape.

DEREK MAHON
'After the *Titanic*'

(*Collected Poems*, 1999)

They said I got away in a boat
And humbled me at the enquiry. I tell you
   I sank as far that night as any
Hero. As I sat shivering on the dark water
   I turned to ice to hear my costly
Life go thundering down in a pandemonium of
   Prams, pianos, sideboards, winches,
Boilers bursting and shredded ragtime. Now I hide
   In a lonely house behind the sea
Where the tide leaves broken toys and hat-boxes
   Silently at my door. The showers of
April, flowers of May mean nothing to me, nor the
   Late light of June, when my gardener
Describes to strangers how the old man stays in bed
   On seaward mornings after nights of
Wind, takes his cocaine and will see no one, repeat no one.
   Then it is I drown again with all those dim
Lost faces I never understood. My poor soul
   Screams out in the starlight, heart
Breaks loose and rolls down like a stone.
   Include me in your lamentations.

His claim notwithstanding, the Titanic *calamity failed to make the proud Shaw humble or the joker Shaw serious. Although he seems to confuse demands with the failure to answer those demands, he was right to resent the paeans of patriotic and patriarchal praise that drowned out common sense. (Nansen, Amundsen and Abruzzi were contemporary explorers, handy counter-examples of the xenophobia that the* Titanic *unmoored.)*

GEORGE BERNARD SHAW
'The *Titanic*: Some Unmentioned Morals'

(*Daily News* (London), 14 May 1912)

Why is it that the effect of a sensational catastrophe on a modern nation is to cast it into transports, not of weeping, not of prayer, not of sympathy with the bereaved nor congratulations of the rescued, not of poetic expression of the soul purified by pity and terror, but of a wild defiance of inexorable Fate and undeniable Fact by an explosion of outrageous romantic lying?

What is the first demand of romance in a shipwreck? It is the cry of Women and Children First. No male creature is to step into a boat as long as there is a woman or child on the doomed ship. How the boat is to be navigated and rowed by babies and women occupied in holding the babies is not mentioned. The likelihood that no sensible woman would trust either herself or her child in a boat unless there was a considerable percentage of men on board is not considered. Women and children first: that is the romantic formula. And never did the chorus of solemn delight at the strict observance of this formula by the British heroes on board the *Titanic* rise to sublimer strains than in the papers containing the first account of the wreck by a surviving eyewitness, Lady Duff Gordon. She described how she escaped in the captain's boat. There was one other woman in it, and ten men: twelve all told. One woman for every five men. Chorus: 'Not once or twice in our rough island story', etc., etc.

Second romantic demand. Though all the men (except the foreigners, who must all be shot by stern British officers in attempting to rush the boats over the bodies of the women and children) must be heroes, the captain must be a super-hero, a magnificent seaman, cool, brave, delighting in death and danger, and a living guarantee that the wreck was nobody's fault, but, on the contrary, a triumph of British navigation. Such a man Captain [E. J.] Smith was enthusiastically proclaimed on the day when it was reported (and actually believed, apparently) that he had shot himself on the bridge, or shot the first officer, or been shot by the first officer, or shot anyhow to bring the curtain down effectively. Writers who had never heard of Captain Smith to that hour wrote of him as they would hardly write of Nelson. The one thing positively known was that Captain Smith had lost his ship by deliberately and knowingly steaming into an ice field at the highest speed he had coal for. He paid the penalty; so did most of those for whose lives he was responsible. Had he brought them and the ship safely to land, nobody would have taken the smallest notice of him.

Third romantic demand. The officers must be calm, proud, steady, unmoved in the intervals of shooting the terrified foreigners. The verdict that they had surpassed all expectations was unanimous. The actual evidence was that Mr Ismay was told by the officer of his boat to go to hell, and that boats which were not full refused to go to the rescue of those who were struggling in the water in cork jackets. Reason frankly given: they were afraid. The fear was as natural as the officer's language to Mr Ismay: who of us at home dare blame them or feel sure that we should have been any cooler or braver? But is it necessary to assure the world that only Englishmen could have behaved so heroically, and to compare their conduct with the hypothetic dastardliness which lascars or Italians or foreigners generally – say Nansen or Amundsen or the Duke of Abruzzi – would have shown in the same circumstances?

Fourth romantic demand. Everybody must face death without a tremor; and the band, according to the Birkenhead precedent, must play 'Nearer, my God, to Thee', as an accompaniment to the invitation to Mr Ismay to go to hell. It was duly proclaimed that thus exactly it fell out. Actual evidence: the captain and officers were so afraid of a panic that, though they knew the ship was sinking, they did not dare to tell the passengers so – especially the third-class passengers – and the band played Rag Times to reassure the passengers, who, therefore, did not get into the boats, and did not realize their situation until the boats were gone and the ship was standing on her head before plunging to the bottom. What happened then Lady Duff Gordon has related, and the witnesses of the American enquiry could hardly bear to relate.

I ask, What is the use of all this ghastly, blasphemous, inhuman, braggartly lying? Here is a calamity which might well make the proudest man humble, and the wildest joker serious. It makes us vainglorious, insolent and mendacious. At all events, that is what our journalists assumed. Were they right or wrong? Did the Press really represent the public? I am afraid it did. Churchmen and statesmen took much the same tone. The effect on me was one of profound disgust, almost of national dishonour. Am I mad? Possibly. At all events, that is how I felt and how I feel about it. It seems to me that when deeply moved men should speak the truth. The English nation appears to take precisely the contrary view. Again I am in the minority. What will be the end of it? – for England, I mean. Suppose we came into conflict with a race that had the courage to look facts in the face and the wisdom to know itself for what it was. Fortunately for us, no such race is in sight. Our wretched consolation must be that any other nation would have behaved just as absurdly.

The patriotic Doyle had found himself on the opposite side of the Boer War from Shaw and now they traded fire again. That Officer Lowe did not know he was addressing Bruce Ismay somewhat weakens Doyle's case on that point.

SIR ARTHUR CONAN DOYLE
The Whole Wonderful Epic

(*Daily News*, 20 May 1912)

I have just been reading the article by Mr Bernard Shaw upon the loss of the *Titanic*, which appeared in your issue of May 14th. It is written professedly in the interests of truth, and accuses everyone around him of lying. Yet I can never remember any production which contained so much that was false within the same compass. How a man could write with such looseness and levity of such an event at such a time passes all comprehension. Let us take a few of the points. Mr Shaw wishes – in order to support his perverse thesis, that there was no heroism – to quote figures to show that the women were not given priority in escape. He picks out, therefore, one single boat, the smallest of all, which was launched and directed under peculiar circumstances, which are now matter for enquiry. Because there were ten men and two women in this boat, therefore there was no heroism or chivalry; and all talk about it is affectation. Yet Mr Shaw knows as well as I know that if he had taken the very next boat he would have been obliged to admit that there were 65 women out of 70 occupants, and that in nearly all the boats navigation was made difficult by the want of men to do the rowing. Therefore, in order to give a false impression, he has deliberately singled out one boat; although he could not but be aware that it entirely misrepresented the general situation. Is this decent controversy, and has the writer any cause to accuse his contemporaries of misstatement?

His next paragraph is devoted to the attempt to besmirch the conduct of Capt. Smith. He does it by his favourite method of 'suggestio falsi' – the false suggestion being that the sympathy shown by the public for Capt. Smith took the shape of condoning Capt. Smith's navigation. Now everyone – including Mr Bernard Shaw – knows perfectly well that no defence has ever been made of the risk which was run, and that the sympathy was at the spectacle of an old and honoured sailor who has made one terrible mistake, and who deliberately gave his life in reparation, discarding his lifebelt, working to the last for those whom he had unwillingly injured and finally swimming with a child to a boat into which he himself refused to enter. This is the fact, and Mr Shaw's assertion that the wreck was hailed as a 'triumph of British navigation' only shows – what surely needed no showing – that a phrase stands for more than truth with Mr Shaw. The same remark applies to his 'wrote of him as they would hardly write of Nelson'. If Mr Shaw will show me the work of any responsible journalist in which Capt. Smith is written of in the terms of Nelson, I will gladly send £100 to the Fabian Society.

Mr Shaw's next suggestion – all the more poisonous because it is not put into so many words – is that the officers did not do their duty. If his vague words mean anything they can only mean this. He quotes as if it were a crime the words of [Fifth Officer Harold Godfrey] Lowe to Mr Ismay when he interfered with his boat. I could not imagine a finer example of an officer doing his duty than that a subordinate should dare to speak thus to the managing director of the Line when he thought that he was impeding his life-saving work. The sixth officer [James P. Moody] went down with the captain, so I presume that even Mr Shaw could not ask him to do more. Of the other officers I have never heard or read any cause for criticism. Mr Shaw finds some cause for offence in the fact that one of them discharged his revolver in order to intimidate some foreign immigrants who threatened to rush the boats. The fact and the assertion that these passengers were foreigners came from several eyewitnesses. Does Mr Shaw think it should have been suppressed? If not what is he scolding about?

Finally, Mr Shaw tries to defile the beautiful incident of the band by alleging that it was the result of orders issued to avert panic. But if it were, how does that detract either from the wisdom of the orders or from the heroism of the musicians? It was right to avert panic, and it was wonderful that men could be found to do it in such a way.

As to the general accusation that the occasion has been used for the glorification of British qualities, we should indeed be a lost people if we did not honour courage and discipline when we see it in its highest form. That our sympathies extend beyond ourselves is shown by the fact that the conduct of the American male passengers, and very particularly of the much-abused millionaires, has been as warmly eulogized as any single feature in the whole wonderful epic.

But surely it is a pitiful sight to see a man of undoubted genius using his gifts in order to misrepresent and decry his own people, regardless of the fact that his words must add to the grief of those who have already had more than enough to bear.

Shaw keeps the heat on while restricting his topics wisely to journalists'
ignorant hyperbole and Captain Smith's lack of restraint. (R. B. Cun-
ninghame Graham was a writer, traveller and Member of Parliament;
Grace Darling rescued five people from a steamboat wreck in 1838;
Shaw's uncle was a medical officer on ships of the Inman Line.) In a
brief reply in the Daily News, *25 May, Doyle bowed out of the exchange*
and accused Shaw of needlessly hurting the feelings of others.

GEORGE BERNARD SHAW
Beating the Hysterics

(*Daily News*, 22 May 1912)

I hope to persuade my friend Sir Arthur Conan Doyle, now that
he has got his romantic and warm-hearted protest off his chest, to read
my article again three or four times, and give you his second thoughts
on the matter; for it is really not possible for any sane man to disagree
with a single word that I have written.

I again submit that when news of a shipwreck arrives without particulars, and journalists immediately begin to invent particulars, they are
lying. It is nothing to the point that authentic news may arrive later on,
and may confirm a scrap or two of their more obvious surmises. The
first narratives which reached us were those by an occupant of a boat
in which there were ten men, two women, and plenty of room for more,
and of an occupant of another boat which, like the first, refused to
return to rescue the drowning because the people in it were avowedly
afraid. It was in the face of that information, and of that alone, that
columns of raving about women and children first were published. Sir
Arthur says that I 'picked out' these boats to prove my case. Of course
I did. I wanted to prove my case. They did prove it. They do prove it.
My case is that our journalists wrote without the slightest regard to the
facts; that they were actually more enthusiastic in their praise of the
Titanic heroes on the day when the only evidence to hand was evidence
of conduct for which a soldier would be shot and a Navy sailor hanged
when later news came in of those officers and crews who did their best;
and that it must be evident to every reasonable man that if there had
not been a redeeming feature in the whole case, exactly the same

'hogwash' (as Mr Cunninghame Graham calls it in his righteous disgust) would have been lavished on the veriest dastards as upon a crew of Grace Darlings. The captain positively lost popularity when the deliberate and calumnious lie that he had shot himself was dropped. May I ask what value real heroism has in a country which responds to these inept romances invented by people who can produce nothing after all but stories of sensational cowardice? Would Sir Arthur take a medal from the hands of the imbecile liars whom he is defending?

Sir Arthur accuses me of lying; and I must say that he gives me no great encouragement to tell the truth. But he proceeds to tell, against himself, what I take to be the most thundering lie ever sent to a printer by a human author. He first says that I 'quoted as if it were a crime' the words used by the officer who told Mr Ismay to go to hell. I did not. I said the outburst was very natural, though not in my opinion admirable or heroic. If I am wrong, then I claim to be a hero myself; for it has occurred to me in trying circumstances to lose my head and temper and use the exact words attributed (by himself) to the officer in question. But Sir Arthur goes on to say: 'I could not imagine a finer example of an officer doing his duty than that a subordinate should dare to speak thus to the managing director of the line when he thought he was impeding his life-saving work.' Yes you could, Sir Arthur; and many a page of heroic romance from your hand attests that you have often imagined much finer examples. Heroism has not quite come to that yet; nor has your imagination contracted or your brain softened to the bathos of seeing sublimity in a worried officer telling even a managing director (godlike being!) to go to hell. I would not hear your enemy libel you so. But now that you have chivalrously libelled yourself, don't lecture me for reckless mendacity; for you have captured the record in the amazing sentence I have just quoted.

I will not accept Sir Arthur's offer of £100 to the Fabian Society for every hyper-Nelsonic eulogy of the late Captain Smith which stands in the newspapers of those first days to bear out my very moderate description of them. I want to see the Fabian Society solvent, but not at the cost of utter destitution to a friend. I should not have run the risk of adding to the distress of Captain Smith's family by adding one word to facts that speak only too plainly for themselves if others had been equally considerate. But if vociferous journalists will persist in glorifying the barrister whose clients are hanged, the physician whose patients die, the general who loses battles, and the captain whose ship goes to the bottom, such false coin must be nailed to the counter at any cost. There have been British captains who have brought their ships safely through ice fields by doing their plain duty and carrying out their instructions. There have been British captains who have seen to it that their crew knew their boats and their places in their boats, and who, when it became necessary to take to those boats, have kept discipline in the face of death, and not lost one life that could have been saved. And often enough nobody has said 'Thank you' to them for it, because they have not done mischief enough to stir the emotions of our romantic journalists. These are the men whom I admire and with whom I prefer to sail.

I do not wish to imply that I for a moment believe that the dead man actually uttered all the heartbreaking rubbish that has been put into his mouth by fools and liars; nor am I forgetting that a captain may not be able to make himself heard and felt everywhere in these huge floating (or sinking) hotels as he can in a cruiser, or rally a mob of waiters and dock labourers as he could a crew of trained seamen. But no excuse, however good, can turn a failure into a success. Sir Arthur cannot be ignorant of what would happen had the *Titanic* been a King's ship, or of what the court-martial would have said and done on the evidence of the last few days.

Owing to the fact that a member of my family was engaged in the Atlantic service, and perhaps also that I happen to know by personal experience what it is like to be face to face with death in the sea, I know what the risk of ice means on a liner, and know also that there is no heroism in being drowned when you cannot help it. The captain of the *Titanic* did not, as Sir Arthur thinks, make 'a terrible mistake'. He made no mistake. He knew perfectly well that ice is the only risk that is considered really deadly in his line of work, and, knowing it, he chanced it and lost the hazard. Sentimental idiots, with a break in the voice, tell me that 'he went down to the depths': I tell them with the impatient contempt they deserve, that so did the cat. Heroism is extraordinarily fine conduct resulting from extraordinarily high character. Extraordinary circumstances may call it forth and may heighten its dramatic effect by pity and terror, by death and destruction, by darkness and a waste of waters; but none of these accessories are the thing itself; and to pretend that they are is to debase the moral currency by substituting the conception of sensational misfortune for inspiring achievement.

I am no more insensible to the pity of the catastrophe than anyone else; but I have been driven by an intolerable provocation of disgusting and dishonourable nonsense to recall our journalists to their senses by saying bluntly that the occasion has been disgraced by a callous outburst of romantic lying. To this I now wish to add that if, when I said this, I had read the evidence elicited by Lord Mersey's enquiry as to the *Californian* and the *Titanic's* emergency boat, I should probably have expressed myself much more strongly. I refrain now only because the facts are beating the hysterics without my help.

Conrad sounds a Shavian note of disabusing realism in his second
Titanic essay when he dismisses the heroism aboard and its journalistic
crying up. But professional brotherhood had caused him to defend
Captain Smith in his earlier essay – it is the commercial corruption of
seamanship that galls him. In the sensitive matter of the band, his realism
takes the form of rough compassion.

JOSEPH CONRAD
The Unsentimental Truth

('Certain Aspects of the Admirable Inquiry into the Loss of the *Titanic*',
English Review, July 1912)

I am not a soft-headed, humanitarian faddist. I have been ordered
in my time to do dangerous work; I have ordered others to do dangerous
work; I have never ordered a man to do any work I was not prepared
to do myself. I attach no exaggerated value to human life. But I know
it has a value for which the most generous contributions to the Mansion
House and 'Heroes' funds cannot pay. And they cannot pay for it,
because people, even of the third class (excuse my plain speaking), are
not cattle. Death has its sting. If Yamsi's manager's head were forcibly
held under the water of his bath for some little time, he would soon
discover that it has. Some people can only learn from that sort of
experience which comes home to their own dear selves.

I am not a sentimentalist; therefore it is not a great consolation to
me to see all these people breveted as 'Heroes' by the penny and
halfpenny Press. It is no consolation at all. In extremity, in the worst
extremity, the majority of people, even of common people, will behave
decently. It's a fact of which only the journalists don't seem aware.
Hence their enthusiasm, I suppose. But I, who am not a sentimentalist,
think it would have been finer if the band of the *Titanic* had been
quietly saved, instead of being drowned while playing – whatever tune
they were playing, the poor devils. I would rather they had been saved
to support their families than to see their families supported by the
magnificent generosity of the subscribers. I am not consoled by the
false, written-up, Drury Lane aspects of that event, which is neither
drama, nor melodrama, nor tragedy, but the exposure of arrogant folly.

There is nothing more heroic in being drowned very much against your will, off a holed, helpless, big tank in which you bought your passage, than in dying of colic caused by the imperfect salmon in the tin you bought from your grocer.

And that's the truth. The unsentimental truth stripped of the romantic garment the Press has wrapped around this most unnecessary disaster.

The bandsmen entered Titanic legendry immediately after Bride's tribute to them in his interview with the New York Times. They became the symbolic vessels of a generalized and harmonious grief; they transformed the last minutes aboard Titanic into a funeral ceremony, at least in the popular imagination. Better, then, that they played ragtime and waltzes to keep the spirits up and then a hymn when doom was imminent. To the familiar candidates for last tune (the hymns 'Nearer My God to Thee' and 'Autumn' and the waltz 'Songe d'Automne') has been added W. B. Bradbury's hymn 'He Leadeth Me' to the tune 'Aughton'.

JOHN MAXTONE-GRAHAM
The Last Gig

(Violet Jessop, *Titanic Survivor*, 1997)

Later on, [orchestra leader and violinist Wallace] Hartley was instructed to move his players forward into the boat deck lobby atop the main staircase. The seven [including one pianist] could continue playing as before because an upright piano was located permanently there. After having completed several selections, Hartley moved his men once more. Temporarily dismissed, they all trooped below, all the way down to E deck, to don overcoats and lifejackets before reassembling at their third venue of the night, outdoors on the port side of boat deck, just aft of the first-class entrance vestibule.

For this final performance, only a string sextet played, since the remaining pianist would also have to have dropped out without a piano being available outdoors on the deck. Since none of the musicians survived, we shall never know how those two idled pianists filled their last hour. Did they remain with their colleagues or might they have wandered off, investigating their chances of entering a lifeboat? My sense is that they probably stayed within reach, bonded, even *in extremis*, to their fellow professionals. Shipboard musicians to the present tend to stick together.

It has often occurred to me how difficult it must have been for those remaining instrumentalists to play out on deck. Of the six, Roger Bricoux and Jack Woodward were cellists and Fred Clarke a bass player. Whereas Clarke habitually played on his feet, the two cellists would have needed seats. What, if anything, did they sit on? Would Hartley have had them bring chairs outdoors or did they remain standing? Cellists I have discussed this with suggest that playing on their feet would have been difficult even if they only plucked a pizzicato accompaniment. Cellist Timothy Eddy of the Bach Aria Group tried playing for me while standing but announced after a few measures that he did so 'only with discomfort'. Some present-day jazz cellists have their instruments equipped with extra-long spikes for playing on their feet but it seems unlikely that such a refinement existed in 1912.

For violinists Hartley and Jock Hume as well as George Krins, the ship's only violist, there must have been different problems. One can only guess at the awkwardness of playing while clad in overcoats and lifejackets; keeping the instruments tucked beneath their chins cannot have been easy. Moreover, although there was doubtless ambient light from deck lights as well as spill from the lounge's forward windows, they must have had to play largely from memory, not necessarily difficult for professional palm court or cafe musicians. Moreover, if they had needed sheet music parts, the question of music stands arises – were any brought out on deck? We simply do not know. One necessary adjustment, common to all six string players, was the necessity of retuning their instruments once they emerged into the cold; low temperatures raise havoc with cat gut.

When Wallace Hartley's body was pulled from the sea and brought aboard the *Mackay-Bennett*, his music case was still strapped across his chest. Although, in the absence of music stands, it was unlikely that any parts would have been distributed that night, perhaps Hartley took the case with him either out of habit or because it contained sheets that he valued. I wonder what music was in it; might it have told us something, if not of the actual final selections, at least what Hartley had *wished* to play? As it was, the musicians seem to have played popular ragtime airs, familiar tunes to which passengers had danced or listened ever since Southampton.

What did they play at the end? My dear friend and colleague, Walter Lord, doyen of *Titanic* historians, hypothesizes persuasively in his *The Night Lives On* that it was neither *Nearer My God to Thee* (which Jessop and several others claimed to have heard) nor the hymn tune *Autumn* but a waltz. The waltz in question, although written by Englishman Archibald Joyce, had a French name, *Songe d'Automne* (Autumn Dream).

It was *Titanic*'s surviving radio operator Harold Bride's offhand response later in New York that created the persistent confusion about that hymn tune. When asked by reporters what the band had played, he merely said 'Autumn', titular English shorthand for the longer, more challenging French name.

Two separate, fragmentary accounts of the musicians' final moments remain. At the British Enquiry, Steward Edward Brown testified: 'I do not remember hearing them stop.' But stop they did and surviving passenger A. H. Barksworth conjures up a final image:

'I do not wish to detract from the bravery of anybody but I might mention that when I first came on deck, the band was playing a waltz. The next time I passed where the band had been stationed, the members had thrown down their instruments, and were not to be seen.'

That precious stringed instruments were precipitously abandoned by their owners tells the tale: Hartley's gallant band had played to the very end.

In fact, I have two taped recordings of *Songe d'Automne*, appropriately recorded at sea by subsequent ship's musicians. The first version is played with piano accompaniment, as though in *Titanic*'s lounge, and the second just by strings, so that it sounds just the way it must have sounded out on deck that night. It is a bittersweet composition, with themes that are alternately lilting and pensive.

LOUIS VON ESCH
'Autumn' (music)

God of mercy and compassion,
    Look with pity on my pain;
Hear a mournful, broken spirit
    Prostrate at Thy feet complain;
Many are my foes and mighty;
    Strength to conquer have I none;
Nothing can uphold my goings
    But Thy blessed Self alone.

Saviour, look on Thy beloved,
    Triumph over all my foes;
Turn to heavenly joy my mourning,
    Turn to gladness all my woes;
Live or die, or work, or suffer,
    Let my weary soul abide,
In all changes whatsoever,
    Sure and steadfast by Thy side.

When temptations fierce assault me,
    When my enemies I find,
Sin and guilt, and death and Satan,
    All against my soul combined,
Hold me up in mighty waters,
    Keep my eyes on things above –
Righteousness, divine atonement,
    Peace and everlasting love.

After the sinking it was remembered that W. T. Stead had identified in Hymns That Have Helped *the Prince of Wales's favourite hymn – 'Nearer My God to Thee'. The* Etude, *an American music magazine, credited Stead with choosing 'Autumn' for the band to play as the ship sank. In his anthology Stead captured the importance of hymns to Victorian and Imperial England; it is fitting that the* Titanic *tragedy should provoke a crescendo of interest in the hymn that was played.*

W. T. STEAD
Hymns that Help

(*Hymns That Have Helped*, 1897)

T he songs of the English-speaking people are for the most part hymns. For the immense majority of our people today the only minstrelsy is that of the hymn-book. And this is as true of our race beyond the sea as it is of our race at home.

Of the making of collections of hymns there is no end. But so far as I have been able to discover, no collection of hymns has ever been made based upon the principle of including in it only those hymns which have been most helpful to the men and women who have most influenced their fellow-men. Yet surely those hymns which have most helped the greatest and best of our race are those which bear, as it were, the hallmark of Heaven.

The root idea of this Hymnal is to select the hymns, not by the fine or finical ear of the critic in the study, or even by the exalted judgement of the recluse in the cloister, but by the recorded experience of mankind. Here and thus did this hymn help me: that is the best of all possible arguments in favour of believing that it will prove helpful under similar circumstances to similar characters. The hymn may be doggerel poetry, it may contain heretical theology, its grammar may be faulty and its metaphors atrocious, but if that hymn proved itself a staff and a stay to some heroic soul in the darkest hours of his life's pilgrimage, then that hymn has won its right to a place among the sacred songs through which God has spoken to the soul of man.

Who is there among the men and women of this generation who has not, at some time or other, experienced the strange and subtle influence of sacred song? Hymns have rung in the ears of some of us while still wandering idly in the streets of the City of Destruction, stern and shrill as the bugle-blast that rouses the sleeping camp to prepare for the onslaught of the foe. Their melody has haunted the ear amid the murmur of the mart and the roar of the street. In the storm and stress of life's battle the echo of their sweet refrain has renewed our strength and dispelled our fears. They have been, as it were, the voices of the angels of God, and when we have heard them we could hear no other sound, neither the growling of the lions in the path nor the curses and threatenings of the fiends from the pit. Around the hymn and the hymn tune how many associations gather from the earliest days, when, as infants, we were hushed to sleep on our mother's lap by their monotonous chant! At this moment, on the slope of the Rockies, or in the sweltering jungles of India, in crowded Australian city, or secluded English hamlet, the sound of some simple hymn tune will, as by mere magic spell, call from the silent grave the shadowy forms of the unforgotten dead, and transport the listener, involuntarily, over land and sea, to the scene of his childhood's years, to the village school, to the parish church. In our pilgrimage through life we discover the hymns which help. We come out of trials and temptations with hymns clinging to our memory like burrs. Some of us could almost use the hymnbook as the key to our autobiography. Hymns, like angels and other ministers of grace, often help us and disappear into the void. It is not often that the hymn of our youth is the hymn of our old age. Experience of life is the natural selector of the truly human hymnal.

There is a curious and not a very creditable shrinking on the part of many to testify as to their experience in the deeper matters of the soul. It is an inverted egotism, – selfishness masquerading in disguise of reluctance to speak of self. Wanderers across the wilderness of Life ought not to be chary of telling their fellow-travellers where they found the green oasis, the healing spring, or the shadow of a great rock in a desert land. It is not regarded as egotism when the passing steamer signals across the Atlantic wave news of her escape from perils of iceberg or fog, or welcome news of good cheer. Yet individuals shrink into themselves, repressing rigorously the fraternal instinct which bids them communicate the fruits of their experience to their fellows. Therein they deprive themselves of a share in the communion of saints, and refuse to partake with their brother of the sacramental cup of human sympathy, or to break the sacred bread of the deeper experiences.

7
The Man's Game

I am willing to remain and play the man's game if there are not enough
boats for more than the women and children. I won't die here like a
beast.   Benjamin Guggenheim

*To Senator Smith's question if 'Women and children first' were the rule
of the sea, Second Officer Lightoller famously replied: 'The rule of human
nature.' But in 1912 nature and convention in gender relations were
exactly what were being hotly debated, and the Titanic sinking wonder-
fully focused the debate. Were women right to follow the rule of Women
and children first, to accept the self-sacrifice of men?*

*The Woman Question immediately established itself as a context
for Titanic. Did male chivalry ('boats') render full suffrage ('votes')
redundant, or was it still an instrument to keep women from full equality?
The complexity of the issue asserted itself. There were strong career
women, such as Lady Duff Gordon and Helen Churchill Candee, both
survivors, who thought that to accept the chivalrous sacrifices of the
men was to display a higher nature. In any case the facts of feminine
involvement in rescue efforts were not always easy to agree upon. There
were well-attested incidents in which women sacrificed themselves for
others, and a few others in which women did the work of men in the
lifeboats – most famously the Countess of Rothes (the 'plucky little
Countess') and Margaret (Molly) Brown. But on the question of women
urging crew to return or not to return to the wreck scene, it seems
reluctance to return was commoner.*

*Race-consciousness joined class- and gender-consciousness to help
define European and North American cultures in the age of Titanic. In
Europe it was stimulated partly by imperialism. Not just in Britain but
also in the USA a self-conscious Anglo-Saxonism had developed. Even
the Masses exhibited ambivalence about 'Asiatic' immigration into*

America, and the Literary Digest *of November 1912 carried a feature on 'Foreign America'. For their part, the British were consciously trying to ally themselves with the USA, through racial identity, and distinguish themselves from the Germans. For their part, some Americans such as Alma White wished to distinguish themselves from what they saw as an effete British society (of which Ismay was a representative). Beside Britain lay an Ireland – the Ireland that thought of Ulster's industry that produced* Titanic *as alien – that was separating itself from England, partly on racial grounds; it saw itself as Celtic and different. The work of the major contemporary English writers too had a high quotient of race-consciousness: Conrad, D. H. Lawrence, Forster, Wells, Kipling, Shaw.*

In the light of all this, the race reaction during and after the sinking of Titanic *is not surprising. What is surprising, though, is the depth and creativity of black reaction in the United States to the sinking of the great ship on which no black passengers as far as we know sailed.*

As Lucile ('modiste'), Lady Duff Gordon wrote fashion columns: one appeared in the San Francisco Examiner *the day* Titanic *struck the iceberg. In her autobiography she remembered the fashionable opportunity of the hearing and added: 'I caught sight of the Duchess of Wellington and Lady Eileen Wellesley, Margot Asquith, Prince Maurice of Battenberg, Prince Albert of Schleswig-Holstein . . .' Lord Mersey rounded upon Counsel for the third-class passengers at the British enquiry, for suspecting Sir Cosmo Duff Gordon of bribing crewmen (in their seriously underfilled lifeboat) not to return to the wreck scene to look for survivors.*

My Beautiful Nightdress

(*Daily Sketch*, 21 May 1912)

Feminine interest was again accentuated in yesterday's proceedings at the Scottish Hall when the evidence of the Duff Gordons was concluded.

By the time Lord Mersey and the assessors took their seats the ladies' galleries were lined with spectators, while the floor-space was crowded, numbers of prominent Society people again putting in an appearance.

The ladies chiefly wore light costumes, flower-decked hats and white blouses being conspicuous, for the day, though dull, was warm. Many of those fortunate enough to secure places commanding uninterrupted views of the witness table settled down comfortably in their seats, took off their hats and jackets and coats, adjusted their opera-glasses and looked fully prepared to see and hear every thing for the whole day without so much as bestirring themselves for lunch.

It was noticeable that the fashionable cerise colour which had prevailed among the fair listeners last week was now superseded by shades of purple and mauve. It was noticeable too that many clergymen took their places in the audience.

It was just a quarter before noon when Lady Duff Gordon entered the box at the call of the Attorney-General. She was dressed in black, with a touch of white at her neck and bosom, and from her black hat fell a black veil over her shoulders.

Looking pale, but perfectly self-possessed, Lady Duff Gordon put her narrative into a few crisp sentences, and was under examination for little more than twenty minutes altogether. Standing erectly at the table, she would turn her head slightly to Sir Rufus Isaacs to catch his questions, and then would turn to Lord Mersey to give her answers in a light, clear voice, which gave no hint of any emotional memories of the horror of shipwreck through which she had passed. There was just a little catch in the breath and a note of dismay as she told the Court that she had quite made up her mind she 'was going to be drowned'.

Nodding her head emphatically, Lady Duff Gordon declared it was 'not a case of one getting into the boat but of being pitched in'. One smiled at the womanlike stress which the witness laid on the politeness of the ship's officer who had given permission to her husband and herself to board the boat.

. . . She stated that she was pressed to get into two boats, but refused to leave her husband. 'After three boats had gone down,' she said, 'my husband and myself and Miss Francatelli (her secretary) were left standing on the deck. There were no other people on the deck at all visible, and I quite made up my mind that I was going to be drowned. Then suddenly we saw this little boat in front of us – this little thing' – pointing to its model on the *Titanic* model at her elbow – 'and we saw some sailors and an officer apparently giving them orders.

'I said to my husband: Ought we not to be doing something? He said: Oh, we must wait for orders. We stood there quite some time while the men were fixing things up. Then my husband went forward and said: Might we get into this boat? and the officer said in a very polite way: Oh certainly do, I will be very pleased.

'Somebody hitched me up from the back and pitched me into the boat, and I think Miss Francatelli was pitched in, and then my husband was pitched in. It was not a case of getting in at all, it was too high. They pitched us in this way into the boat.' (Lady [Duff] Gordon illustrated the method used to get her into the boat by placing her hand under her shoulders.) 'Then two American gentlemen got pitched in.' As far as Lady Duff Gordon could remember the order given to the boat was 'You will row away about 200 yards.' She heard no order that the boat was to go back if called.

Lady Duff Gordon said that she was terribly seasick in the boat.

She saw the ship go down. Before it sank she heard terrible cries. After it sank she never heard a cry. 'My impression was,' she said, 'there was absolute silence.'

You knew there were people in the *Titanic*, didn't you? – No, I was thinking nothing about it.

Did you say it might be dangerous to go back; you might get swamped? – No.

With regard to an article under her signature in a newspaper Lady Duff Gordon said that the signature was a forgery. She denied she had made many statements it contained and explained that it was written by a friend (who had supper with her in New York) from things that she had said.

Samuel Collins and Robert William Pusey, two firemen, who were also in the boat, said that they heard no suggestion that the boat should go back. Pusey told how the promise of a gift to the crew came to be made. He said: 'I heard Lady Duff Gordon say: There is my beautiful nightdress gone, and I said Never mind about your nightdress as long as you have got your life. Then a man said: We have lost our kit and our pay will be stopped, and then it was that the promise was made to give £5 each for a new kit.'

When Pusey left the box Lord Mersey said: 'And now we have finished with No. 1 boat, I hope.'

*The anarchist and feminist Emma Goldman was in Denver when news
of the* Titanic *disaster reached her. She wanted a display of equality
aboard the sinking ship. Whereas she sees the women who accepted
male chivalry as displaying their 'training', she sees the self-sacrifice of
the crew and steerage men as displaying 'human nature'. But were the
engineers, stokers and wireless operators who stayed at their posts
exhibiting training or nature or both? Were first-class men who willingly
stayed on board when the lifeboats left displaying human nature too,
as well as training in chivalry?*

EMMA GOLDMAN
'Suffrage Dealt Blow by Women of *Titanic*'

(*Denver Post*, 21 April 1912)

Barring all sensational and conflicting reports of the *Titanic*
horrors there are two features which seem to have been overlooked
altogether. One is, the part woman has played in the terrible disaster,
which to say the least, is in keeping with centuries of her training as a
mere female.

With all the claims the present-day woman makes for her equality
with man, her great intellectual and emancipatory achievements, she
continues to be as weak and dependent, as ready to accept man's tribute
in time of safety and his sacrifice in time of danger, as if she were still
in her baby age.

'The men stood aside to let the ladies go first.' What about the ladies?
What about their love superior to that of the men? What about their
greater goodness? Their demand to equal rights and privileges? Is this
to be found only at the polls, or on the statutes? I fear me very much
that the ladies who have so readily accepted the dictations of the men,
who stood by when the men were beaten back from the lifeboats, have
demonstrated their utter unfitness and inferiority, not merely to the
title of man's equal, but to her traditionary fame of goodness, love and
self-sacrifice.

It is to be hoped that some there were among the steerage victims at least, who preferred death with those they loved to life at the expense of the loved ones.

The second feature is this: To die for those we love is no small matter in a world where each is for himself and the devil take the hindmost. But to die for those far removed from us by a cold and cruel social and material gulf – for those who by their very position must needs be our enemies – for those who, a few moments before the disaster, probably never gave a thought to the toilers and pariahs of the ship – is so wonderful a feat of human nature as to silence forever the ridiculous argument against the possibilities of human nature. The average philistine forever prates of how human nature must be coerced and beaten; how it must be kept in check and disciplined. How little he knows of the grandeur of human nature has never been so magnificently demonstrated as by the crew of the *Titanic*, the sailors, stokers, workers and drones belonging to the disinherited of the earth!

With neither club or statute to compel them, I wonder what induced these men to go to their death with greater fortitude than do soldiers on the battlefield? Why, it is human nature, stripped of all social artifice, of the deadening and dulling chase for material gains. Human nature, come into its own! Into its deep social kinship which so far has only expressed itself in great stress but which points to still greater possibilities for the future, when man shall no longer his brother maim!

This contemporary response is a clever piece of vindictive irony with a crudely felicitous found rhyme.

CLARK MCADAMS
'Enough Said'

(*St Louis Despatch*)

'**V**otes for Women!'
   Was the cry,
Reaching upward
   To the sky.
Crashing glass,
   And flashing eye –
'Votes for women!'
   Was the cry.

'Boats for women!'
   Was the cry,
When the brave
   Were come to die.
When the end was drawing nigh –
   'Boats for women!'
Was the cry.

Life has many
   Little jests
Insignificant
   As tests.
Doubt and bitterness
   Assail
But 'Boats for women!'
   Tells the tale.

Though appearing in a feminist-socialist magazine, the writer is able to praise the chivalrous while seeing chivalry as an aspect of a social system that must be condemned.

'Masculine Chivalry'

(*Progressive Woman* (Chicago), May 1912)

When the great steamer *Titanic* went down recently it carried with it something like 1,500 human beings, the great majority of them men. Reports have it that about 800 women and children were saved, and something like 80 men, besides the sailors who manned the lifeboats.

We know that these women and children were saved because the men stood back and – gave their lives instead. That is a terrible test of 'chivalry' at a time like this. Men who feel themselves of importance in the world of affairs, step aside and give unknown women and children precedence in a life-and-death test.

We are filled with something akin to awe when we think of the personal struggles that must have filled each breast as its owner watched his last hope of life slipping away from him, saw some frail woman taking his place in the lifeboats and felt the darkness closing in about him.

But they did it. And yet most of those men, no doubt, stubbornly opposed the idea of the rights of women in participation in governmental affairs. Exploited them in industry, voted for the white slave pen, sent the daughter to the street, the son to the army, the husband to tramp the streets for a job! Four hundred immigrant women were saved. What of the lives of these poor women once they reach New York?

It is a strange situation, and one which no doubt requires the deep and unfathomable processes of the masculine brain to account for. No woman has yet been able to understand it. And, if you please, the women are beginning to say they are willing to exchange the chivalry for the right to help run a government that will build safer ships, safer mines and mills and factories, establish more departments for human welfare and think less of the profits and the gaudy display of the few at the cost of so many lives.

Chivalry, no doubt, has its attractive, romantic side, but just plain common sense would serve social progress so much better!

Candee was the centre of an admiring male circle in first class that included Archibald Gracie. This crisp report was followed on 4 May by a short story in Collier's Weekly, *'Sealed Orders', in which Candee lightly fictionalized the tragedy and opposed the irresistible power of God with the 'virility immortal' of the noble Anglo-Saxon men. Candee was an independent non-feminist, author of* How Women May Earn a Living *(1900); she lived to visit and describe exotic places in* New Journeys in Old Asia *(1927) and survived until the age of ninety.*

HELEN CHURCHILL CANDEE
'God's Noblemen Aid Women and Children'

(*San Francisco Examiner*, 20 April 1912)

. . . The action of the men on the *Titanic* was noble. They stood back in every instance that I noticed and gave the women and children the first chance to get away safely.

Particularly heroic was the conduct of Isidor Straus, Major Archibald Butt, John Jacob Astor and Henry B. Harris. They formed a group. Most of the passengers were on the stern of the *Titanic*, for the leak was forward, and it was known that if she sank it would be bow first.

An officer of the *Titanic* ordered Mrs Straus into a boat. She said:

'I will not leave my husband. We've been together all these years, and I'll not leave him now.'

It brought tears to our eyes to witness her great devotion for her husband.

Mr Harris insisted that his wife get into a lifeboat. She refused at first, but was finally forced into the boat.

As we put away I observed Mrs Straus waving her handkerchief at us. The *Titanic* was then settling. Her stern was out of the water, and she was going down bow first. There must have been 1,400 persons gathered together on the stern.

I saw Colonel Astor helping get the women and children into the boats. Then he went below, remaining there several minutes. I believe he was searching for more women and children.

Finally he came back again. He was on deck when the *Titanic* sank, I believe, for when I last saw him he was still aiding in the work of rescue.

Major Butt was one of God's noblemen. I saw him working desperately to get the women and children into boats.

What need can there be of recounting the heroic deeds performed by those men who remained on the *Titanic*? To dwell upon them only sickens the heart, with the realization of how they perished.

THE SHIP THAT WILL NEVER RETURN

(The Loss of the "Titanic.")

SONG

AND

POEM

Written & Composed

by

F. V. ST. CLAIR.

COPYRIGHT   LONDON.   ALL RIGHTS RESERVED.

E. MARKS & SON,

125, MARE STREET, HACKNEY, N.E.

Overnight, *Titanic* became the most sung about ship in history; Edwardian sentimentality dominated sheet music.

Religious disaster songs became popular among black street and country singers in the twentieth century, part of the tradition of 'ballet' singing. The Titanic *wreck was made to measure: no other event was as celebrated in black religious songs as this. One week after the sinking, a blind preacher was selling a song about the ship's loss. Abbe Niles collected 'The* Titanic' *from Rabbit Brown in New Orleans; 'but as he is not easy to understand, I translate it in full'.*

RABBIT BROWN
'The *Titanic*'

(*Bookman*, March–August 1928)

'Twas on the ten of April, on a sunny afternoon
The *Titanic* left South Hamilton, each as happy as bride and
    groom.
Noone thought of dangier, or what their fate may be,
Ontell a gruesome iceburig cost fifteen hundred perished in the
    sea.

It was earily Monday morning, just about the break of day,
Captain Smith called for help from the *Carpathia*, and it was
    many miles away,
Everyone was cawm an' silent, asked each other what that
    trouble may be;
Not thinking that death was looiking, there upon that Northern
    sea.

The *Carpathia* received the wi'less, 'S. O. S., in distress,
Come at once, we are sinking, make no delay and do your bes'.
Get your lifeboats all in readiness, 'cause we're goin' down very
    fast.
We have saved the women and children, and try to hold out to
    the last.'

You know, at last they called on the passengers, told 'em to
    hurry to the deck;

Then they realized that the mighty *Titanic* would undoubtedly
  be a wreck.
They lowe'd lifeboats one by one, takin' women an' children
  from the stawt –
The po' men they were left to care for themself, but they sho'
  played a hero's pawt.

You know, they stood out on that sinkin' deck, and they was all
  in great despair;
You know, accidents may happen most any time, an' we know
  not when an' where;
The music played as they went down, on that dark blue sea,
An' you could hear the sound of that familiar hymn, singin'
  Nero my Gawd to Thee:

'Nero my Gawd to Thee, Nero my Gawd to Thee,
Nero my Gawd to Thee, Nero to Thee!
Though like a wanderer, as the sun goes down,
Thou wilt be over me –' Just then the *Titanic* went down.

*Leadbelly sings about a dignified black absentee, Jack Johnson, heavy-
weight champion of the world. Leadbelly moves across from the religious
disaster song to the secular song of sharper social comment. He wrote
to Moses Asch: 'There was not no Negroes died on that ship. But Jack
Johnson went to get on board. "We are not hauling no coal," (they said)
... it was so much Jim Crow he could not have no go.'*

LEADBELLY (HUDDIE LEDBETTER)
'Titanic'

(*Leadbelly: A Collection of World-Famous Songs*, ed. John and Alan Lomax,
1959)

Captain Smith, when he got his load,
Might 'a' heared him holl'in', 'All aboa'd!'
Cryin', 'Fare thee, *Titanic*, fare thee well.'

Captain Smith, when he got his load,
Might 'a' heared him holl'in, 'All aboa'd!'
Cryin', 'Fare thee, *Titanic*, fare thee well!'

Jack Johnson wanted to get on boa'd;
Captain Smith hollered, 'I ain' haulin' no coal.'
Cryin', 'Fare thee, *Titanic*, fare thee well!'

It was midnight on the sea,
Band playin', 'Nearer My God to Thee'.
Cryin', 'Fare thee, *Titanic*, fare thee well!'

Titanic was sinking down,
Had them lifeboats aroun'.
Cryin', 'Fare thee, *Titanic*, Fare thee well!'

Had them lifeboats aroun',
Savin' the women, lettin' the men go down.
Cryin', 'Fare thee, *Titanic*, fare thee well!'

When the women got out on the land,
Cryin', 'Lawd, have mercy on my man.'
Cryin', 'Fare thee, *Titanic*, fare thee well!'

Jack Johnson heard the mighty shock,
Might 'a' seen the black rascal doin' th' Eagle Rock.
Cryin', 'Fare thee, *Titanic*, fare thee well!'

Black man oughta shout for joy,
Never lost a girl or either a boy.
Cryin', 'Fare thee, *Titanic*, fare thee well!'

Ellen Williamson in When We Went First Class *(1977) tells the story of upset passengers on* Titanic *in Cherbourg who had seen 'a black-faced stoker peering at them through a hole in a smokestack of an adjacent ship'. Another report was of a grinning stoker peering down from* Titanic*'s fourth (dummy) funnel while the ship was in Queenstown. These stokers became confused with the stoker Bride said tried to steal Phillips's lifebelt. Marshall in his punctual book on the tragedy identified the thieving stoker as a 'negro' amid a series of other errors.*

LOGAN MARSHALL
The Negro Stoker

(*Sinking of the* Titanic *and Great Sea Disasters*, 1912)

On board the *Titanic*, the wireless operator, with a lifebelt about his waist, was hitting the instrument that was sending out C. Q. D., messages, 'Struck on iceberg, C. Q. D.'

'Shall I tell captain to turn back and help?' flashed a reply from the *Carpathia*.

'Yes, old man,' the *Titanic* wireless operator responded. 'Guess we're sinking.'

An hour later, when the second wireless man came into the boxlike room to tell his companion what the situation was, he found a negro stoker creeping up behind the operator and saw him raise a knife over his head. He said afterwards – he was among those rescued – that he realized at once that the negro intended to kill the operator in order to take his lifebelt from him. The second operator pulled out his revolver and shot the negro dead.

'What was the trouble?' asked the operator.

'That negro was going to kill you and steal your lifebelt,' the second man replied.

'Thanks, old man,' said the operator. The second man went on deck to get some more information. He was just in time to jump overboard before the *Titanic* went down. The wireless operator and the body of the negro who tried to steal his belt went down together.

In one song, 'De Titanic*', a below deck-hand tells the Captain the ship is sinking, only to be told 'Go back, Bill, an' shut yo' mouth,/ Got forty-eight pumps to keep de water out!' Bill, the Travelling Coon and the celebrating Jack Johnson come together in the black rhythmically spoken rhyming poem called the 'Toast' (related to jive-talk, rap, the talking blues and the 'Dozens'), the hero of which is Shine. In the* Titanic Toast, *adversity is turned into advantage, a symbolic reversal of the black–white power relationship in the United States.*

BOBBY LEWIS (PERFORMER)
'Shine'

(Deep Down in the Jungle: Negro Narrative Folklore from the Streets of Philadelphia, *1963)*

The eighth of May was a hell of a day
When the *Titanic* was sinking away.
Yeah, what a hell of a day, when the news reached the seaport
    town
The *Titanic* was sinking down.
Shine went below deck, eating his peas
Till the water come up to his knees.
Shine went up on deck, said, 'Captain, I was downstairs eating
    my peas
Till the water come up to my knees.'
Captain said, 'Shine, Shine, sit your black ass down.
I got ninety-nine pumps to pump the water down.'
Shine went back down below deck, looking through space
Till the water came up to his waist.
Shine went up on deck, said, 'Captain, I was downstairs looking
    through space
Till the water came up to my waist.'
Captain said, 'Shine, Shine, sit your ass down.
Got ninety-nine pumps to pump the water down.'
Shine went down below deck eating his bread
Till the water came up to his head.

Shine went up on deck, said, 'Captain, I was downstairs eating
   my bread
Till the water came up to my head.'
He said, 'Shine, Shine, sit your ass down.
Got ninety-nine pumps to pump the water down.'
Shine took off his shirt and started to take a dive.
Captain's daughter came over to Shine.
Said, 'Shine, Shine, save poor me.
Give you all the pussy eyes ever did see.'
Shine said, 'Pussy ain't nothing but meat on the bone,
You can fuck it, you can suck it, you can leave it alone.'
Shine jumped in the water and met up with a shark.
Shine said, 'You may be king of the ocean, king of the sea,
You got to be a swimming motherfucker to outswim me.'
And Shine swim on.

Here is Shine by way of Walt Whitman and Allen Ginsberg, a black yawp of triumph, both meaner and more informed than the Titanic Toasts.

ETHERIDGE KNIGHT
'Dark Prophecy: I Sing of Shine'

(*Born of a Woman*, 1980; from *The Essential Etheridge Knight*, 1986)

And, yeah, brothers,
while white / america sings about the unsinkable molly brown
(who was hustling the *titanic*
when it went down)
I sing to thee of Shine
the stoker who was hip enough to flee the fucking ship
and let the white folks drown
with screams on their lips
(jumped his black ass into the dark sea, Shine did,
broke free from the straining steel).
Yeah, I sing to thee of Shine
and how the millionaire banker stood on the deck
and pulled from his pockets a million dollar check
saying Shine Shine save poor me
and I'll give you all the money a black boy needs –
how Shine looked at the money and then at the sea
and said jump in mothafucka and swim like me –
And Shine swam on – Shine swam on –
and how the banker's daughter ran naked on the deck
with her pink tits trembling and her pants roun her neck
screaming Shine Shine save poor me
and I'll give you all the pussy a black boy needs –
how Shine said now pussy is good and that's no jive
but you got to swim not fuck to stay alive –
And Shine swam on Shine swam on –

How Shine swam past a preacher afloating on a board

crying save *me* nigger Shine in the name of the Lord –
and how the preacher grabbed Shine's arm and broke his
   stroke –
how Shine pulled his shank and cut the preacher's throat –
And Shine swam on – Shine swam on –
And when the news hit shore that the *titanic* had sunk
Shine was up in Harlem damn near drunk

Titanic *and her sister ships were seen by their owners and builders as vehicles of the 'Anglo-Saxon' alliance, as this report of the launch of* Titanic *amply shows. Frank T. Bullen (1857–1915) was the author of sea stories,* A Son of the Sea *(1905); the aptly named Saxon Payne was an official of Harland & Wolff, responsible for the Belfast works.*

The Genius of the Anglo-Saxon

(*Belfast Telegraph*, 1 June 1911)

Following the launch, the Pressmen who had travelled from various parts of the United Kingdom to witness it were entertained at luncheon at the Grand Central Hotel as the guests of Messrs Ismay, Imrie & Company, the owners of the two new vessels. A capital repast was served.

Mr J. Shelley representing the hosts, speaking subsequently said on their behalf he would like to thank the Pressmen for their attendance, and he thought they would agree with him that that had been a historic day. (Hear, hear.) So far as the mercantile marine was concerned, they might indeed say that the year 1911 had been an *annus mirabilis*. He was speaking with absolute truth when he said that the association between the White Star line and the members of the Press had always been of the most friendly character. Messrs Ismay, Imrie & Company had always appreciated the kindly support and co-operation the members of the Press had given them on such occasions as that, and he trusted they would have many more such gatherings in future. It seemed to him that as the year passed and as the conditions of life changed, the Anglo-Saxon nations became more closely united as a result of such co-operation as was indicated by the building of ships like the *Titanic* and *Olympic*, which promoted intercourse between the mighty Republic in the West and the United Kingdom. (Applause.) Intercourse of this kind helped to secure a guarantee for the peace and well-being of the world at large to a greater extent than could be done by the efforts of all the Chancellories of Europe. (Hear, hear.)

Mr Frank T. Bullen, the well-known author and lecturer, said Mr Shelley had furnished him with a great surprise that afternoon, because, while he had known him to be a very good fellow and an able organizer, he had never suspected him of being such an eloquent orator. Mr Shelley's reference to the ties which bound together the Anglo-Saxon race had forcibly appealed to him. The full significance of the work that was being done by Messrs Ismay, Imrie & Co. in the building of these large vessels was not understood even by the representatives of the Press. If an ordinary visitor had been in Belfast that day he would not have noticed anything out of the common in their streets, although the launch they had just witnessed signalized one of the greatest triumphs ever recorded in the history of shipbuilding. Two ships now anchored in the waters of the lough had between them a tonnage of 90,000 tons, yet no noise was made about the fact. If such a launch as that in connection with the *Titanic* had taken place in Germany or any other Continental country the streets would have been beflagged, and everyone would have been shouting for joy; but in Belfast they went on their way attending to their little everyday engagements, and saying, 'I don't think I can spare time to see that ship launched; it will be just the same as usual.' That was the peculiar genius of the British race. When he saw the first *Oceanic* with a tonnage of 2,800 register, he felt immensely proud. He had seen many bigger vessels since then, and now they had the *Titanic* and the *Olympic*, the largest ships yet launched. He could say a good deal about the builders, but that was not the time for doing so. He would, however, ask the guests to recognize in the heartiest manner the help that had been rendered them by Mr Shelley, Mr Saxon J. Payne and Mr Workman, of the White Star line. (Applause.)

The health of these three gentlemen having been drunk, Mr Saxon J. Payne responded. He said he did not recognize any distinction between the various sections of the Anglo-Saxon race, and they looked upon the building of the *Titanic* and the *Olympic* as a great Anglo-Saxon triumph. He was glad to say that the trials of the *Olympic* had proved very satisfactory while they had all admired the manner in which the launch of her sister ship was carried out. The two vessels were pre-eminent examples of the vitality and the progressive instincts of the Anglo-Saxon race, and he did not see anything which need give them alarm, regarding the prospects for the future. As a race they were young and strong and vigorous, and by what it had done in assisting the White Star line in its great and commendable enterprise Belfast could lay claim to no small share in the maintenance of the prosperity of the British Empire. (Hear, hear.)

That the building of these great ships could be seen as a contribution to world peace, founded on Anglo-American supremacy, would explain the warm attention Stead – ardent champion of world peace – paid to Harland & Wolff and the leviathans of the sea. This excerpt is from a promotional booklet put out by the White Star Line.

The Progress of the Race

(*White Star Line: Royal Mail Triple-Screw Steamers* Olympic *and* Titanic, 1911)

The advent of these Leviathans of the Atlantic coincides very appropriately with the most important development of modern times – the movement of the British and American people towards the ideal of international and universal peace. Of all the forces contributing to this great and desirable consummation, commerce has been one of the most potent, and as the growth of international trade is largely due to the progress in shipping, it is impossible to over-estimate the service rendered to the Anglo-Saxon race by the enterprise of our Shipowners and Shipbuilders. No better instance of this spirit of enterprise can be produced than the building of the White Star Liner *Olympic* and her sister ship *Titanic*, constructed as they have been side by side at Messrs Harland & Wolff's Ship Yard, Belfast. The spectacle of these two enormous vessels on adjoining slips, representing over 100,000 tons displacement, was altogether unprecedented, and naturally the public interest taken in the vessels on both sides of the Atlantic has been very keen. It has been felt that, great as the triumphs have been in the past in Naval Architecture and Marine Engineering, these two vessels represent a higher level of attainment than had hitherto been reached; that they are in fact in a class by themselves, and mark a new epoch in the conquest of the Ocean, being not only much larger than any vessels previously constructed, but also embodying the latest developments in modern propulsion.

The *Olympic* and *Titanic* are not only the largest vessels in the World; they represent the highest attainments in Naval Architecture and Marine Engineering; they stand for the pre-eminence of the Anglo-Saxon race on the Ocean; for the 'Command of the Seas' is fast changing from a

Naval to a Mercantile idea, and the strength of a maritime race is represented more by its instruments of commerce and less by its weapons of destruction than was formerly supposed. Consequently, these two Leviathans add enormously to the potential prosperity and progress of the race, and the White Star Line have well deserved the encomiums that have been showered upon them for their enterprise and foresight in the production of such magnificent vessels.

*There was a considerable racial mix among the passengers, and there
are copious references in testimony and memoir to swarthy foreigners,
often Italian or 'Latin'. Perhaps among many, racial awareness had
been heightened by the sinking of the P & O liner Oceana in March,
when it was said that Lascars among the crew were useless in the crisis.
But Lowe went too far on the fifth day of the U.S. hearings, and on the
fourteenth day, after representations from the Italian ambassador in
New York, he recanted somewhat in an affidavit.*

'A Lot of Italians, Latin People . . .': Harold Lowe's Testimony and Retraction

(*U.S. Senate Hearings*, 1912)

SENATOR SMITH. One more question and I will let you go.
Did you hear any pistol shots?

MR LOWE. Yes.

SENATOR SMITH. And by whom were they fired Sunday night?

MR LOWE. I heard them, and I fired them.

SENATOR SMITH. Where?

MR LOWE. As I was going down the decks, and that was as I was being
lowered down.

SENATOR SMITH. In lifeboat—

MR LOWE. Lifeboat No. 14.

SENATOR SMITH. What did you do?

MR LOWE. As I was going down the decks I knew, or I expected every
moment, that my boat would double up under my feet. I was quite
scared of it, although of course it would not do for me to mention
the fact to anybody else. I had overcrowded her, but I knew that I
had to take a certain amount of risk. So I thought, 'Well, I shall have
to see that nobody else gets into the boat or else it will be a case'—

SENATOR SMITH. That was as it was being lowered?

MR LOWE. Yes; I thought if one additional body was to fall into that
boat, that slight jerk of the additional weight might part the hooks
or carry away something, no one would know what. There were a

hundred and one things to carry away. Then, I thought, well, I will keep an eye open. So, as we were coming down the decks, coming down past the open decks, I saw a lot of Italians, Latin people, all along the ship's rails – understand, it was open – and they were all glaring, more or less like wild beasts, ready to spring. That is why I yelled out to look out, and let go, bang, right along the ship's side . . .

SENATOR SMITH. I have also a statement from Officer Lowe, of the *Titanic*, which I have been requested to put into the record. This comes to me through the Italian ambassador and contains an explanation by Mr Lowe of the testimony which he gave that he fired his gun, as his boat was being lowered into the water, because of the glaring eyes of Italian immigrants, who he was afraid menaced his safety in lowering the lifeboat. Mr Lowe wants this statement to go into the record, and the Italian ambassador wants it to go in.

The statement referred to is as follows:

This is to certify that I, Harold Godfrey Lowe, of Penralt Barmouth, fifth officer of the late steamship *Titanic*, in my testimony at the Senate of the United States stated that I fired shots to prevent Italian immigrants from jumping into my lifeboat.

I do hereby cancel the word 'Italian' and substitute the words 'immigrants belonging to Latin races'. In fact, I did not mean to infer that they were especially Italians, because I could only judge from their general appearance and complexion, and therefore I only meant to imply that they were of the types of the Latin races. In any case, I did not intend to cast any reflection on the Italian nation.

This is the real truth, and therefore I feel honoured to give out the present statement.

H. G. LOWE,
Fifth Officer late Titanic

WASHINGTON, D. C., *April 30, 1912*

[On the reverse]

The declaration on the other side was made and confirmed this day by Harold Godfrey Lowe, fifth officer of the late steamship *Titanic*, in my presence and in the presence of Signor Guido di Vincenzo, secretary of the legal office of the royal embassy.

Washington, this 30th day of April 1912.

The Royal Ambassador of Italy,

CUSANI

[SEAL.]

THE SECRETARY OF THE LEGAL OFFICE OF THE ROYAL EMBASSY,

G. DI VINCENZO.

8
Anticipations and Realizations

Make it new!
   Ezra Pound

Titanic *both anticipated and realized progressive modernity. A new intense value placed in Euro-American culture on time and space led to recklessness. Introducing the new 'syllabic' typewriter, the* Literary Digest *(May 1912) said: 'The "speed-mania" extends much further than travel, whether on sea or land. Every one, no matter what he may be doing, tries for a speed-record.' If speed was one component of progressive modernity, size was another. From the reckless expansion of countries, through corporate mergers, to the alarming enlargement of ocean liners, the age was mesmerized by titanism. 'We have arrived at a new time,' announced Winston Churchill in 1909, 'and with this new time, strange methods, huge forces and combinations – a Titanic world – have spread all around us.'*

The cult of the machine itself was also a component of progressive modernity. Avant-garde art critics were contemplating 'machine forms' and 'hard mechanical shapes'; the modernist writer Ezra Pound was to see the beauty of machines in energy and function. Harland & Wolff shipyard and the machines within it were a modernist space out of which came a machine aesthetic which the ships composed; the aesthetic appeal of Titanic, *inside and out, is part of the enduring appeal of the ship and its story. 'In the ocean liner,' Henry Adams thought when he visited the Cunard exhibit at the 1893 Chicago Exposition, force, space and time would meet within a generation: 'The ocean liner ran the surest line of triangulation to the future, because it was the nearest of man's products to a unity.'*

This preoccupation with the future may help explain the apparently reactionary interest of the time in the paranormal. After the Titanic tragedy, some passengers claimed that they had been aware of omens that mishap was in the offing. Claims of premonition from the populace arrived at the offices of the Daily Sketch every day after the sinking. Previsions were claimed. Then there was the luck of those travellers who cancelled their passage; such luck could be seen as evidence of the providential. Arnold Bennett noted in his diary: 'Paris, Saturday, April 20th: Yesterday the Selwyns and Calou came to lunch. Only their anxiety to meet us here and hear the rest of my comic novel prevented them from going home with the H. B. Harrises on the Titanic'; it was the best thing the novel accomplished.

The two perspectives, the modernist and the reactionary, were brought to bear on the Titanic disaster. The second perspective remembered foretellings. (It encouraged quantities of humbug, and still does.) The first convened hearings and published reports, and thereafter books and articles, trying to get at the mechanical truth. There was a third perspective, somewhere in between. Titanic had a human meaning over and above its literal life and death. It was a metaphor, comical at times, of extraordinary richness.

The Futurists revelled in the 'morality of speed' and the 'reign of the machine'. Most were painters (theirs an art of motion), but Marinetti was a writer who issued his Futurist Manifesto in 1909. 'Those people who today [1913] make use of the telegraph, the telephone, the phonograph, the train, the bicycle, the motorcycle, the automobile, the ocean liner, the dirigible, the aeroplane ... do not realize that the various means of communication, transportation and information have a decisive influence on their psyche.' The modernist art movements of the day earned that phrase, coming and going with dizzying speed.

F. T. MARINETTI
'Manifesto of Futurism'

(1909)

1. We intend to sing the love of danger, the habit of energy and fearlessness.

2. Courage, audacity and revolt will be essential elements of our poetry.

3. Up to now literature has exalted a pensive immobility, ecstasy and sleep. We intend to exalt aggressive action, a feverish insomnia, the racer's stride, the mortal leap, the punch and the slap.

4. We say that the world's magnificence has been enriched by a new beauty; the beauty of speed. A racing car whose hood is adorned with great pipes, like serpents of explosive breath – a roaring car that seems to ride on grapeshot – is more beautiful than the *Victory of Samothrace*.

5. We want to hymn the man at the wheel, who hurls the lance of his spirit across the Earth, along the circle of its orbit.

6. The poet must spend himself with ardour, splendour and generosity, to swell the enthusiastic fervour of the primordial elements.

7. Except in struggle, there is no more beauty. No work without an aggressive character can be a masterpiece. Poetry must be conceived as a violent attack on unknown forces, to reduce and prostrate them before man.

8. We stand on the last promontory of the centuries! ... Why should we look back, when what we want is to break down the mysterious doors of the Impossible? Time and Space died yesterday. We already live in

the absolute, because we have created eternal, omnipresent speed.

9. We will glorify war – the world's only hygiene – militarism, patriotism, the destructive gesture of freedom-bringers, beautiful ideas worth dying for and scorn for woman.

10. We will destroy the museums, libraries, academies of every kind, will fight moralism, feminism, every opportunistic or utilitarian cowardice.

11. We will sing of great crowds excited by work, by pleasure, and by riot; we will sing of the multicoloured, polyphonic tides of revolution in the modern capitals; we will sing of the vibrant nightly fervour of arsenals and shipyards blazing with violent electric moons; greedy railway stations that devour smoke-plumed serpents; factories hung on clouds by the crooked lines of their smoke; bridges that stride the rivers like giant gymnasts, flashing in the sun with a glitter of knives; adventurous steamers that sniff the horizon; deep-chested locomotives whose wheels paw the tracks like the hooves of enormous steel horses bridled by tubing; and the sleek flight of planes whose propellers chatter in the wind like banners and seem to cheer like an enthusiastic crowd.

A titanic plan to alter the orbit of the earth is the premise of a novel by one of the Titanic's *most famous casualties. A year before Wells's* The Time Machine, *it envisages life in the future (*AD *2000) and imagines pioneering trips to Jupiter and Saturn. 'This is more than ever a mechanical age,' says Astor's historian, and he mentions (Astor's predictions), 300 mph trains, videophones, live television transmission, wind turbines and solar power, divided freeways with phosphorescent lane-markers and variable-speed lanes. By 2000, the English-speaking races have triumphed and the United States and the British Empire have divided half the globe between them.*

JOHN JACOB ASTOR
More than Ever a Mechanical Age

(*A Journey in Other Worlds: A Romance of the Future,* 1894)

'I... n marine transportation we have two methods, one for freight and another for passengers. The old-fashioned deeply immersed ship has not changed radically from the steam and sailing vessels of the last century, except that electricity has superseded all other motive powers. Steamers gradually passed through the five hundred-, six hundred- and seven hundred-foot-long class, with other dimensions in proportion, till their length exceeded one thousand feet. These were very fast ships, crossing the Atlantic in four and a half days, and were almost as steady as houses, in even the roughest weather.

'Ships at this period of their development had also passed through the twin and triple screw stage to the quadruple, all four together developing one hundred and forty thousand indicated horsepower, and being driven by steam. This, of course, involved sacrificing the best part of the ship to her engines, and a very heavy idle investment while in port. Storage batteries, with plates composed of lead or iron, constantly increasing in size, had reached a fair state of development by the close of the nineteenth century.

'During the second decade of the twentieth century the engineers decided to try the plan of running half of a transatlantic liner's screws by electricity generated by the engines for driving the others while the ship was in port, this having been a success already on a smaller scale.

For a time this plan gave great satisfaction, since it diminished the amount of coal to be carried and the consequent change of displacement at sea, and enabled the ship to be worked with a smaller number of men. The batteries could also, of course, be distributed along the entire length, and placed where space was least valuable . . .

'Free to delve in the allurement and fascination of science, emancipated man goes on subduing Nature, as his Maker said he should, and turning her giant forces to his service in his constant struggle to rise and become more like Him who gave the commandments and showed him how he should go.

'Notwithstanding our strides in material progress, we are not entirely content. As the requirements of the animal become fully supplied, we feel a need for something else. Some say this is like a child that cries for the moon, but others believe it the awakening and craving of our souls. The historian narrates but the signs of the times, and strives to efface himself; yet there is clearly a void, becoming yearly more apparent, which materialism cannot fill. Is it some new subtle force for which we sigh, or would we commune with spirits? There is, so far as we can see, no limit to our journey, and I will add, in closing, that, with the exception of religion, we have most to hope from science.'

As well as ill omens, premonitions and providential escapes, there were literary works that could in some sense be regarded as foretellings, coincidental or not: curious anticipations of the fate that befell Titanic. Melville's 'slimy slug' also anticipates Hardy's famous poem. ('Lubbard' is lubber.)

HERMAN MELVILLE
'The Berg: A Dream'

(*John Marr and Other Sailors*, 1888)

I saw a ship of martial build
(Her standards set, her brave apparel on)
Directed as by madness mere
Against a stolid iceberg steer,
Nor budge it, though the infatuate ship went down.
The impact made huge ice-cubes fall
Sullen, in tons that crashed the deck;
But that one avalanche was all –
No other movement save the foundering wreck.

Along the spurs of ridges pale,
Not any slenderest shaft and frail,
A prism over glass-green gorges lone,
Toppled; nor lace of traceries fine,
Nor pendant drops in grot or mine
Were jarred, when the stunned ship went down.
Nor sole the gulls in cloud that wheeled
Circling one snow-flanked peak afar,
But nearer fowl the floes that skimmed
And crystal beaches, felt no jar.
No thrill transmitted stirred the lock

Of jack-straw needle-ice at base;
Towers undermined by waves – the block
Atilt impending – kept their place.
Seals, dozing sleek on sliddery ledges

Slipt never, when by loftier edges
Through very inertia overthrown,
The impetuous ship in bafflement went down

Hard Berg (methought), so cold, so vast,
With mortal damps self-overcast;
Exhaling still thy dankish breath –
Adrift dissolving, bound for death;
Though lumpish thou, a lumbering one –
A lumbering lubbard loitering slow,
Impingers rue thee and go down,
Sounding thy precipice below,
Nor stir the slimy slug that sprawls
Along thy dead indifference of walls.

This poem was not of course a foretelling of the disaster but a response to it. It first appeared in the souvenir programme of the Covent Garden theatrical matinée of 14 May. Hardy's poem is one of his 'satires of circumstance', and the ideas of collision, the convergence of the twain (here in its icy parody of sexual congress) and the Double were established elements of his philosophy.

THOMAS HARDY
'The Convergence of the Twain'
(Lines on the loss of the *Titanic*)

(*Fortnightly Review*, June 1912)

I

In a solitude of the sea
Deep from human vanity,
And the Pride of Life that planned her, stilly couches she.

II

Steel chambers, late the pyres
Of her salamandrine fires,
Cold currents thrid, and turn to rhythmic tidal lyres.

III

Over the mirrors meant
To glass the opulent
The sea-worm crawls – grotesque, slimed, dumb, indifferent.

IV

Jewels in joy designed
To ravish the sensuous mind
Lie lightless, all their sparkles bleared and black and blind.

V
Dim moon-eyed fishes near
Gaze at the gilded gear
And query: 'What does this vaingloriousness down here?' . . .

VI
Well: while was fashioning
This creature of cleaving wing,
The Immanent Will that stirs and urges everything

VII
Prepared a sinister mate
For her – so gaily great –
A Shape of Ice, for the time far and dissociate.

VIII
And as the smart ship grew
In stature, grace and hue,
In shadowy silent distance grew the Iceberg too.

IX
Alien they seemed to be:
No mortal eye could see
The intimate welding of their later history,

X
Or sign that they were bent
By paths coincident
On being anon twin halves of one august event,

XI
Till the Spinner of the Years
Said 'Now!' And each one hears,
And consummation comes, and jars two hemispheres.

In this 1912 rumination, Rider Haggard lightly implies that fictional anticipations like his own might function as warnings. Haggard (1856–1925) was the author of She *(1887) as well as* King Solomon's Mines *(1886).*

SIR H. RIDER HAGGARD
Titanic and the Imagination

(*The Days of My Life: An Autobiography*, vol. II, 1926)

It is curious how often imagination is verified by fact – perhaps . . . because the lines in which it must work are narrow and after all based on fact, perhaps because it does possess some spiritual insight of its own. Many instances have come within my own experience, of which I will quote a few that I chance to remember.

I pass over *King Solomon's Mines*, a work of pure imagination, for in my day very little was known of the regions wherein its scenes were laid, many details of which have been verified by subsequent discovery. In its sequel, *Allan Quatermain*, however, occurs a fine example of the literary coincidence. In this book I invented a mission station at an unexplored spot on the Tana River, which station I caused to be attacked by the Masai. In subsequent editions of the work I inserted the following note, which explains itself:

> By a very strange and sad coincidence, since the above was written, the Masai, in April 1886, massacred a missionary and his wife – Mr and Mrs Houghton – on this same Tana River, and at the *spot described*. These are, I believe, the first white people who are known to have fallen victims to this cruel tribe.

. . . Again, in *Mr Meeson's Will* I set out very fully indeed the circumstances under which a new and splendid liner was lost at sea, and the great majority of those on board of her were drowned owing to lack of boats to accommodate them. In a preface to this story, written in the year 1888, I make the following remark:

The only part of this humble skit, however, that is meant to be taken seriously is the chapter which tells of the loss of the R.M.S. *Kangaroo*. I believe it to be a fair and, in the main, accurate account of what must and one day will happen upon a large and crowded liner in the event of such a collision as that described, or of her rapid foundering from any other cause. It is a remarkable thing that people who for the most part set a sufficient value on their lives, daily consent to go to sea in ships the boats of which could not on emergency possibly contain half their number.

During the present year this prophecy, and indeed the whole scene of the sinking of the *Kangaroo*, has been fearfully fulfilled in the instance of the great White Star liner *Titanic*. If I could think of and foresee such things, how is it that those who are responsible for the public safety have proved themselves so lacking in prevision – that section of the Board of Trade, for instance, whose duty it is to attend to such matters?

I fear we must seek the answer in the character of our nation, whose peculiarity it is to ignore or underrate dangers that are not immediately visible, and therefore never to be ready to meet them. If anyone doubts this, let him study the history of our wars during the last sixty years or so, and even earlier. The Crimea, the Abyssinian Expedition, the first Boer War, the Zulu War, the second Boer War, which was the child of the last two, the Egyptian Wars, have all told the same tale. With the details of three of these I have been acquainted, and they are awful. Only our wealth has brought us out of them – I will not say with honour, but in safety. We declare proudly that 'we always muddle through', but this, after all, is a boast that only fits the lips of the incompetent. What will happen when we are called upon to meet a nation, or nations, of equal or greater strength, that are competent? One can only hope for the best, and that the genius of our people, or of individuals among them, may carry us through in the future as it has done in the past. Meanwhile we blunder on. England, in lives and treasure, pays the bill out of her ample but not bottomless pocket, and everything ends in a rocket-burst of decorations conferred amid the shouts of the devotees of music-halls.

The most famous foretelling in literature of the Titanic *disaster is* Futility, *which was reprinted in 1912 after the disaster as* The Wreck of the Titan, or Futility. *Robertson (1861–1915) was the son of a ship's captain and in the merchant service rose to be first mate. He said that* Futility *was the outcome of automatic writing in one sitting: it came publication-ready from the 'Unknown'. Among the startling anticipations in Robertson's story is the tiny but notorious phrase 'practically unsinkable'.*

MORGAN ROBERTSON
The Wreck of the Titan, Or, Futility

(1898)

She was the largest craft afloat and the greatest of the works of men. In her construction and maintenance were involved every science, profession, and trade known to civilization. On her bridge were officers, who, besides being the pick of the Royal Navy, had passed rigid examinations in all studies that pertained to the winds, tides, currents and geography of the sea; they were not only seamen, but scientists. The same professional standard applied to the personnel of the engine-room, and the steward's department was equal to that of a first-class hotel.

Two brass bands, two orchestras, and a theatrical company entertained the passengers during waking hours; a corps of physicians attended to the temporal, and a corps of chaplains to the spiritual, welfare of all on board, while a well-drilled fire-company soothed the fears of nervous ones and added to the general entertainment by daily practice with their apparatus.

From her lofty bridge ran hidden telegraph lines to the bow, stern engine-room, crow's-nest on the foremast, and to all parts of the ship where work was done, each wire terminating in a marked dial with a movable indicator, containing in its scope every order and answer required in handling the massive hulk, either at the dock or at sea – which eliminated, to a great extent, the hoarse, nerve-racking shouts of officers and sailors.

From the bridge, engine-room, and a dozen places on her deck the ninety-two doors of nineteen watertight compartments could be closed in half a minute by turning a lever. These doors would also close automatically in the presence of water. With nine compartments flooded the ship would still float, and as no known accident of the sea could possibly fill this many, the steamship *Titan* was considered practically unsinkable.

Built of steel throughout, and for passenger traffic only, she carried no combustible cargo to threaten her destruction by fire; and the immunity from the demand for cargo space had enabled her designers to discard the flat, kettle-bottom of cargo boats and give her the sharp dead-rise – or slant from the keel – of a steam yacht, and this improved her behaviour in a seaway. She was eight hundred feet long, of seventy thousand tons' displacement, seventy-five thousand horsepower, and on her trial trip had steamed at a rate of twenty-five knots an hour over the bottom, in the face of unconsidered winds, tides and currents. In short, she was a floating city – containing within her steel walls all that tends to minimize the dangers and discomforts of the Atlantic voyage – all that makes life enjoyable.

Unsinkable – indestructible, she carried as few boats as would satisfy the laws. These, twenty-four in number, were securely covered and lashed down to their chocks on the upper deck, and if launched would hold five hundred people. She carried no useless, cumbersome life-rafts; but – because the law required it – each of the three thousand berths in the passengers', officers' and crew's quarters contained a cork jacket, while about twenty circular life-buoys were strewn along the rails.

In view of her absolute superiority to other craft, a rule of navigation thoroughly believed in by some captains, but not yet openly followed, was announced by the steamship company to apply to the *Titan*: She would steam at full speed in fog, storm and sunshine, and on the Northern Lane Route, winter and summer, for the following good and substantial reasons: First, that if another craft should strike her, the force of the impact would be distributed over a larger area if the *Titan* had full headway, and the brunt of the damage would be borne by the other. Second, that if the *Titan* was the aggressor she would certainly destroy the other craft, even at half-speed, and perhaps damage her own bows; while at full speed, she would cut her in two with no more damage to herself than a paintbrush could remedy. In either case, as the lesser of two evils, it was best that the smaller hull should suffer. A third reason was that, at full speed, she could be more easily steered out of danger, and a fourth, that in case of an end-on collision with an iceberg – the only thing afloat that she could not conquer – her bows would be crushed in but a few feet further at full than at half speed, and at the most three compartments would be flooded – which would not matter with six more to spare.

So, it was confidently expected that when her engines had limbered themselves, the steamship *Titan* would land her passengers three thousand miles away with the promptitude and regularity of a railway train. She had beaten all records on her maiden voyage, but, up to the third return trip, had not lowered the time between Sandy Hook and Daunt's Rock to the five-day limit; and it was unofficially rumoured among the two thousand passengers who had embarked at New York that an effort would now be made to do so.

Eight tugs dragged the great mass to midstream and pointed her nose down the river; then the pilot on the bridge spoke a word or two; the first officer blew a short blast on the whistle and turned a lever; the tugs gathered in their lines and drew off; down in the bowels of the ship three small engines were started, opening the throttles of three large ones; three propellers began to revolve; and the mammoth, with a vibratory tremble running through her great frame, moved slowly to sea.

East of Sandy Hook the pilot was dropped and the real voyage begun. Fifty feet below her deck, in an inferno of noise, and heat, and light, and shadow, coal-passers wheeled the picked fuel from the bunkers to the fire-hold, where half-naked stokers, with faces like those of tortured fiends, tossed it into the eighty white-hot mouths of the furnaces. In the engine-room, oilers passed to and fro, in and out of the plunging, twisting, glistening steel, with oil-cans and waste, overseen by the watchful staff on duty, who listened with strained hearing for a false note in the confused jumble of sound – a clicking of steel out of tune, which would indicate a loosened key or nut. On deck, sailors set the triangular sails on the two masts, to add their propulsion to the momentum of the record-breaker, and the passengers dispersed themselves as suited their several tastes. Some were seated in steamer chairs, well wrapped – for, though it was April, the salt air was chilly – some paced the deck, acquiring their sea legs; others listened to the orchestra in the music-room, or read or wrote in the library, and a few took to their berths – seasick from the slight heave of the ship on the ground-swell . . .

When the watch turned out at midnight, they found a vicious half-gale blowing from the northeast, which, added to the speed of the steamship,

made, so far as effects on her deck went, a fairly uncomfortable whole
gale of chilly wind. The head sea, choppy as compared with her great
length, dealt the *Titan* successive blows, each one attended by sup-
plementary tremors to the continuous vibrations of the engines – each
one sending a cloud of thick spray aloft that reached the crow's-nest on
the foremast and battered the pilot-house windows on the bridge in a
liquid bombardment that would have broken ordinary glass. A fog-bank,
into which the ship had plunged in the afternoon, still enveloped her –
damp and impenetrable; and into the grey, ever-receding wall ahead,
with two deck officers and three lookouts straining sight and hearing to
the utmost, the great racer was charging with undiminished speed.

At a quarter past twelve, two men crawled in from the darkness at
the ends of the eighty-foot bridge and shouted to the first officer, who
had just taken the deck, the names of the men who had relieved them.
Backing up to the pilot-house, the officer repeated the names to a
quartermaster within, who entered them in the log-book. Then the men
vanished – to their coffee and 'watch-below'. In a few moments another
dripping shape appeared on the bridge and reported the crow's-nest
relief.

'Rowland, you say?' bawled the officer above the howling of the wind.
'Is he the man who was lifted aboard, drunk, yesterday?'

'Yes, sir.'

'Is he still drunk?'

'Yes, sir.'

'All right – that'll do. Enter Rowland in the crow's-nest, quartermaster,' said the officer; then, making a funnel of his hands, he roared
out: 'Crow's-nest, there.'

'Sir,' came the answer, shrill and clear on the gale.

'Keep your eyes open – keep a sharp lookout.'

'Very good, sir.'

'Been a man-o'-war's-man, I judge, by his answer. They're no good,'
muttered the officer. He resumed his position at the forward side of
the bridge where the wooden railing afforded some shelter from the
raw wind, and began the long vigil which would only end when the
second officer relieved him, four hours later. Conversation – except in
the line of duty – was forbidden among the bridge officers of the *Titan*,
and his watchmate, the third officer, stood on the other side of the large
bridge binnacle, only leaving this position occasionally to glance in at
the compass – which seemed to be his sole duty at sea. Sheltered by

one of the deck-houses below, the boatswain and the watch paced back and forth, enjoying the only two hours respite which steamship rules afforded, for the day's work had ended with the going down of the other watch, and at two o'clock the washing of the 'tween-deck would begin, as an opening task in the next day's labour.

By the time one bell had sounded, with its repetition from the crow's-nest, followed by a long-drawn cry – 'all's well' – from the lookouts, the last of the two thousand passengers had retired, leaving the spacious cabins and steerage in possession of the watchmen; while, sound asleep in his cabin abaft the chart-room, was the captain, the commander who never commanded – unless the ship was in danger; for the pilot had charge, making and leaving port, and the officers, at sea.

Two bells were struck and answered; then three, and the boatswain and his men were lighting up for a final smoke, when there rang out overhead a startling cry from the crow's-nest:

'Something ahead, sir – can't make it out.'

The first officer sprang to the engine-room telegraph and grasped the lever. 'Sing out what you see,' he roared.

'Hard aport, sir – ship on the starboard tack – dead ahead,' came the cry.

'Port your wheel – hard over,' repeated the first officer to the quarter-master at the helm – who answered and obeyed. Nothing as yet could be seen from the bridge. The powerful steering-engine in the stern ground the rudder over; but before three degrees on the compass card were traversed by the lubber's-point, a seeming thickening of the darkness and fog ahead resolved itself into the square sails of a deep-laden ship, crossing the *Titan*'s bow, not half her length away.

'H–l and d–' growled the first officer. 'Steady on your course, quarter-master,' he shouted. 'Stand from under on deck.' He turned a lever which closed compartments, pushed a button marked – 'Captain's Room', and crouched down, awaiting the crash.

There was hardly a crash. A slight jar shook the forward end of the *Titan* and sliding down her foretopmast-stay and rattling on deck came a shower of small spars, sails, blocks and wire rope. Then, in the darkness to starboard and port, two darker shapes shot by – the two halves of the ship she had cut through; and from one of these shapes, where still burned a binnacle light, was heard, high above the confused murmur of shouts and shrieks, a sailorly voice:

'May the curse of God light on you and your cheese-knife, you brass-bound murderers.'

The shapes were swallowed in the blackness astern; the cries were hushed by the clamour of the gale, and the steamship *Titan* swung back to her course. The first officer had not turned the lever of the engine-room telegraph.

The boatswain bounded up the steps of the bridge for instructions.

'Put men at the hatches and doors. Send every one who comes on deck to the chart-room. Tell the watchman to notice what the passengers have learned, and clear away that wreck forward as soon as possible.' The voice of the officer was hoarse and strained as he gave these directions, and the 'aye, aye, sir' of the boatswain was uttered in a gasp . . .

'Ice,' yelled the lookout; 'ice ahead. Iceberg. Right under the bows.' The first officer ran amidships, and the captain, who had remained there, sprang to the engine-room telegraph, and this time the lever was turned. But in five seconds the bow of the *Titan* began to lift, and ahead, and on either hand, could be seen, through the fog, a field of ice, which arose in an incline to a hundred feet high in her track. The music in the theatre ceased, and among the babel of shouts and cries, and the deafening noise of steel, scraping and crashing over ice, Rowland heard the agonized voice of a woman crying from the bridge steps: 'Myra – Myra, where are you? Come back.'

Seventy-five thousand tons – dead weight – rushing through the fog at the rate of fifty feet a second, had hurled itself at an iceberg. Had the impact been received by a perpendicular wall, the elastic resistance of bending plates and frames would have overcome the momentum with no more damage to the passengers than a severe shaking up, and to the ship than the crushing in of her bows and the killing, to a man, of the watch below. She would have backed off, and, slightly down by the head, finished the voyage at reduced speed, to rebuild on insurance money, and benefit, largely, in the end, by the consequent advertising of her indestructibility. But a low beach, possibly formed by the recent overturning of the berg, received the *Titan*, and with her keel cutting the ice like the steel runner of an ice-boat, and her great weight resting on the starboard bilge, she rose out of the sea, higher and higher – until the propellers in the stern were half exposed – then, meeting an easy, spiral rise in the ice under her port bow, she heeled, overbalanced and crashed down on her side, to starboard.

The holding-down bolts of twelve boilers and three triple-expansion engines, unintended to hold such weights from a perpendicular flooring, snapped, and down through a maze of ladders, gratings and fore-and-aft bulkheads came these giant masses of steel and iron, puncturing the sides of the ship, even where backed by solid, resisting ice; and filling the engine- and boiler-rooms with scalding steam, which brought a quick, though tortured death, to each of the hundred men on duty in the engineer's department.

Amid the roar of escaping steam, and the bee-like buzzing of nearly three thousand human voices, raised in agonized screams and callings from within the inclosing walls, and the whistling of air through hundreds of open dead-lights as the water, entering the holes of the crushed and riven starboard side, expelled it, the *Titan* moved slowly backward and launched herself into the sea, where she floated low on her side – a dying monster, groaning with her death-wound . . .

On the first floor of the London Royal Exchange is a large apartment studded with desks, around and between which surges a hurrying, shouting crowd of brokers, clerks and messengers. Fringing this apart-ment are doors and hallways leading to adjacent rooms and offices, and scattered through it are bulletin-boards, on which are daily written in duplicate the marine casualties of the world. At one end is a raised platform, sacred to the presence of an important functionary. In the technical language of the 'City', the apartment is known as the 'Room', and the functionary, as the 'Caller', whose business it is to call out in a mighty sing-song voice the names of members wanted at the door, and the bare particulars of bulletin news prior to its being chalked out for reading.

It is the headquarters of Lloyds – the immense association of under-writers, brokers and shipping-men, which, beginning with the customers at Edward Lloyd's coffee-house in the latter part of the seventeenth century, has, retaining his name for a title, developed into a corporation so well equipped, so splendidly organized and powerful, that kings and ministers of state appeal to it at times for foreign news.

Not a master or mate sails under the English flag but whose record, even to forecastle fights, is tabulated at Lloyds for the inspection of prospective employers. Not a ship is cast away on any inhabitable coast of the world, during underwriters' business hours, but what that mighty sing-song cry announces the event at Lloyds within thirty minutes.

One of the adjoining rooms is known as the Chartroom. Here can be found in perfect order and sequence, each on its roller, the newest charts of all nations, with a library of nautical literature describing to the last detail the harbours, lights, rocks, shoals and sailing directions of every coast-line shown on the charts; the tracks of latest storms; the changes of ocean currents, and the whereabouts of derelicts and icebergs. A member at Lloyds acquires in time a theoretical knowledge of the sea seldom exceeded by the men who navigate it.

Another apartment – the Captain's room – is given over to joy and refreshment, and still another, the antithesis of the last, is the Intelligence office, where anxious ones enquire for and are told the latest news of this or that overdue ship.

On the day when the assembled throng of underwriters and brokers had been thrown into an uproarious panic the Crier's announcement that the great *Titan* was destroyed, and the papers of Europe and America were issuing extras giving the meagre details of the arrival at New York of one boat-load of her people, this office had been crowded with weeping women and worrying men, who would ask, and remain to ask again, for more news. And when it came – a later cablegram, – giving the story of the wreck and the names of the captain, first officer, boatswain, seven sailors, and one lady passenger as those of the saved, a feeble old gentleman had raised his voice in a quavering scream, high above the sobbing of the women, and said:

'My daughter-in-law is safe; but where is my son, – where is my son, and my grandchild?' Then he had hurried away, but was back again the next day, and the next . . .

The 'Napoleon of newsmen' can seem to dominate the story of Titanic. From the Old World to the New *(1892) contained a fictional episode involving* S S Majestic *navigated by Captain Edward J. Smith (with whom Stead had travelled on that liner) which follows another ship that strikes an iceberg in mid-Atlantic. Stead believed life stretched beyond the grave and in* How I Know the Dead Return *(1909) used the east-west passage of an Atlantic liner and marconigrams in an extended metaphor to explain how the dead communicate. After he drowned on* Titanic *Stead communicated his experience to a medium, and his daughter Estelle published it as* The Blue Island, *with a prefatory letter from another devotee of spiritualism, Sir Arthur Conan Doyle. Stead is disappointingly undetailed about his experiences just before and just after* Titanic *went down.*

W. T. STEAD
The Story Stead Could Not File By Deadline

(*The Blue Island: Experiences of a New Arrival beyond the Veil*, through the hand of Estelle Stead, 1922)

Of my actual passing from earth to spirit life I do not wish to write more than a few lines. I have already spoken of it several times and in several places. The first part of it was naturally an extremely discordant one, but from the time my physical life was ended there was no longer that sense of struggling with overwhelming odds; but I do not wish to speak of that.

My first surprise came when – I now understand that to your way of thinking I was then dead – I found I was in a position to help people. From being in dire straits myself, to being able to lend a hand to others, was such a sudden transition that I was frankly and blankly surprised. I was so taken aback that I did not consider the why and the wherefore at all. I was suddenly able to help. I knew not how or why and did not attempt to enquire. There was no analysis then; that came a little later.

I was also surprised to find a number of friends with me, people I knew had passed over years before. That was the first cause of my realizing the change had taken place. I knew it suddenly and was a trifle alarmed. Practically instantaneously I found myself looking for myself. Just a moment of agitation, momentary only, and then the full and glorious realization that all I had learnt was true. Oh, how badly I needed a telephone at that moment! I felt I could give the papers some headlines for that evening. That was my first realization; then came a helplessness – a reaction – a thought of all my own at home – they didn't know yet. What would they think of me? Here was I, with my telephone out of working order for the present. I was still so near the earth that I could see everything going on there. Where I was I could see the wrecked ship, the people, the whole scene; and that seemed to pull me into action – I could help! . . . And so in a few seconds – though I am now taking a long time to tell you, it was only a few seconds really – I found myself changed from the helpless state to one of action; HELPFUL not helpless – I was helpful, too, I think.

I pass a little now. The end came and it was all finished with. It was like waiting for a liner to sail; we waited until all were aboard. I mean we waited until the disaster was complete. The saved – saved; the dead – alive. Then in one whole we moved our scene. It was a strange method of travelling for us all, and we were a strange crew, bound for we knew not where. The whole scene was indescribably pathetic. Many, knowing what had occurred, were in agony of doubt as to their people left behind and as to their own future state. What would it hold for them? Would they be taken to see Him? What would their sentence be? Others were almost mental wrecks. They knew nothing, they seemed to be uninterested in everything, their minds were paralysed. A strange crew indeed, of human souls waiting their ratings in the new land.

A matter of a few minutes in time only, and here were hundreds of bodies floating in the water – dead – hundreds of souls carried through the air, alive; very much alive, some were. Many, realizing their death had come, were enraged at their own powerlessness to save their valuables. They fought to save what they had on earth prized so much.

The scene on the boat at the time of striking was not pleasant, but it was as nothing to the scene among the poor souls newly thrust out of their bodies, all unwillingly. It was both heartbreaking and repellent. And thus we waited – waited until all were collected, until all was ready, and then we moved our scene to a different land.

It was a curious journey that. Far more strange than anything I had anticipated. We seemed to rise vertically into the air at terrific speed.

As a whole we moved, as if we were on a very large platform, and this was hurled into the air with gigantic strength and speed, yet there was no feeling of insecurity . . . We were quite steady. I cannot tell how long our journey lasted, nor how far from the earth we were when we arrived, but it was a gloriously beautiful arrival. It was like walking from your own English winter gloom into the radiance of an Indian sky. There, all was brightness and beauty. We saw this land far off when we were approaching, and those of us who could understand realized that we were being taken to the place destined for all those people who pass over suddenly – on account of its general appeal. It helps the nerve-racked newcomer to fall into line and regain mental balance very quickly. We arrived feeling, in a sense, proud of ourselves. It was all lightness, brightness. Everything as physical and quite as material in every way as the world we had just finished with.

Our arrival was greeted with welcomes from many old friends and relations who had been dear to each one of us in our earth life. And having arrived, we people who had come over from that ill-fated ship parted company. We were free agents again, though each one of us was in the company of some personal friend who had been over here a long while.

A prodigious number of metaphors were spawned by the Titanic. *The American left-wing magazine* Masses *saw* Titanic *as a 'true miniature' of the commercial state 'built and bossed by a few colossi bestriding the busy multitude and ordering the intricacies of production and distribution'. The 'insanity of luxury' and the 'insanity of speed' drive both ship and society. Chesterton offers a milder version of this angry metaphor.*

G. K. CHESTERTON
The Swift Poetry of Peril

(*Illustrated London News*, 27 April 1912)

The tragedy of the great shipwreck is too terrific for any analogies of mere fancy. But the analogy which springs to the mind between the great modern ship and our great modern society that sent it forth – this analogy is not a fancy. It is a fact; a fact perhaps too large and plain for the eye easily to take in. Our whole civilization is indeed very like the *Titanic*; alike in its power and its impotence, its security and its insecurity. Technically considered, the sufficiency of the precautions are a matter for technical enquiry. But psychologically considered, there can be no doubt that such vast elaboration and system induce a frame of mind which is inefficient rather than efficient. Quite apart from the question of whether anyone was to blame, the big outstanding fact remains: that there was no sort of sane proportion between the extent of the provision for luxury and levity, and the extent of the provision for need and desperation. The scheme did far too much for prosperity and far too little for distress – just like the modern State. Mr Veneering, it will be remembered, in his electoral address, 'instituted a new and striking comparison between the State and a ship'; the comparison, if not new, is becoming a little too striking. By the time you have made your ship as big as a commonwealth your commonwealth does become very like a ship – rather like a sinking ship.

For there is a real connection between such catastrophes and a certain frame of mind which refuses to expect them. A rough man going about the sea in a small boat may make every other kind of mistake: he may obey superstitions; he may take too much rum; he may get drunk; he may get drowned. But, cautious or reckless, drunk or sober, he cannot forget that he is in a boat and that a boat is as dangerous a beast as a wild horse. The very lines of the boat have the swift poetry of peril; the very carriage and gestures of the boat are those of a thing assailed. But if you make your boat so large that it does not even look like a boat, but like a sort of watering-place, it must, by the deepest habit of human nature, induce a less vigilant attitude of the mind. An aristocrat on board ship who travels with a garage for his motor almost feels as if he were travelling with the trees of his park. People living in open-air cafés sprinkled with liqueurs and ices get as far from the thought of any revolt of the elements as they are from that of an earthquake under the Hotel Cecil. The mental process is quite illogical, but it is quite inevitable. Of course, both sailors and passengers are intellectually aware that motors at sea are often less useful than lifeboats, and that ices are no antidote to icebergs. But man is governed not only by what he thinks but by what he chooses to think about; and the sights that sink into us day by day colour our minds with every tint between insolence and terror. This is one of the worst evils in that extreme separation of social classes which marks the modern ship – and State.

But whether or no our unhappy fellow-creatures on the *Titanic* suffered more than they need from this unreality of original outlook, they cannot have had less instinct of actuality than we have who are left alive on land: and now that they are dead they are much more real than we. They have known what papers and politicians never know – of what man is really made, and what manner of thing is our nature at its best and worst. It is this curious, cold, flimsy incapacity to conceive what a *thing* is like that appears in so many places, even in the comments on this astounding sorrow. It appears in the displeasing incident of Miss Sylvia Pankhurst, who, immediately after the disaster, seems to have hastened to assure the public that men must get no credit for giving the boats up to women, because it was the 'rule' at sea. Whether this was a graceful thing for a gay spinster to say to eight hundred widows in the very hour of doom is not worth enquiry here. Like cannibalism, it is a question of taste. But what chiefly astonishes me in the remark is the utter absence which it reveals of the rudiments of political thought. What does Miss Pankhurst imagine a 'rule' is – a sort of basilisk? Some hundreds of men are, in the exact and literal sense of the proverb, between the devil and the deep blue sea. It is their business, if they can make up their minds to it, to accept the deep sea and resist the devil.

What does Miss Pankhurst suppose a 'rule' could do to them in such extremities? Does she think the captain would fine every man sixpence who expressed a preference for his life? Has it occurred to her that a hundredth part of the ship's population could have thrown the captain and all the authorities into the sea? But Miss Pankhurst's remark, though imbecile, is informing. Now I see the abject and idolatrous way in which she uses the word 'rule', I begin to understand the abject and idolatrous way in which she uses the word 'vote'. She cannot see that wills and not words control events. If ever she is in a fire or shipwreck with men below a certain standard of European morals, she will soon find out that the existence of a rule depends on whether people can be induced to obey it. And if ever she has a vote in the very low state of European politics, she will very soon find out that its importance depends on whether you can induce the man you vote for to obey his mandate or to keep any of his promises. It is vain to rule if your subjects can and do disobey you. It is vain to vote if your delegates can and do disobey you.

But, indeed, a real rule can do without such exceptions as the Suffragettes; *de minimis non curat lex*. And if the word 'rule' be used in the wider sense of an attempt to maintain a certain standard of private conduct out of respect for public opinion, we can only say that not only is this a real moral triumph, but it is, in our present condition, rather a surprising and reassuring one. It is exactly this corporate conscience that the modern State has dangerously neglected. There was probably more instinctive fraternity and sense of identical interests, I will not say, on an old skipper's vessel, but on an old pirate's, than there was between the emigrants, the aristocrats, the journalists or the millionaires who set out to die together in the great ship. That they found in so cruel a way their brotherhood and the need of man for the respect of his neighbour, this is a dreadful fact, but certainly the reverse of a degrading one. The case of Mr Stead, which I feel with rather special emotions, both of sympathy and difference, is very typical of the whole tragedy. Mr Stead was far too great and brave a man to require any concealment of his exaggerations or his more unbalanced moods; his strength was in a flaming certainty, which one only weakens by calling sincerity, and a hunger and thirst for human sympathy. His excess, we may say, with real respect, was in the direction of megalomania; a childlike belief in big empires, big newspapers, big alliances – big ships. He toiled like a Titan for that Anglo-American combination of which the ship that has gone down may well be called the emblem. And at the last all these big things broke about him, and somewhat bigger things remained: a courage that was entirely individual; a kindness that was entirely universal. His death may well become a legend.

In this editorial-cum-infomercial in the Telegraph's *Territorial Army corner, Anglo-Saxonism (of which Stead was a champion) and British Imperialism are welded one more time in the most patriotic of* Titanic *metaphors.*

'A *Titanic* Lesson'

(*Daily Telegraph*, 22 April 1912)

Amidst all our sorrow it comes as a great relief to learn definitely that England still breeds men who will in the hour of danger surrender their lives to save the women and children. Some of us had begun to wonder whether that fine spirit of heroism on which our Empire has been builded had not run to premature decay.

When the hour of peril comes, Englishmen still face it as of old. If ever the war clouds burst upon our islands England will still be able to find hundreds of thousands of noble hearts willing to die for those they hold dear, but the pity is that in these days of peace we cannot find our full quota of 300,000 men willing to learn how to defend them. Let the appeal to duty, so nobly responded to by every Briton aboard the *Titanic*, make a special appeal to every one of the same stock to do his duty. It is not enough that we should send in our cheques and postal orders to the various distress funds; heroism goes deeper than the pocket, and is rarer than minted sovereigns. Let the men of Great Britain show their appreciation of the conduct of the *Titanic*'s passengers and crew by an act that will go deeper than the pocket, and even, perchance, touch that vein of unselfish devotion to duty which should lie at the bottom of every British heart.

We, too, are members of the crew of a great ship – the mightiest and noblest ship that ever sailed the sea of Empire – the British ship of State. Some of us have learnt to believe our ship unsinkable, and invasion unthinkable. We have learnt to laugh to scorn the idea of danger upon the high sea of foreign politics. Let us learn our lesson afresh, and take it to heart. Whatever happens, let it find us prepared, not only to die – but to do. It may so chance that before many voyages are completed this great ship of State of ours, that we call the British Empire, may pile herself upon some unsuspected iceberg of European complication;

let us be at least prepared. There are few men worthy of the name who, in such a predicament, would like to be numbered amongst the 'passengers' of the ship of State – they would all wish to take their places with the crew – to die, perhaps, but at least to help. There is only one way in which citizens can help when the good vessel is staggering under the shock of war, and that is by knowing how to take their places in the ranks.

Do not let us lose this sad opportunity of driving home into the minds of our 'passenger' citizens which road their plain duty lies. When the sudden danger comes it will be too late for them to learn how to be of service; the utmost they can then hope to do is to sacrifice their lives for their women and children. Is it not far better that, whilst there is yet time, they should learn how to sell their lives more dearly!

Let every Territorial who reads this page ask some civilian friend now – before it is too late – to learn to do his duty by the ship of State by joining the crew of the Territorial Army. If only some small percentage of men answer to this appeal, then those brave hearts who went down a week ago will not have died in vain. Not only will that have saved their fellow-passengers from death, and the fair fame of Anglo-Saxon courage from tarnish, but they will have bequeathed to their brethren on shore a priceless message of courage and of duty – a bequest that may well save that Empire from shipwreck in troublous times ahead.

The anticipation of Nature's subjugation can be found on the pages of Wells and other writers contemporary with Titanic. *The sinking of* Titanic *was commonly seen at the time as representing with the vividness of natural or divine lesson, the retributive power of Nature over mankind and his scientific hubris. The picture of the* ILN's *science writer of Nature as a carnivore is one that has faded in our own time.*

ANDREW WILSON
Nature and Catastrophe

(*Illustrated London News*, 11 May 1912)

The terrible calamity of the wreck of the *Titanic* will now, I suppose, overshadow in our minds the equally tragic loss of the *Eurydice* and the *Birkenhead*. The memory of an old catastrophe tends naturally to be replaced by the recollection of tragedy of recent date. The Messina earthquake is far more real to us than was or is the earthquake of Lisbon, though the damage done in the last-named cataclysm was infinitely greater. In the sphere of shipbuilding, as in other matters, we of today are far ahead in scientific culture and in its application to the wants of modern life than were even our fathers, but it must strike us all very forcibly that, with all our calculations, reasonings, experiments and so forth, the elemental forces of Nature now and then smash our most cherished schemes and exploits into fragments. Man requires ever to be at war with Nature. He is continually contravening or ignoring her laws to expedite his own affairs. The aviator, the locomotive driver, the balloonist, the builder of ships, the wireless-telegraphic inventor, and even the doctor, are all at war with Nature when we come to think of it. They triumph over Nature, and get their own way, in a sense, in spite of gravitation and every other law or condition which is impressed on the world's face. What we call 'invention' is another name for conquering the conditions Nature has made her own, and by whose standard she abides. This view of man as a warrior against the established order of the universe is very apt to escape us when we become lost in admiration of the latest achievement to save time or to annihilate space.

Careful as man may be in the conduct of his 'many inventions', Nature frequently retaliates by a display of forces against the fury of which humanity is often incapable of defending itself. A cyclone, a volcanic eruption, its neighbour the earthquake, a plague suddenly developed – and we are practically lost. Even an ice floe may work destruction of appalling extent, though it may legitimately be argued that man's knowledge of ocean ice should be fairly complete, and that he can 'get even' with Nature by noting the results of observation of oceanic ice-movements. I trust this latter point will be thoroughly investigated when the history of the *Titanic* disaster comes to be fully comprehended. If a relatively few miles of course-alteration would have kept the big liner out of the reach of the ice floe which ripped her side – a not unreasonable supposition – why was the ordinary course pursued? No exigencies of millionaire life could warrant the incurring of any risk whatever in respect of fast voyaging, if such were the case, and the many other souls on board demanded equal care. I apportion no blame here; I am merely thinking that, if I had been a passenger, and had known the choice lay between an ice-safe route meaning a day or two's longer voyage, and a short cut with the risk of ice, I should not have felt very comfortable had I learnt the decision was to keep north in place of going south.

It is open for us to argue that great catastrophes are utilized by science to improve our safety and diminish our risks. True, but the price paid is very high. You say you need more boats, for example, but a British Admiral points out that no number of boats will be of any service, provided you cannot launch them safely and preserve them in a rough sea. He falls back on the unsinkable ship, but then chance, as in the case of the *Titanic*, may mean a ripping away by the edge of an ice floe of one side of the ship. Again, are we not allowing a state of megalocephaly – in plain words, 'swelled head' – to dominate the whole matter of ocean transport? Why these great ships, fitted with every luxury, and necessitating special docks? To me, the disaster symbolizes the work of Nature, the quiet watchful carnivore, ready to strike out with its paw. Man's duty is to keep, as far as he can, out of reach of the stroke.

9
War and Peace

Analogies have been drawn between the attitudes that sailed and sank Titanic *and those that created World War I. The military subtext of the rivalry between British and German shipbuilders and shipping lines might seem confirmed by the way the great liners, including* Olympic, *were conscripted into service after 1914. A score of years had to pass before the wreck of the* Titanic *significantly entered the imagination, and when it did, it was the German imagination. The ship represented capitalist decadence in both Robert Prechtl's novel,* Titanensturz *(1937) and Herbert Selpin's wartime, anti-British motion picture* Titanic *(1943). A generation later,* Titanic *occupied the symbolic Cold War site of struggle between the USA and the Soviet Union (popularly in the 1976 bestseller and 1980 Hollywood film,* Raise the Titanic*).*

In peacetime, lesser talents have sported in the debris field. Versifiers were quickly on the scene; poets' corners became clearing-houses for bad, deeply felt verse. In May 1912 were published The Chief Incidents of the *Titanic* Wreck Treated in Verse *by Edwin Drew (27 indifferent poems), and* Solidaridad en el Dolor (Catástrofe del *Titanic*): Poema Filosófico-Moral en tres Partes y en Romance Heroico *by B. V. Silva. Major poetic achievements came later.*

Songwriters were not behindhand, for 112 pieces of Titanic *music (excluding blues, ballads and gospel) were registered for copyright in the USA in 1912;* Titanic *is the most sung disaster in American history. An unperformed 'music drama',* Titanic, *by Platon G. Brounoff (1863– 1924, a Russian-born American composer), has been lost. The Englishman Gavin Bryars's 1969 composition,* The Sinking of the *Titanic, reworked in 1994, is a haunted subaqueous music; Ronan Magill has composed* Titanic: An Atmospheric Poem in Five Pictures for Piano Solo *(1997), a work of versatile tonalities. Familiar German readings of the* Titanic *disaster inform Wilhelm Dieter Siebert's opera,* Untergang der *Titanic, performed in the Deutsche Oper, Berlin, in 1979 and staged as* The Sinking of the *Titanic in Los Angeles in 1980. The performative summons of* Titanic *is loud because the maiden voyage was itself a brash, quasi-theatrical event, a première. The summons is answered in* Titanic, *a Broadway musical of 1997.*

The disaster, early and late, hugely inspired (or commercially required) movies, three in 1912 alone: Saved from the *Titanic (USA);* In Nacht und Eis *(Germany);* Titanic Wreck *(USA). In 1929/1930, E. A. Dupont made three versions of* Atlantic. *Later full-length screen narratives include* Titanic *(USA, 1953),* A Night to Remember *(UK, 1958) and* Titanic *(USA, 1997).*

There have been two notable American plays, Christopher Durang's absurdist drama, Titanic *(1974) and Jeffrey Hatcher's* Scotland Road *(1993, named after the longitudinal passage the crew used on* Titanic*). French playwright Jean-Pierre Ronfard's* Le Titanic *(1986) recruits Hitler, Sarah Bernhardt and Charlie Chaplin to increase the already vast historical displacement of* Titanic.

G. B. Shaw was scathing about the 'romance' of Titanic *but was spared the cheap romances and potboiler fictions that bubble up from the wreck. Among serious novels,* Every Man for Himself *(1996) by Beryl Bainbridge and* Psalm at Journey's End *(Norwegian, 1990; English, 1996) by Erik Fosnes Hansen have been the most acclaimed, the latter a fictionalization of the bandsmen whose lives converge at the crossroads of two European eras.*

The ship has been a magnet both for amateur painters and for professional marine artists who have turned portraiture of Titanic *into a popular, middlebrow genre. Among the notable serious essays in painting are the German artist Max Beckmann's* The Sinking of the Titanic, *and the Ulster artist Charles Dixon's* Titanic Fitting Out at Belfast, *both painted in 1912.*

The demand for *Titanic* survivors' stories began immediately and was
sustained through the three waves of popular interest in the disaster.

Until the 1980s, the Titanic *disaster was mediated chiefly through Walter Lord's famous 1955 book which had 'discovered'* Titanic *for a new generation: it was adapted for television by George Roy Hill and John Whedon (a Writers Guild of America-prize play in 1956) and for the cinema by Eric Ambler in 1958. Biel reads the book as a modernist narrative, but one whose modernism is limited by a nostalgia induced by Cold War anxiety.*

STEVEN BIEL
Titanic in the Cold War

(*Down with the Old Canoe: A Cultural History of the* Titanic *Disaster*, 1996)

What was *A Night to Remember* nostalgic *for*? Certainly not class or ethnic prejudice. But Lord also mentioned the disappearance of 'some nobler instincts' – chivalry and noblesse oblige – and recognized, in retrospect, that 'the women and children first idea was still very stirring' at the time he wrote the book. Tales of old-fashioned chivalry possessed obvious appeal in a postwar culture that celebrated the 'traditional' family and sacralized the roles of male breadwinner and female homemaker. These roles, as Elaine Tyler May has shown, 'represented a source of meaning and security in a world run amok'. Lord sounded a common Cold War theme when he waxed nostalgic about confidence and certainty, and though he debunked the most egregious myths about Butt and Astor, *A Night to Remember* told a new generation about how men protected women in times of danger. (Five years later, in *The Good Years*, he refined the end-of-an-era idea to give it more of a reformist bent and made the Great War rather than the *Titanic* the watershed event. 'These years were good,' he wrote, 'because, whatever the trouble, people were sure they could fix it', an attitude no longer possible after the experience of world war. As alternatives to 'Good', he suggested 'Confident', 'Buoyant', 'Spirited' and 'Golden'.)

Above and beyond its stated objects of nostalgia, Lord's narrative yearned for time itself. Review after review linked the book's excitement to its profusion of characters and, more specifically, to the ways in which Lord depicted '[w]hat they saw and felt and did at a particular moment' – 'the human side of the *Titanic* story'. Unlike the 1912 accounts, which described heroism and cowardice in terms of gender, class and ethnicity, *A Night to Remember* revealed a spectrum of behaviour among 'men and women, rich and poor, officers and crew'. How people 'acted', said the *New York Times*, 'is the core of Mr Lord's account, and explains its fascination, a pull as powerful in its way as the last downward plunge of the ship itself'. If what another reviewer called 'legendary acts of gallantry' stood out most dramatically, what really mattered was the ability – the time – to think and feel and act in any way. 'What would it be like to be aboard a sinking ocean liner?' began a *Newsweek* piece titled 'The Fabric of Disaster'. The night was 'a mixture of overconfidence, heroism and stupidity', or, in a slightly different trinity, 'devotion, gallantry and stupidity'. While noting Lord's 'restraint', the *Christian Century* observed that 'the terrible drama of this existential situation par excellence' – the fashionable Jean-Paul Sartre had even made his way into book reviews – 'comes smashing through all the author's reticence'. In place of irony Lord posed a mimetic challenge to his readers: How would I have acted in the same situation?

Time to act: This is what links *A Night to Remember*'s modernism and nostalgia. Lord's method of stretching time to leap from point to point in space postponed the inevitable so that readers could see, over and over again, that the *Titanic* disaster happened slowly. Lord maintained 'suspense . . . against a known conclusion' – suspense in the most literal sense, interruption and delay. The *Titanic* took two hours and forty minutes to sink, and Lord's narrative, with its combination of quick jumps and recurrence, managed to move at a fast pace while dramatizing the disaster's full duration. The minute-by-minute, multiple-perspective technique and the end-of-an-era theme fused to create a double sense of lost time. Simultaneously wistful and anxious, *A Night to Remember* spoke of a bygone age in which disasters gave people time to die.

In the 1950s there was good reason to be nostalgic for this older kind of disaster. Nostalgia, as Fred Davis has noted, 'thrives . . . on the rude transitions wrought by such phenomena as war, depression, civil disturbance and cataclysmic natural disasters – in short, those events that cause masses of people to feel uneasy and to wonder whether the world and their being are quite what they always took them to be.' The *Titanic* resonated in the fifties because it provided a nostalgic alternative to a world in 'crude transition' to the atomic age. Just as the 'return' to the nuclear family and 'traditional' gender roles seemed to offer security amid the constant threat of nuclear war, so did the *Titanic* provide shelter in the 'memory' of a safer time and even in the recollection of a quainter kind of disaster. In addition to observing that *A Night to Remember* depicted the passengers and crew in a range of emotions and a variety of actions, reviewers uncritically accepted Lord's idea that the disaster marked a point of radical discontinuity. 'It was,' wrote one, 'the end of an era of security and the beginning of a time of danger and disbelief.' A technological catastrophe, despite all reassurances about its impossibility, ushered in a new era of anxiety and fear; 'the unpredictable undid the most confidently predicted'; nothing was fail-safe.

The real rude transition had occurred more recently. A truly modern technological disaster would not give its victims time to die, would not necessarily allow for survivors, might not even have an aftermath. The *Titanic*, like all objects of nostalgia, was at once current and distant – a 'means for engaging the present' and an emblem of discontinuity. 'There is an even-keel, golden-mean gentility about most of the action which makes the whole event far more remote than 44 years would ordinarily make anything,' the *Christian Century* shrewdly observed. 'But the desperation in the context of the action makes it contemporary enough to keep you up as long as it takes to finish the book the night you start it.' Time to die was something remote; desperation was contemporary.

Few directly mentioned the bomb, but it loomed nevertheless. The *Reader's Digest* condensation was bracketed by articles entitled 'Inside the H-Bomb Plant' and 'The Fearsome Atomic Submarine'. The most intriguing reference appeared in the last line of *Time*'s review of *A Night to Remember*: 'This air age, when death commonly comes too swiftly for heroism or with no survivors to record it, can still turn with wonder to an age before yesterday when a thousand deaths at sea seemed the very worst the world must suffer.' . . .

Lord's book took a particularly imaginative approach to the time-to-die and end-of-an-era themes. The TV version, with its huge cast and elaborate staging, similarly stretched time by juxtaposing simultaneous moments throughout the ship's expanse. A reviewer summed up George Roy Hill's technique: 'A narration delivered by Claude Rains was used to bridge the almost limitless number of sequences that made up the comprehensive picture of life aboard the doomed liner.' Rains announced the time – 11.40, 11.45, midnight, 12.15, 12.20, 12.24, 12.42, and so on until 2.20 – as scenes shifted from first class to steerage, from the bridge to the wireless room, from the *Titanic*'s boiler room to the *Californian*'s radio cabin. (Commercial breaks also added to the suspension of time, if not to the suspense of the drama.) As in the book, there were no dominant characters; the show displayed a range of responses. Unlike the book, the broadcast ended with the ship going down rather than with the *Carpathia*'s arrival. It focused exclusively on the slowly dawning awareness of the disaster's seriousness: the preparations for escape or death. 'With no fixed policy to guide them,' Rains explained, the passengers 'behaved as the moment and their characters dictated'. In 1956 preparation no longer necessarily meant making things right with God, though the band played the hymn 'Autumn' in the TV version. Now it was the mere possibility of prep-aration – loading boats, saying good-bye, contemplating, brooding, even panicking – that gave the broadcast its dramatic intensity. *Variety* observed how the '[s]kilful interlacing of shots from every quarter of the ship delineated the initial confidence in the ship's unsinkability and then captured the varied moods of resignation, panic, cowardice and heroism as the truth became known'. After the 'freezing waters of the North Atlantic closed over the grave of the *Titanic*' came the denouement. Rains, seated at a book-covered desk, ran down the list of contingencies and declared with consummate British authority, 'Never again has man been so confident. An age had come to an end.' Fade out.

The 1958 British film production of *A Night to Remember* (which was more successful in the United States than was the Hollywood *Titanic*) economically covered the gamut of behaviour from Ismay to the Strauses to a composite steerage hero named Murphy, but it also featured a central character, Second Officer Charles Lightoller (Kenneth More), whom the script called upon to announce the end of an era while sitting atop an overturned collapsible lifeboat in the black and freezing Atlantic. 'I know what the sea can do. But this is different,' Lightoller tells Colonel Gracie. 'Because we hit an iceberg?' Gracie enquires. 'No,' explains Lightoller. 'Because we were so sure. Because even though it's happened, it's still unbelievable. I don't think I'll ever feel sure again. About anything.' While these pronouncements of the Age of Anxiety gave the broadcast and film their currency, their poig-nancy came from the elaborate dramas of awareness and preparation. The movie took what Lord thought was the enormous liberty of allowing the band's cellist to sing 'Nearer My God to Thee', but what mattered more than absolute accuracy was the tempo of the music – unhurried, deliberate – and the possibility of resolutions. (In contrast with its content, promotional strategies for the film were distinctly modern. American exhibitors were encouraged to try a variety of tie-ins, including souvenir books, contests through local radio and TV, 'quiz mats' about the disaster in newspapers, swizzle sticks in the shape of the *Titanic*, and department store window displays featuring movie stills and posters and juxtaposing 1958 fashions with 1912 fashions. For all its ambivalence about modernity, *Titanic* nostalgia was also a shrewd marketing ploy.) . . .

Other 'rediscoveries' of the disaster conveyed the time-to-die theme with less creativity than *A Night to Remember*. Jack Weeks's 'tragic saga of incredible folly and incredible courage' – a non-fiction piece in *Holiday* magazine that coincided with the release of the Webb–Stanwyck movie – simply listed 'the customary performances of confusion, inadequacy, stupidity and selfishness', and, of course, 'beautiful courage'. Richard O'Connor's *Down to Eternity* had the double misfortune of being published less than two months after *A Night to Remember* and not being nearly as good a book. With its glossy cover painting of Clifton Webb, it tried to capitalize on the resurgent interest in the disaster generated by the film. O'Connor too emphasized the variety of 'human behaviour' and the possibility of human drama – the long opening chapter was called 'Dramatis Personae' – though his cast of characters was smaller than Lord's and he sacrificed credibility by repeating the old legends about Astor, Butt and a heroic Newfoundland that dog-paddled for hours to help guide the lifeboats to the *Carpathia*. Still, *Down to Eternity* shared with other fifties Titanica the dual sense of continuity and discontinuity. The book was advertised with the slogan 'The Night a World Ended', and O'Connor explicitly stated that the disaster marked a sharp historical break: 'Even across the comparatively short interval of four decades, the Edwardians seem almost like a lost tribe to be studied from the viewpoint of an anthropologist, so little did they apparently have in common with the tense and fearful man of the present.' The disaster brought out the contrast between Edwardian confidence and modern anxiety, but it also signalled the realization that unimaginable technological catastrophes were still possible. Here again the *Titanic* was both unlike and like the bomb, a far cry from its threat of instantaneous destruction yet its ancestor in terms of misplaced assurance and extraordinary hubris: 'So the Edwardians contemplated, when they were not completely deaf to, a warning signal that they and their works – no matter how massive, how convenient, how defiant of the forces that have always waited at the world's edge to remind man of his frailty, whether an iceberg or a man-made device that can destroy cities in a flash of solar energy – were only of the earth, earthly.'

The politics of nostalgia are ambiguous. A deep feeling of dissatisfaction with the present combines with a sense of historical disjunction so absolute that there is nothing to do but regret the loss. Lord sealed off a compelling discussion of historical contingency by chalking everything up to fate. Later he regretted the loss of faith in the possibility of human-directed change and reform. Despite such fatalism, the rediscovery of the *Titanic* served at least in part as a political critique – an implicit challenge to the Cold War gospel of progress. The fascination with an archetype of technological hubris indicated serious doubts about the equation of technology and advancement. While many fifties Americans were reading about or watching the *Titanic* disaster, the atomic establishment was telling the public about 'the sunny side of the atom'. More broadly, the nostalgia for security reflected an ambivalence about the achievements of the 'affluent society' and the burgeoning national security state. Locating security in the remote, pre-*Titanic* past called into question the claims that defence-based abundance had provided Americans with permanent safety and comfort.

Margaret ('Molly') Tobin Brown took turns at the oars with two other women in lifeboat No. 6. Decades later her Titanic *exploit was connected to her earlier adventures in Colorado to produce the legend of Unsinkable Molly. In the 1960 musical she is the American Dream incarnate – 'stamped American from stem to stern'. Europe welcomes her as it did the World War II saviours from the New World (she is energy amid effeteness), and European nobility comes to visit her in Denver, like western Europe bowing to American power after the war. Even in a* Titanic *lifeboat, she is a wish-fulfilling American desire to see Russia off the Cold War premises. (Shamus is her father.)*

MEREDITH WILLSON AND RICHARD MORRIS
Stamped American from Stem to Stern

(The Unsinkable Molly Brown, 1960)

Scene 10

The mid-Atlantic.

Time: Shortly after 2.30 a.m., 15 April 1912.

At Rise: The stage is screened in mist. Centre stage there is a very crowded lifeboat. In the far distance we see a luxury liner, her lights ablaze. She is sinking. We hear the sounds of the ship's whistle and the roll of water. MOLLY *is in the lifeboat, dressed in a full-length chinchilla coat and high boots. The confusion of the passengers in the lifeboat almost causes it to sink. A* MALE PASSENGER *stands up rocking the boat from side to side endangering all.*

MALE PASSENGER: We're going to sink. There are too many of us.
  It's too crowded. We're going to sink, I tell you!
MOLLY [*Standing up*]: SIT DOWN, YOU JACKASS!
[*She whips a .45 from out of the folds of her chinchilla and fires in the air, then points the gun at the hysterical man*]
  I said, sit, 'fore I colour the Atlantic with your yellow guts!
[MALE PASSENGER *sits*]
  Now, pick up that oar and let's get the hell outta here!
[*The* MAN *reluctantly starts to row. Next to* MOLLY *there is a drenched*

WOMAN *holding her crying* CHILD. MOLLY *peels out of her chinchilla
and throws it over the* MOTHER *and* CHILD]

MOLLY [*To* MOTHER]: Sorry 'bout the cussin' in front of the kid.

[*A wounded* SAILOR *collapses over his oar.* MOLLY *quickly moves
him to one side and takes over his oar*]

MOLLY: Oops. Move over baby.

[*Starting to row*]

Pull, folks, pull . . .

MOTHER: He's right, isn't he? We're too crowded. We're going to sink.

MOLLY: Not with Molly Brown aboard. I was born in a cyclone in
Hannibal, Missouri. That was my start and this sure in hell ain't
gonna be my finish.

MOTHER: But they'll never find us. There are no flares. They'll never
find us.

MOLLY: Honey, we got built-in flares. We ain't down yet. Come on,
now, come on, we all got so much livin' and lovin' to do – Work them
oars.

SAILOR: The lady's right. Pull, pull.

MOLLY [*Her face lighting up*]: 'Lady' . . . 'lady' . . . Well, I made it.
Sittin' in a rowboat in the middle of the ocean, I *finally* made it. All
together, pull . . . pull.

[*Belting as she rows*]

Belly up, belly up to the bar, boys

SING, damn it . . .

[*The* PASSENGERS *start to sing along with* MOLLY]

MOLLY & PASSENGERS [*Building in spirit and volume*]:

Belly up, belly up to the bar, boys

If it isn't your day –

[*Pointing at a quiet group*]

What's the matter . . . ya mad at music?

MOLLY & ALL [*At the top of their lungs*]:

A quart and a pint mixed up just right

Will cure you right away . . .

[MOLLY *continues to lead the group with everything she's got . . . and
that's plenty. With her setting the example, the* PASSENGERS *row and
sing and sing and row as the lights fade*]

Music Bridge:

Scene 11

Upper hallway of the BROWNS' *Denver mansion.*

Time: Late April.

At Rise: ROBERTS *enters, staggering under an enormous basket of flowers.* SHAMUS *enters carrying a newspaper.*

SHAMUS [*Proudly holding up the paper*]: She did better'n the sports page this time. She made headlines, my girl did.
[*Pointing to paper*]
That says 'Molly' and that says 'Brown', don't it?

ROBERTS [*Looking around flowers*]: Yes, sir . . . Mrs Brown asked me if you'd like some flowers in your room, Mr Tobin. I simply can't find a place for any more downstairs. These are from the Governor.

SHAMUS: Fine, fine.
[*Holding up the paper*]
What's that say?

ROBERTS: 'Heroine.'

SHAMUS: Go on, man. Go on.

ROBERTS [*Puts the basket of flowers down. Takes the paper from* SHAMUS *and reads the account with a formal air*]: 'Heroine of Sea Disaster. The occupants of Lifeboat Number Six sang the praise of Denver's own Mrs J. J. Brown. They credited her with keeping their lifeboat afloat. They said "Mrs Brown rowed steadily for seven and one half hours."'

SHAMUS [*Proud at last*]: Taught her to row back in Missouri.

ROBERTS [*Continues reading*]: 'When interviewed at her home yesterday, the Denver woman made light of her heroism: "Hell, I got Tobin guts and Brown luck – with that combination who wouldn't be unsinkable?" The unsinkable Mrs Brown will be decorated by the French Government for her courage. When asked about the medal, she said, "A girl can always use another piece of jewellery."'

*Among serious poets, Harriet Monroe and Thomas Hardy early
responded to the fate of* Titanic. *The large-scale poems were by E. J.
Pratt, Anthony Cronin and Hans Magnus Enzensberger. Written in the
five-beat lines of English epic poetry, Pratt's poem attempts epic scale
and succeeds at least in being a well-paced verse telling of the story
from a number of angles (like Lord's later book). The use of dialogue,
technical ship's terms and quotations indicates the mainstream modernism of Pratt's 1033-line poem.*

E. J. PRATT
The Titanic

(1935; from *Complete Poems*, 1989)

The Band

> East side, West side, all around the town,
> The tots sang 'Ring-a-Rosie'
> 'London Bridge is falling down',
> Boys and girls together . . .

The cranks turn and the sixth and seventh swing
Over and down, the 'tiller' answering
'Aye, Aye, sir' to the shouts of officers –
'Row to the cargo ports for passengers.'
The water line is reached, but the ports fail
To open, and the crews of the boats hail
The decks; receiving no response they pull
Away from the ship's side, less than half full.
The eighth caught in the tackle foul is stuck
Half-way. With sixty-five capacity,
Yet holding twenty-four, goes number three.

The sharp unnatural deflection, struck
By the sea-level with the under row
Of dipping port-holes at the forward, show

How much she's going by the head. Behind
The bulkheads, sapping out their steel control,
Is the warp of the bunker press inclined
By many thousand tons of shifting coal.

The smoothest, safest passage to the sea
Is made by number one – the next to go –
Her space is forty – twelve her company:
'Pull like the devil from her – harder – row!
The minute that she founders, not a boat
Within a mile around that will not follow.
What nearly happened at Southampton? So
Pull, pull, I tell you – not a chip afloat,
God knows how far, her suction will not swallow.'

> *Alexander's rag-time band . . .*
> *It's the best band in the land . . .*

Voices From the Deck:
'There goes the Special with the toffs. You'll make
New York tonight rowing like that. You'll take
Your death o'cold out there with all the fish
And ice around.'
　　　　　　　　'Make sure your butlers dish
You up your toddies now, and bring hot rolls
For breakfast.'
　　　　　　　　'Don't forget the finger bowls.'

The engineering staff of thirty-five
Are at their stations: those off-duty go
Of their free will to join their mates below
In the grim fight for steam, more steam, to drive
The pressure through the pumps and dynamo.
Knee-deep, waist-deep in water they remain,
Not one of them seen on the decks again.
The under braces of the rudder showing,
The wing propeller blades begin to rise,
And with them, through the hawse-holes, water flowing –
The angle could not but assault the eyes.
A fifteen minutes, and the fo'c'sle head
Was under. And five more, the sea had shut

The lower entrance to the stairs that led
From C deck to the boat deck – the short cut
For the crew. Another five, the upward flow
Had covered the wall brackets where the glow
Diffusing from the frosted bulbs turned green
Uncannily through their translucent screen.

This poem is the fifth of a six-poem sequence called Of Commerce and
Society. *Hill once wrote: 'Was not the* Titanic *disaster partly the result
of rhetoric? A sinkable ship was called "Unsinkable"; and the realists
and practical men, who are always the blindest dreamers of this world,
were swamped by a slogan.' In one reading of this dense little ode, the
archaic sea is eager to capsize the ambitions of human commerce: it is
the gods who trade in the terse realities behind façades whom we should
be appeasing, in 1912, in 1958, always.*

GEOFFREY HILL
'Ode on the Loss of the *Titanic*'

(*For the Unfallen: Poems 1952–1958*, 1959)

Thriving against façades the ignorant sea
Souses our public baths, statues, waste ground:
Archaic earth-shaker, fresh enemy:
('The tables of exchange being overturned');

Drowns Babel in upheaval and display;
Unswerving, as were the admired multitudes
Silenced from time to time under its sway.
By all means let us appease the terse gods.

Dante is a ghost at the comedy of Titanic, *and he haunts Enzensberger's thirty-three canto post-modernist poem.* Titanic *is to bear the weighty cargo of twentieth-century history: an almost impossible tonnage, but from the leftist angle a manageable pattern emerges. Unlike Pratt, Enzensberger gives his borrowed forms a self-consciousness: the poem comments upon itself and in Canto twenty-seven we read 'There was no such thing as the sinking of the* Titanic./ *It was just a movie, an omen, a hallucination'.*

HANS MAGNUS ENZENSBERGER
The Sinking of the Titanic

(1980)

First Canto

There is someone who listens, who waits,
holds his breath, very close by,
here. He says: This is *my* voice.

Never again, he says,
is it going to be as quiet,
as dry and warm as it is now.

He hears himself
in his gurgling head.
He says: There is no one here

but me. This must be *my* voice.
I wait, I hold my breath,
I listen. The distant rumour

in my ears, antennae
of soft flesh, means nothing.
It is just the beat

of my blood in the veins.
I have been waiting for a long time,
holding my breath.

White noise in the earphones
of my time machine.
Mute cosmic static.

Nobody knocks or cries for help.
No radio signal.
Either this is the end,

I tell myself, or else
we have not yet begun.
Here we are! Now!

A scraping sound. A creaking. A crack.
This is it. An icy fingernail
scratching at the door and stopping short.

Something gives.
An endless length of canvas,
a snow-white strip of linen

being torn, slowly at first
and then more and more briskly
being rent in two with a hissing sound.

This is the beginning.
Listen! Don't you hear it?
Hold fast, for God's sake!

Then there is silence again.
Only a thin tinkle is to be heard
in the cupboards,

a trembling of crystal,
more and more faintly
and dying away.

Do you mean to say
that was all?
Yes. We've had it.

This was the beginning.
The beginning of the end
is always discreet.

It is now 11.40 p.m.
on board. There is a gash
of two hundred yards

underneath the waterline
in the steel-plated hull, slit
by a gigantic knife.

The water is rushing
into the bulkheads.
Thirty yards above sea level

the iceberg, black and silent, passes,
glides by the glittering ship,
and disappears in the dark.

. . .

Fourth Canto

Those were the times! I believed
in every word I wrote, and I wrote
The Sinking of the Titanic.
It was a good poem.
I remember exactly
the way it began, with a sound.
'A scraping sound,' I wrote,
'stopping short. Silence.' No,
it wasn't like that. 'A thin jingling,'
'a clatter of silver.' Yes,
that's the way I began, I think.
More or less. And so forth.
I quote from memory.
I forget the rest.

What a pleasant feeling it was
to be ingenuous! I didn't want to admit to myself
that the tropical party was all over.
(What do you mean by party? It was need,
you bloody fool, need and necessity.)
A few wretched years afterward,

now, it's all finished,
there are plenty of shoes,
plenty of light bulbs and unemployed,
brand-new machines and regulations.
I feel the cold in my bones,
an anachronism
within an anachronism.

I can smell the coke burning.
It is here I reside,
in the most hideous city of Europe,
amongst slowly rotting Prussian princes
and members of the Central Committee,
in bitter, anguished, national seediness,
and I remember, and recollect
my recollections. Don't worry,
I used to tell myself, it's just a fata morgana,
in actual fact the island of Cuba
does not reel under our feet.

And I was right then,
because at that time nothing foundered
except my poem
about the sinking of the *Titanic*.
It was a poem pencilled
in a notebook, wrapped up
in black oilcloth, I had no copy,
because on the entire island of Cuba
there was not one sheet of carbon paper
to be found. Do you like it? I asked
Maria Alexandrovna, and then
I put it into a buff Manila envelope.
It was shipped from Havana harbour
in a mailbag for Paris
which never turned up again.

We all know the rest of the story.
Outside it is snowing. I try
to take up the thread, and sometimes,
now, for example, I think I have found it.

I pull. The veil is rent in two
with a hissing sound, and in the broad daylight
I recognize all of them:
the mulatto girls, the Captain
with his white whiskers, Dante
(1265–1321), Jerome, the stoker
(first name unknown) (1888?–1912),
the Old Master from Umbria
with his paint-stained fingernails,
born in such and such a year
and died thereafter,
Maria Alexandrovna (1943–) –

All of them, those
who froze to death, those who drowned,
1217 altogether, it is said, or 1500,
according to others. Go on squabbling,
maggots! Argue, deathwatch beetles,
about their numbers!
I for one know them all,
even the five Chinese, flattened
like flour bags against the planks
of the lifeboat. I think I know them,
I think they are still alive,
but I would not take an oath on it.

And so I am sitting here, wrapped up
in blankets, while outside the snow
is coming down. I am playing around
with the end, the end of the *Titanic*.
I've nothing better to do.
I have time, like a God.
I have nothing to lose. I deal
with the menu, the radiograms, the drowning men.
I collect them, I pick them up
from the black, icy waters of the past.

Debris, broken sentences,
empty fruit crates, heavy Manila bags,
buff-coloured, soaked, soiled by the brine,

I fetch verses from the waves,
from the dark, warm waves
of the Caribbean,
teeming with sharks,
with dismembered verses, with life belts
and swirling souvenirs.

Cinema's romance with *Titanic* has rarely flagged.

10
Sea of Controversy

Round the decay
Of that colossal wreck, boundless and bare
The lone and level sands stretch far away.
Percy Bysshe Shelley, 'Ozymandias'

Titanic *memorabilia in the shape of promotional ware existed before the maiden voyage. In the Edwardian era there was a craze for collecting postcards in Britain;* Titanic *postcards that celebrated or promoted the ship were followed after her sinking by commemorative postcards, some of them quasi-religious and betraying late Victorian sentimental religiosity. The ship had begun her posthumous career, one that went into partial eclipse (like postcards themselves) until the 1950s. Over the years there have been memorial wall plaques and statues (one of the most impressive of which is the Women's* Titanic *Memorial in Washington, D.C., unveiled in 1931). The desire to grieve and commemorate was tainted by commerce and early there were commemorative chinaware, badges and tobacco tins.*

It was with the first revival of 'Titanicism' that Titanic *societies began.* Titanic *Enthusiasts of America, formed in 1963, became the* Titanic *Historical Society Inc. in 1974 (out of Indian Orchard, Massachusetts). These societies belong to the history of clubs, enthusiasms and pastimes but occasionally skirt the borders of cult and religion.* Titanic *enthusiasts have recently found a new happy hunting ground, the green pastures of the Internet on which they can sport among* Titanic *websites and join online* Titanic *Societies and unbridle their obsession through games and discussions.*

Titanic *museums, formal venues for the display of memorabilia, for stopping* Titanic *in time, opened and became secular churches for* Titanic *enthusiasm. Maritime museums have always been drawn to* Titanic, *and*

*larger museums, maritime or no, have deemed it wise to open permanent
Titanic exhibits, as in Belfast, Halifax and Vancouver.*

*As soon as the ship sank there were those who contemplated its actual
recovery, including the Astor, Guggenheim and Widener families who
wanted the wreck raised. Methods of salvage were dreamed up over the
ensuing decades, but it was not until 1985 that the wreck was located
and filmed – which set in motion the second revival of Titanicism.
Subsequent study of the wreck has been an incentive to deep-water
exploration and to its associated technology. With the retrieval of artefacts, the ship has become a laboratory for the study of seabed corrosion.
Dives have also suggested answers to why the ship sank so quickly:
inferior steel in the ship's plates that allowed them to fracture, inferior
iron rivets that permitted the seams to open readily, six thin slices along
the hull across watertight holds – these are hypotheses based on forensic
analysis of recovered material.*

*But the removal of items from the ship's debris field and the granting
of exclusive rights to do so to an American company has made the waters
around the wreck a sea of controversy. Is the site a graveyard (the U.S.
Congress declared the area a Memorial Site), an archaeological site
or corporate property belonging to the salvors-in-possession? Titanic,
troubling the living stream as it has done from its conception, has
instigated soul-searchings among museum curators, court judges, relatives of Titanic dead, the few remaining survivors, Titanic society
members and marine archaeologists.*

Two research centres, in Woods Hole, Massachusetts and Toulon, France;
two remarkable men, Robert Ballard and Jean-Louis Michel; two
research ships, Knorr *and* Le Suroit; *and two new underwater vehicles,*
Argo *and* S A R, *found* Titanic *on 1 September 1985. Ballard had contem-*
plated discovery of the ship since the 1970s. This excerpt displays the
exuberant nicknaming camaraderie of the successful expedition and the
religious feeling Ballard has always maintained he felt at the site.

ROBERT D. BALLARD WITH RICK ARCHBOLD
The Discovery of *Titanic*

(*The Discovery of the* Titanic, 1995)

At lunchtime on August 31 [1985], after a minor delay to make
some adjustments to *Argo*, we began the eighth pass. The weather was
getting steadily worse and the sea was beginning to build; it seemed
only a matter of time before the storm hit. Evening came and still
nothing. All was quiet in the ranks and I had begun to face defeat. In
only five days we would have to head home. Alone in my cabin after
dinner, I washed my face and stared into the mirror. The specially
designed *Titanic* patch – a gift from Jean-Louis Michel – sewn on the
breast of my blue jumpsuit stared back at me. Each member of the
scientific party had proudly sewn on one of these as we had sailed out
of the Azores. That now seemed light-years away. Could it have been
less than three weeks ago?

Whatever happened I knew I'd still be wearing the patch when we
sailed into our home port at Woods Hole. Right then, however, I hoped
our return would be under cover of darkness.

I went back to the control van, where the Crash Crew had just come
on watch. Line nine was now in progress. Maybe Martin and Bernard
would redeem their earlier humiliation and be the ones to spot the first
sign of wreckage. But I doubted it. Wearily, I laid out the next line on
the plotting table so navigator Cathy Offinger would know which course
to follow when it came time to begin line ten. Our coverage of the new
search area was now nearly complete. I noted that line nine would
take us directly to the northeastern limit of previous S A R coverage,

overlapping the portion they had missed – that sliver of bottom one mile wide and five miles long.

I stayed in the van until the midnight watch change. Jean-Louis and the other members of the Watch of Quiet Excellence came tumbling in, still rubbing their eyes and holding warm cups of coffee, breaking the quiet mood with a sudden infusion of noise and energy. With the changing of the guard, seven separate and simultaneous conversations filled the command centre as the outgoing member of each station reported status to his replacement. The pleasant hubbub was occasionally punctuated by calls coming in over the speakers hooked up to the bridge, all underscored with the never-ending background noise of printers printing and sonars pinging. Then, after ten or fifteen minutes, the old watch was gone and the new watch settled down to work. This was always the quietest time of all – before the music and gossip returned. So began the graveyard shift of September 1, 1985.

During his watch, Jean-Louis was to continue line nine until *Argo* crossed over into the area already covered by SAR and then head north one mile to begin line ten, which should happen not long before the watch changed at 4 a.m. Since the injury to *Argo*'s cable, Jean-Louis and Earl had maintained their reputation as the master flyers who covered more ground than the other watches – they had simply changed their style, speeding the ship up (and paying out the full length of undamaged cable) until *Argo* kited to maximum viewing height, then slowing it down again.

With Jean-Louis in charge and Harris's Heroes in the van, I knew *Argo* was in good hands. Now it was time for me to take a break. But before I left, I heard Billy Lange make his nightly forecast. The last couple of nights he'd taken to predicting exactly when the *Titanic* would be found. He'd pick a spot on the chart and estimate when *Argo* would be there. Tonight, he said, they would find the ship between 2 and 2.30. The *Titanic* sank at 2.20 a.m. Lange was getting superstitious, I thought, but I hoped against hope that tonight he would be right. As I left the van, 'I Heard It Through the Grapevine' played softly on the stereo.

Back in my cabin, propped up in my bunk in warm flannel pyjamas, I picked up Chuck Yeager's autobiography. As I began to read, my mind soon left the ocean depths and was soaring into the stratosphere.

Unbeknownst to me, a drama was beginning to play itself out in the control van below. About 12 minutes before 1 a.m., Bill Lange turned to Stu Harris and said, 'What are we going to do to keep ourselves awake tonight?' All they'd seen so far was more mud, endless miles of bland, featureless bottom. Stu didn't answer. His eyes were glued to the *Argo* monitor. He had seen a new kind of image. 'There's something,' he said simply, as he pointed to the TV screen. Suddenly, every member of the sleepy watch became alive and alert, but no one could believe that it wasn't just another false alarm, or a practical joke. Had Zoo Crew fever infected the Watch of Quiet Excellence?

But no. Stu switched *Argo*'s camera from forward-looking camera to down-looking and a few seconds later, Bill Lange exclaimed, 'Wreckage!' And sure enough, there on the video screen were the unmistakable images of things man-made. A few seconds later, Stu added his exultant note: 'Bingo!'. and then the van echoed with a chorus: 'Yeah!' followed by shrieks and war whoops.

Moments later, Lieutenant Rey on the sonar reported, 'I'm getting a hard contact.' For a few minutes there was nothing more to see save for a few small glacial boulders. Had they been seeing things after all? A discussion started as to whether they should go wake Ralph White so he could start filming. Then, at two minutes to one, more small definite debris fragments began to appear. They decided to go get Ralph.

After the long, tedious, fruitless search and yesterday's minor mutiny, no one wanted to drag me out of the sack on a false alarm. Nothing is more embarrassing than to become a member of the 'I Saw a Flare Club'. Bill Lange was the first to suggest that 'Someone should go get Bob', but no one made a move. By four minutes past one, everyone in the van had become convinced something was up, but as all sorts of wreckage streamed past, no one wanted to leave. Now Stu Harris said, 'Let's go get Bob', but still there were no volunteers. Ironically, the ship's cook, who had never before ventured into the van, now wandered in. He sure had picked a hell of a moment to take his first peek. The van crew immediately pressed him into service and sent him up to rouse me.

While the cook headed aft and up to my quarters, something new appeared amid the unrecognizable wreckage passing on the video screen. It was perfectly circular . . . 'A boiler?' someone mused. 'It's a boiler!' Bill Lange sang out. Now there could be absolutely no doubt. But Jean-Louis still wouldn't believe what his eyes were telling him. He opened the book containing a facsimile of the now-famous 1911 *Ship-builder* article on the *Olympic* and the *Titanic* and turned to the page with the pictures of the boilers. He looked from page to screen and back again, repeating over and over, as if to convince himself, 'Yes, it *ees* a boiler.'

When the cook stuck his head through the door of my cabin, I was still busy breaking the sound barrier with Yeager. Finally, I'd gotten the *Titanic* out of my mind. 'The guys think you should come down to the van,' he said. It took a couple of seconds for the import of his words to penetrate, then I sprang out of my bunk, Yeager's book flying, pulled on my jumpsuit over my pyjamas, and practically knocked the cook out of the way in my haste to get to the van. I must have run the three decks down and aft in about thirty seconds.

When I burst into the van, Stu informed me that *Argo* had just passed over a massive ship's boiler. The initial elation in the room had subsided to a simmer, but was still ready to boil over again. Quickly, they replayed the tape and sure enough I saw the image of a big ship's boiler – *Titanic*'s. I didn't yelp or shout. In fact, for a few seconds, I didn't say anything. Then, totally at a loss for words, I simply kept repeating in a quiet but incredulous voice, 'God damn. God damn . . .'

I turned to Jean-Louis. The look in his eyes said everything. The *Titanic* had been found. We'd been right all along. Then he said softly, 'It was not luck. We earned it.'

Our hunt was almost over. Somewhere very near us lay the RMS *Titanic*.

Around us the van again erupted in whoops and shouts. I went around and congratulated the members of the watch, shaking hands, patting people on the back. But in the midst of my elation, I began to realize the danger we were in. Larger and larger pieces of wreckage were now passing under *Argo* and Earl had to winch in to avoid hitting them. We didn't yet know where the main wreck was. If large pieces of it were intact, they would loom up quite suddenly – too suddenly for even Grumpy to avoid. I cautioned the watch, 'Be careful now about the altitude.' But we were all so mesmerized by what we were seeing that it was some minutes before I converted the warning into a command.

As the images on the video screen grew more and more vivid – large pieces of twisted hull plating, portholes, a piece of railing turned on its side – for the first time since I had started on this quest twelve years before, the full human impact of the *Titanic*'s terrifying tragedy began to sink in. Here at the bottom of the ocean lay not only the graveyard of a great ship, but the only fitting monument to the more than 1,500 people who had perished when she went down. And we were the very first people in seventy-three years to come to this precise spot to pay our respects. Images from the night of the disaster – a story I now knew by heart – flashed through my mind with painful intensity.

At 1.13 a.m. – eight minutes after *Argo* passed over the boiler – I snapped out of my reverie and gave the order to raise *Argo* to its strobing altitude of 80 to 100 feet. I was being careful, but I didn't realize until later just how dangerous our situation was. Unwittingly, we were coming into the wreck at the worst spot. I would never have flown *Argo* through that place in the way that I did, knowing what I know now. It was as if we were towing our sled through downtown Manhattan after World War III. We were only about twelve feet above the *Titanic*'s deck.

Word had now spread through the ship and people were pouring into the van. The place was becoming a madhouse. With *Argo*'s running lights turned off, the newcomers saw not a real-time image of the bottom, but a series of snapshots taken every eight seconds – a sort of disco effect. By 1.25, we had crossed the debris field and I decided to pull *Argo* up. In this northwestern corner of our new search area, the tracking was poor. I wanted to put in a new transponder net before surveying the wreckage in detail. Besides, bedlam had erupted in the van – it was time for celebration before getting back to work – and people had started to pass around paper cups of Mateus wine purchased in the Azores. At least the stuff was bubbly. It was the closest we came to champagne.

I won't soon forget that scene of triumph and jubilation. Emory Kristof clapped me on the back and then went back to snapping pictures. Ralph White filmed furiously away. Jean-Louis grinned broadly. Everybody was talking at once, congratulating each other, while trying to pay attention to the job at hand.

Then, at the height of this victory celebration, our mood suddenly crashed as if *Argo* had again hit bottom. Someone – I don't remember who – pointed up to the twin clocks, one with Zulu (Greenwich time) and one with local time on it and said something like 'Oh my God!' It was approaching 2 a.m. local time, very close to the exact hour of the *Titanic*'s sinking. That was all it took to break our mood. Here we were just catching our breaths at the peak of elation and suddenly we felt awkward, even sad. Part of our vulnerability may have been due to the fact that for the first time since the search had started we were without a purpose. All at once the professional was replaced by the human being. The van became quiet.

I said something like, 'I don't know how you people feel, and I don't want to impose my feelings on you all, but I know that in about twenty minutes I'm going out on the fantail. If anyone wants to join me, they're welcome. If not, that's okay.' That was it. Then I walked out of the van.

I don't remember exactly what I did for the next twenty minutes. I just found a quiet corner to be alone with my thoughts. And I imagine a lot of others did the same. When I got to the fantail, quite a few people had gathered. I raised the Harland & Wolff flag, the emblem of the Belfast shipyard that had built the *Titanic*. I wasn't trying to be theatrical about it, it just seemed the right thing to do. The storm that had appeared to threaten us had passed by at a safe distance and the weather was beautiful: the sky was clear and filled with stars, the sea calm. Except for the moon, it was just like the night the *Titanic* went down. I spoke only a few words: 'I really don't have much to say, but I thought we might just observe a few moments of silence.'

It was one thing to have won – to have found the ship. It was another thing to be there. That was the spooky part. I could see the *Titanic* as she slipped nose first into the glassy water. Around me were the ghostly shapes of the lifeboats and the piercing shouts and screams of people freezing to death in the water.

Our little memorial service lasted five, maybe ten minutes. Then I just said, 'Thank you all. Now let's get back to work.'

The writer believes Titanic *has now made the metaphoric journey from coffin-ship to historical site and is therefore a suitable place of secular pilgrimage and scientific study. At some point you take off the glasses through which you see distress and don a second pair through which you see history, science and incidental economic opportunity.*

WILLIAM F. BUCKLEY, JR.
'Down to the Great Ship'

(*New York Times*, 18 October 1987)

After being asked one final time whether I suffered from claustrophobia, I was directed to the shoulder-wide opening of the little submarine, leading to vertical iron railing-steps descending into the tubular control centre of the *Nautile*.

It is the $20 million diadem of I F E R M E R, a scientific offshoot of the French Government – an underwater exploratory vessel built with titanium, six feet in diameter at its widest point and weighing only 18 tons. It can descend to depths of 20,000 feet. The chief pilot occupies the berth on the port side. Behind him, sitting on an abbreviated chair, is the co-pilot. The starboard berth is for the 'observer', in this case me. Each of us has a porthole built of one-foot thick plastic. The co-pilot, in addition, has two sets of 8-inch television screens. The first set looks ahead via remote video, one camera video trained to look dead ahead, the other, to pivot. The second set of videos portrays at close range and at longer range the exact operation of the mechanical arms operating from the side of the *Nautile*, designed to pick up objects from the sea bed. With aid of the video, the operator can exactly instruct the arms.

The overhead hatch is now tightly sealed and as you look about you, you close your eyes slowly, hoping this will not be the moment you contract claustrophobia. Once lifted and positioned by crane and halyard, the *Nautile* is dragged by cable to the launching end of the *Nadir*, the mother ship, dropped into the ocean, and towed by the *Nadir* and by frogmen on a rubber Zodiac a short distance through the water. The descent begins.

At about 2.20 a.m., losing finally its fight to stay afloat, 2 hours 40 minutes after it glanced the iceberg, the *Titanic*'s stern rose up so high that the huge ship was almost vertical over the water. It paused there, appeared, in the description of some witnesses in their lifeboats, to shudder, and then eased back to an angle of about 45 degrees, as if cocking itself to spring ahead on its long descent. Seconds later it catapulted into its plunge, with its live company of some 1,500 people, including the eight-piece band, which had been performing for the condemned right up until it was no longer possible to stand up. Like everyone else, they were wearing life preservers. It is calculated that it took the *Titanic* approximately 10 minutes to reach bottom and that it was travelling, when it hit the ocean floor, at a speed of 20 miles per hour.

To descend the same distance, two and a half miles to the ocean floor, the *Nautile* takes 90 minutes, which means a descent at just less than 1.66 miles per hour. You try to sit up, which requires you to raise your knees six inches or so – there is no room to stretch them out. You have been advised not to eat breakfast, and dutifully you have not.

It is 11.30 a.m., 30 minutes after our descent began, lunch time aboard the *Nautile*. The co-pilot, Pierre Yves, brings out the two little packages wrapped in aluminium foil. The first course is a hard-boiled egg. Do I wish any salt? *'S'il vous plaît, oui.'* Then there is cold roast beef and French bread. Followed by cheese and a plum or a peach.

'Do you have anything to drink?' I ask abstractly. Answer: yes; they have water. But it is not thereupon proffered, though you are left believing that a direct request would produce the plastic bottle. It isn't any lack of French hospitality, it is just that it would be such an awful *dérangement* if the observer along the way experienced an undeniable call of nature. Just the physical gyrations necessary to accomplish this bring to mind a Marx Brothers three-in-a-bed sequence. You pass.

What to do, as the pilot and co-pilot exchange rapid, technical French? I had arrived on the *Nautile* with two bulging plastic bags, causing the chief pilot, Georges, to frown and ask, Did I really need all that – *équipage*? Embarrassed, I had pulled out the larger of my three flash-lights, and three of my six cassette tapes. But that did leave me with (1) two small flashlights; (2) a book (a thriller to distract me, during the long descent and the long ascent; (3) a little dictating machine (I might want to make notes, and there is hardly room for even the smallest lap top), which dictating machine serves also as a Walkman, for which, (4) I was left with three cassettes. The second parcel carried (5) a thick white sweater to augment protection from the 38-degree cold at ocean-floor level already provided by long winter underwear, regular sweater and the fire-resistant coveralls provided by the French; (6) a little can of Right Guard, in case the chill exercised less than all its usual functions; and then (7) a set of kneepads furnished by Ralph White, my new best friend, an American professional jack-of-all-trades, a genial member of the entrepreneur's team who knew more about diving, history, mechanics, ships, airplanes and the sea than anyone I had ever met.

Why kneepads, for heaven's sake? You will see, Ralph said; and indeed I would see. When you are lying with your nose against the porthole you need to put your left knee somewhere, since there is no room to stretch out. So it ends up on the narrow knurled ice-cold titanium bottom strip between you and Georges. Try then bringing up your knee when it is protected only by underwear, pants, and fire suit for a half hour against the cold grid; and then give thanks to the Lord for Ralph. The kneepads plus gloves for hands that would become cold and, (8) perhaps most important, an inflatable rubber pillow, this to lay over the little metal bar that runs either under your chest while you are lying down, or else under your back when reclining during the vertical passages. There are moments when you wonder whether an extra million dollars might not have been dredged up to cushion that bisecting rod.

But the great moment is coming. We will reach bottom at 3,784 metres, and Georges will turn on the outside beams when we reach 3,550 metres. We are in place, standing guard by our portholes. The lights flash on. Nothing to see, though the water is startlingly clear, diaphanous to the extent of our light's beam, an apparent 25 to 30 feet ahead, never mind that it is pitch dark out there.

Then, gradually, it happens: We descend slowly to what looks like a yellow-white sandy beach, sprinkled with black rocklike objects. These, it transpires, are pieces of coal. There must be 100,000 of them in the area we survey, between the bow of the ship and the stern, a half-mile back. On my left is a man's outdoor shoe. Left shoe. Made, I would say, of suede of some sort. I cannot quite tell whether it is laced up. And then, just off to the right a few feet, a snow-white teacup. Just sitting there, thank you, on the sand. I liken the sheer neatness of the tableau to a display that might have been prepared for a painting by Salvador Dali. Will we, I ask Georges anxiously, pause to scoop up the shoe?

No. The expedition does not pick up articles of personal clothing.
What about the teacup?
Only if it is embroidered in blue. The distinction, I learn, is that the

blue-bordered china is rarer than the plain white, which was used by the 712 steerage passengers. The 337 first-class passengers had the fancier, blue-bordered china. Enough of the former has been picked up in the 26 previous dives. Time is limited, and we will not use it up on redundancies.

On and on we float, our bottom resting sometimes six inches from the ocean floor, sometimes a metre or two. We are looking for targets of opportunity, which is why I am expected to keep looking hard to starboard, but also specifically for a piece of the command mechanism from the bridge (the signal handles brought back sharply by First Officer William Murdoch when he reversed engines, moments after the iceberg was sighted dead ahead). The control mechanism has been photographed lying on the ocean floor in the area we are now covering, and instructions are being radioed from above ('130 degrees, proceed for 60 metres') to direct us to our quarries. And then a portion of a leaded window, missing from a reconstruction of an ornamental *vitrine* window that had been a part of the luxuriant decorations in first class. And a man's leather satchel, contents unknown.

We were below, searching and scooping, for six and one half cold hours. Ralph said I would find it surprising how quickly the time passed. That was not exactly what I felt after two or three hours. But the sensation, in microcosm, was vivid, exhilarating and uncomplicated by any philosophical misgivings about our mission. I did not feel any kinship to the voyeur; no more than when, a year earlier, I ogled at the tombs in the Nile or, a dozen years ago, at the catacombs in Lima beneath the great cathedral, where the bones of thousands of Incas lie.

I was a passive part of an archaeological venture that was also an adventure – only about 150 men and women in the world have dived as deep in the water as I have now done. The excavation is singular because it is being conducted in a part of the planet heretofore thought totally inaccessible, let alone accessible to people who have in mind actually collecting an inventory of items that, for 75 years, have lain on the ocean floor, objects last seen by men and women two-thirds of whom died a quite awful death, victims of the hubris of an assortment of thoughtless naval architects, cocky seamen and mindless money-men.

Finally the moment came to terminate our sortie, to begin our slow ascent. After a few minutes, permission was requested over the radio (permission granted) to jettison one of our two lead weight ballasts, permitting a sharp increase in our rate of ascent.

I tried to sit up, just to find something different to do with my bones. But I had to lean just slightly forward. Otherwise, I might lean just slightly back, in which case I might brush up against one of those hundred toggle switches behind me and, who knows, flip the one that would toss me out between the shoe and the teacup – the pressure out there was 6,000 pounds per square inch.

Time to use the Walkman? But to recover the satchel, dig out the relevant parts and wire in my ears, represented a series of exertions on the order of stopping to change one's socks while climbing to the top of Mount Everest.

So I half-froze, half-continued trying to read my stubbornly unprepossessing thriller with my flashlight between my teeth, my hands behind me, supporting my arched back, and exchanged every now and then a drollery, in my kitchen-French, with the pilots.

I looked for the one hundredth time at the fast-changing depth-meter. This time it joyfully told me that we had just about reached the surface. I knew we were within 50 metres when the little sub began to roll, reflecting surface turbulence. It seemed an age before the frogmen were there to secure us to the halyard coming down from the ship's crane. But eventually we were airborne into the mother-ship's womb. The hatch was turned, and I climbed out; a Superman grin on my face, I have to admit.

To some, Ballard is a 'marine cowboy', a restless explorer of the deeps who occasionally comes up for moral and rhetorical air. But this is an eloquent plea for an end to salvage of Titanic *and a beginning of our respectful 'telepresence' at the wreck. Ballard is a technological visionary at home with the thought of virtual travel and even with warfare waged virtually (which still, as we know from the 1991 Gulf War, yet kills and maims people). Ballard repeated his concerns about salvage in the Epilogue to the 1995 edition of* The Discovery of the Titanic.

ROBERT D. BALLARD
'Statement Before the [U.S.] House Merchant Marine and Fisheries Committee 29 October 1985'

(*Oceanus*, 1985)

Since man has built ships, nature and man himself have sent many of those crafts of commerce and of war back to the bottom of the sea. Those that sank in the deep sea were felt lost forever while those sinkings which occurred in shallow water have, at times, been the focus of intense search and recovery operations. Since Alexander the Great descended to the bottom of the sea in the first crude diving bell, salvaging the treasures of the sea has become a part of our folklore. To many Americans, underwater treasure hunters and salvagers are marine cowboys with the wind blowing in their faces and the wild seas to ride.

We have followed their exploits in the news and seen little harm in their actions except when they have clearly destroyed wrecks of historical value. This conflict of interest between salvagers and marine historians and archaeologists is at the centre of public attention. Resting in 13,000 feet of water off the North American coast is the greatest shipwreck in man's history, the RMS *Titanic* and, unlike most shallow water wrecks, it is in excellent condition.

The chances that a ship sinking in shallow water will end up like the *Titanic* are small. Many ships which sink in shallow water have struck a reef and are severely damaged or went aground in a storm and were violently pounded against a reef or a rocky coastline. Once the remains of these ships came to rest, their wooden planks are food for the worm boring organisms that live in the shallow waters of the world's oceans. The metallic objects began to rust in the oxygen-rich waters and encrusting organisms flourished in the sun-bathed surface layers slowly turning man-made outlines into mounds of coral or current-swept sand dunes. In many cases, all that remains is the cargo itself and the treasure hunters see no conflict in the salvage efforts.

I am neither an archaeologist nor treasure hunter; I am a marine scientist and explorer. I am not here to enter the debate as much as I am here to point out that the technological genius most Americans are so proud of has entered the deep sea in full force and placed before us a new reality. In short, the great pyramids of the deep are now accessible to man. He can either plunder them like the grave robbers of Egypt or protect them for the countless generations which will follow ours.

Unlike the shallow reefs off Florida which reduce a wreck to an unrecognizable mound of encrusted coral, the deep sea is a preserving environment. Ships in the deep were, in many cases, sent to the bottom without having sustained any major structural damage. They either took on water during a storm and sank, or like the *Titanic*, had a hole punched in their hull. In the deep sea, shipwrecks enter a world of total darkness which makes the growth of plants impossible. Without plants, few animals can be found, creating a desert-like world with an organism here and another one there. The freezing temperatures of the deep sea further inhibit biological activity as does the extreme pressure. The pressure at the *Titanic* site is more than 6,000 pounds per square inch. Far from land, the rate of sedimentation in the deep sea is measured at an inch or so per thousand years. And in some deep sea environments like the historically travelled Mediterranean Sea, the bottom waters are poor in oxygen further making the deep sea a giant preserving refrigerator.

Some would say, so what. If the deep sea is a great preserver of man's history, what good does it do us if it is left in total darkness beyond the reach of man's enquiring mind. My answer is it isn't and each day we are moving at a faster and faster pace to make it easily accessible to the general public. The technology we used to find the *Titanic* is the vanguard of the very technology man will use to find, document and revisit historic pieces of preserved history in the deep sea. Known as 'telepresence', this technology in cruder form has been with us for many years. Going to the movies or turning on the television or picking up the phone are all forms of telepresence. The ability to project your thoughts, your eyes, and eventually your hands, is each day becoming an increasing reality. Exploration in the deep sea is not driving this technology, but it is beginning to benefit from it. The space programme with its robots on Mars and Venus, the military with its desire to remove humans from the risks of combat, and the commercial world with their evolving television coverage and the proliferation of multiple cinemas, are the driving forces of telepresence technology. Cinemas are becoming smaller and eventually more personalized. Commercial companies are beginning to build small cinemas inside flight simulators for a life-like trip through the Universe.

I strongly believe that if the *Titanic* is left alone that within the next few years, beginning as early as next year, robotic vehicles will be able to enter its beautifully designed rooms and document in colour its preserved splendour. No salvage operation in the world could duplicate this feat.

The *Titanic* is just one such example. Literally thousands of ships lie in the deep sea awaiting mankind. The question is, will he come to plunder or to appreciate? This is a debate which grows louder, not quieter. Technologists, like myself, can only cause this problem and suggest its possible impact, but Congress must take the necessary actions and, in my case, hopefully before the *Titanic* is destroyed.

The issue of the role of maritime museums in the bitterly contested underwater terrain of Titanic *salvage was brought to the surface in 1994 when the National Maritime Museum in Greenwich mounted an exhibition of 150 items recovered by the American salvors, RMS Titanic Inc. The Head of Exhibitions and Display at the National Maritime Museum defended the Museum's display of* Titanic *debris field artefacts in its* Wreck of the Titanic *exhibit in the teeth of gale-force opposition. The ethics of corporate partnership and sponsorship in public educational activities are an issue throughout European and American societies.*

STEPHEN DEUCHAR
'The Case for the National Maritime Museum'

(Titanic *International*, 1994)

I would like to say immediately that the National Maritime Museum's decision to mount the exhibition on October 94 to April 95 was taken neither swiftly nor lightly. We canvassed opinion in many quarters: other museums, families of survivors, families of those who died, archaeologists, conservators, *Titanic* societies, maritime societies, and members of the public. Many views emerged – most for, some against, all offered sincerely and politely. I recall with particular gratitude a meeting with Edward and Karen Kamuda and Don Lynch of the [American] Titanic Historical Society at the Museum last autumn, where together we tried to unravel some of the complex issues involved and ended in amicable agreement to disagree. Such is the stuff of healthy debate.

In the end, the Museum's fourteen Trustees, chaired by Admiral of the Fleet the Lord Lewin and including HRH Prince Philip, decided early in 1994 that the NMM could not and should not forgo the opportunity to influence the future destiny of these artefacts by playing a part in determining the way they are to be displayed and interpreted, and the way they are to be preserved for posterity. For it seems to us that two critical questions emerge from all the debate that has taken place. First, do objects closely associated with the wreck of the *Titanic* help to explain, elucidate and evoke contact with this most famous of maritime stories, and, second, should steps be taken to ensure that any objects raised from the wrecksite are not sold off, are properly preserved and are kept together as an integrated collection eventually in a permanent home? The answers to both these questions is, we strongly believe, yes.

Because of this, we have decided to proceed in the exhibition project with the New York-based company RMS Titanic, Inc., and as part of our agreement to set up an International Advisory Committee (with representatives from the UK, USA, Canada, Sweden, Norway and France) to help us make the right decisions along the possibly circuitous and difficult road to establishing a Titanic Memorial Museum.

Of course we respect the views of those who think differently on these two issues, or who think that other considerations are more important. In particular we accept that calling a wrecksite a 'gravesite' will always elicit a strong emotive response; and we are aware that the more rational contrary view may fall on deaf ears. But that contrary view exists and gathers momentum nonetheless: let us remember that the real tragedy took place on the surface, and that the vast seabed debris field (between the two parts of the separated hull) from where the artefacts have been recovered is not a 'gravesite' but an archaeological site of considerable importance cradling the material fragments of one of history's most famous episodes and, as such, an incomparable resource for reconstructing a picture of international society in 1912 across all social classes. Of course our belief that the past is tenuous and intangible without the preservation and presentation of its physical remnants may seem a narrow, museum-centred view of the world. But we can only get on with our job. Our instincts in museums are to find and preserve the finest evidence of the past and to present it selectively and searchingly to our public.

If, as has become clear in professional circles, there is now a growing acceptance of the archaeological importance of the wrecksite, the NMM acknowledges that there is still some residual suspicion about the methods and techniques of artefact recovery employed during the 1987 and 1993 expeditions undertaken by IFREMER (the French national oceanographic research agency who worked with Robert Ballard in 1985 in locating the wreck) in conjunction with RMS Titanic, Inc. Such suspicion, like much suspicion, has proved unfounded: the NMM's own archaeologist has been given free access to IFREMER's records and we find to our pleasure that the site mapping and recovery operations were undertaken with scrupulous regard to archaeological good practice; indeed the care and professionalism, backed up by remarkable technology, with which they were conducted sets new standards in the field of nautical archaeology.

Likewise, some rather bizarre allegations made against the standards of artefact conservation and preservation in Norfolk, Virginia, following the 1993 expedition, have proved wholly without foundation. Our own Head of Conservation has recently inspected all the 1993 material (currently at conservation laboratories in France) and is highly impressed by the standards that are being maintained whilst the full conservation programme, to museum standards, is planned. We cannot help feeling that, despite the evidence, some people really want to believe that things have been done badly by RMS Titanic, Inc.! My impression is that some people who aren't involved in the project really wish they could be; this often causes ill-feeling and the truth can get badly distorted. In fact the NMM – which has enjoyed a first-hand, not a second-hand or third-hand view – has been consistently impressed by all aspects of the conduct of the company and its personnel since we first made contact with them two and a half years ago. They are striving to do things properly.

Of course the company and its shareholders, who have spent some $12 million to date in recovering and conserving the artefacts, hope to recover their outlay and make a profit in the end. And I am aware that there are always dangers when commercial and cultural imperatives become entwined. But very little deep-ocean archaeology takes place these days without partnerships with commerce: for without capital these expeditions simply would not get underway, and, without the expeditions, shipwrecks would remain as heritage out-of-reach – their artefacts lost to our culture and the physical reality of history slipping, crumbling away.

To their credit and our reward, RMS Titanic, Inc. has rescued about 2,600 objects from the *Titanic* site – a tiny, tiny fraction of the whole, but in fact a great financial liability in themselves. For once retrieved they have to be conserved, catalogued, interpreted, and displayed: on top of the expenditure so far, millions more will be spent before the international version of the Greenwich exhibition is launched. It is a very heavy, pretty risky, investment. It is fair to hope our partners succeed in getting their money back; it may take them some time. They may not make their fortune. Probably, far more money has already been made from the *Titanic* story by others – through films, books, videos and the mountains of merchandise generated over the decades . . .

We think it is our duty as the world's leading maritime museum to set out the facts and the issues very clearly and very objectively; rather than shirking controversy we aim to explore it, allowing the public proper access to the facts. Above all we believe that the artefacts displayed in the Greenwich exhibition, in the subsequent touring exhibition and finally in a Titanic Memorial Museum, are the most powerful and most fitting tribute to the *Titanic* story that the NMM can ever make. There is no better way to do it and we are proud to be involved.

11
Ship of State

For decades Titanic *was a source of embarrassment to her owners and builders. Little wonder: sinkings do not encourage shipbuilding orders. The decades' long official reticence began as early as March 1913 when Father Frank Browne SJ – who sailed on* Titanic *from Southampton to Queenstown, taking marvellous photographs along the way – wished to give illustrated lectures on the great ship. White Star requested him to desist 'as we do not wish the memory of this calamity to be perpetuated'.*

Titanic *was the product of a long intertwined culture of industrialism, entrepreneurship, the Calvinist work ethic, meritocratic ideas, Ulster–Scots application and Victorian English progressivism. It is no coincidence that Edward Harland wrote the chapter entitled 'Shipbuilding in Belfast – Its Origin and Progress' for* Men of Invention and Industry (1897) *by Samuel Smiles, he of self-help fame. 'If all true patriots would go and do likewise,' Harland ended, 'there would be nothing to fear for the prosperity and success of Ireland.'*

But there was something to fear – Irish nationalism. The first vote on the Third Irish Home Rule Bill in the British House of Commons was taken the very day people in Belfast were reading of the loss of Titanic. *Members of the Institution of Mechanical Engineers visited Belfast in July 1912, wishing to see for themselves where such behemoths as* Titanic *were created, but knew public interest was fastened on the question of whether or not Ireland would be granted Home Rule, provoking possibly armed resistance by Protestant unionists.*

It was the political fever that softened the blow to Ulster pride of the loss of Titanic. *In any case, actively religious Protestants were, like their American counterparts, in two minds about the luxury and materialism the ship seemed to embody and many were not surprised to see the hand of the Lord in its destruction, as the sermons in Protestant churches across the north of Ireland on the Sunday after the disaster showed.*

After the partitioning of the island into Northern Ireland and Irish Free State in 1921, Titanic sank into the Unionist subconscious. The founding of the new state and the foundering of the ship became confused. The splendidly arrogant Stormont Parliament building could be seen as a stationary Titanic. The new state was always in danger of being sunk by the chillingly impersonal 'iceberg' dynamics of Irish nationalism.

Whereas Irish-American reaction to the disaster was unambiguous, hostile reaction by Irish Catholics did not materialize until after the setting up of Northern Ireland and they found themselves marooned in a Protestant, Unionist statelet. It was later that Catholic Titanic folklore surfaced, for example that the registration number of Titanic, if read in a mirror, formed the words No Pope. Catholics came to see Orange hubris in the disaster as American blacks saw white hubris.

Nowadays, for a number of reasons, the reluctance in Northern Ireland to celebrate Titanic has melted and embarrassment has given way to renewed pride. Titanic is a ship that is coming in for everyone.

*Andrews is one of the few unblemished heroes of the sinking. Despite
the bizarre claim by an American woman in the 1940s that she had
been rescued by Andrews who (bribed by Ismay to make himself scarce)
took her with him into hiding after the disaster, the story grew that
Andrews stayed pondering Norman Wilkinson's commissioned painting
over the smoking-room mantelpiece,* The Approach of the New World.
*Andrews was a much-loved engineering genius. His place in Irish culture
at the time – as a Unitarian, Unionist and staunch Empire-man – is
complex. The Irish nationalists Sir Horace Plunkett and Erskine Childers
paid high tribute to his mind and mastery. (Bullock (1865–1935) was
a noted Irish novelist.)*

SHAN F. BULLOCK
The Death of Thomas Andrews

(*Thomas Andrews Shipbuilder,* 1912)

It is almost certain that Andrews, who knew the ship as no one
else did, realized at his first sight of her wounds – a three hundred feet
gash, six compartments open to the sea and perhaps twenty feet of
water in one or more of them – that she was doomed. Possibly with
some of his faithful assistants, probably with Captain Smith, he had
made a thorough examination of the damaged side, reporting to the
Captain as result of his examination that the ship could not live more
than an hour and a half, and advising him to clear away the boats.

How this order was carried out, with what skill and unselfishness on
the part of Captain Smith and his officers, has been told elsewhere in
full detail; nor is it necessary to record further here than that eventually,
after two hours of heroic work, a total of 652 lives left the *Titanic* in
eighteen boats. Subsequently 60 more were rescued from the sea, or
transferred from the collapsibles, making a sum total of 712 rescued by
the *Carpathia.* 712 out of 2,201: it seems tragically few! Yet at midnight
it may have seemed to Andrews that fewer still could be saved, for not
even he hoped that his ship could live for two hours and twenty minutes
more.

As he came up from the grim work of investigation he saw Miss Sloan
and told her that as an accident had happened it would be well, just by

way of precaution, to get her passengers to put on warm clothing and their lifebelts and assemble on the boat deck. But she read his face, 'which had a look as though he were heart broken', and asked him if the accident were not serious. He said it was very serious; then, bidding her keep the bad news quiet for fear of panic, he hurried away to the work of warning and rescue.

Another stewardess gives an account of Andrews, bareheaded and insufficiently clad against the icy cold, going quietly about bidding the attendants to rouse all passengers and get them up to the boats.

Overhearing him say to Captain Smith on the upper deck, 'Well, three have gone already, Captain,' she ran to the lower stairway and to her surprise found water within six steps of her feet. Whereupon she hurried above to summon help, and returning met Andrews, who told her to advise passengers to leave the upper deck.

Ten minutes went. The water had crept further up the stairway. Again Andrews came to her and said, 'Tell them to put on warm clothing, see that everyone has a lifebelt and get them all up to the boat deck.'

Another fifteen minutes went. The top of the stairway was now nearly awash. A second time Andrews came. 'Open up all the spare rooms,' he ordered. 'Take out all lifebelts and spare blankets and distribute them.'

This was done. Attendants and passengers went above to the boat deck. But returning for more belts, the stewardess again met Andrews. He asked her whether all the ladies had left their rooms. She answered 'Yes, but would make sure.'

'Go round again,' said he; and then, 'Did I not tell you to put on your lifebelt. Surely you have one?'

She answered 'Yes, but I thought it mean to wear it.'

'Never mind that,' said he. 'Now, if you value your life, put on your coat and belt, then walk round the deck and let the passengers see you.'

'He left me then,' writes the stewardess, 'and that was the last I saw of what I consider a true hero and one of whom his country has cause to be proud.'

In how far Andrews' efforts and example were the means of averting what might well have been an awful panic, cannot be said; but sure it is that all one man could do in such service, both personally and by way of assisting the ship's officers, was done by him. 'He was here, there and everywhere,' says Miss Sloan, 'looking after everybody, telling the women to put on lifebelts, telling the stewardesses to hurry the women up to the boats, all about everywhere, thinking of everyone but himself.'

Others tell a similar story, how calm and unselfish he was, now pausing on his way to the engine-room to reassure some passengers, now earnestly begging women to be quick, now helping one to put on her lifebelt – 'all about everywhere, thinking of everybody but himself'.

It is certain also that on the boat deck he gave invaluable help to the officers and men engaged in the work of rescue. Being familiar with the boats' tackle and arrangement he was able to aid effectively at their launching; and it was whilst going quietly from boat to boat, probably in those tragic intervals during which the stewardess watched the water creep up the stairway, that he was heard to say: 'Now, men, remember you are Englishmen. Women and children first.'

Some twenty minutes before the end, when the last distress signal had been fired in vain, when all that upper deck and the fore deck as well were ravaged by the sea, there was a crush and a little confusion near the place where the few remaining boats were being lowered, women and children shrinking back, some afraid to venture, some preferring to stay with their husbands, a few perhaps in the grip of cold and terror. Then Andrews came and waving his arms gave loud command:

'Ladies, you must get in at once. There is not a minute to lose. You cannot pick and choose your boat. Don't hesitate. Get in, get in!'

They obeyed him. Do they remember today, any of them, that to him they, as so many more, may owe their lives?

A little way back from that scene, Miss Sloan stood calmly waiting and seeing Andrews for the last time. She herself was not very anxious to leave the ship, for all her friends were staying behind and she felt it was mean to go. But the command of the man, who for nearly two hours she had seen doing as splendidly as now he was doing, came imperatively. 'Don't hesitate! There's not a moment to lose. Get in!' So she stepped into the last boat and was saved.

It was then five minutes past two. The *Titanic* had fifteen minutes more to live.

Well, all was done now that could be done, and the time remaining was short. The forecastle head was under water. All around, out on the sea, so calm under those wonderful stars, the boats were scattered, some near, some a mile away or more, the eyes of most in them turned back upon the doomed ship as one by one her port lights, that still burnt row above row in dreadful sloping lines, sank slowly into darkness. Soon the lines would tilt upright, then flash out and flash bright again; then, as the engines crashed down through the bulkheads, go out once more, and leave that awful form standing up against the sky, motionless, black, preparing for the final plunge.

But that time was not yet. Some fifteen minutes were left; and in those minutes we still have sight of Andrews.

One met him, bareheaded and carrying a lifebelt, on his way to the bridge perhaps to bid the Captain goodbye.

Later, an assistant steward saw him standing alone in the smoking-room, his arms folded over his breast and the belt lying on a table near him. The steward asked him, 'Aren't you going to have a try for it, Mr Andrews?'

He never answered or moved, 'just stood like one stunned'.

What did he see as he stood there, alone, rapt? We who know the man and his record can believe that before him was home and all the loved ones there, wife and child, father and mother, brothers and sister, relatives, friends – that picture and all it meant to him then and there; and besides, just for a moment maybe, and as background to all that, swift realization of the awful tragedy ending his life, ending his ship.

But whatever he saw, in that quiet lonely minute, it did not hold or unman him. Work – work – he must work to the bitter end.

Some saw him for the last time, down in the engine-room, with Chief Engineer Bell and Archie Frost and the other heroes, all toiling like men to keep the lights going and the pumps at work.

Others saw him, a few minutes before the end, on the boat deck, our final and grandest sight of him, throwing deck chairs overboard to the unfortunates struggling in the water below.

Then, with a slow long slanting dive, the *Titanic* went down, giving to the sea her short-spanned life and with it the life of Thomas Andrews.

So died this noble man. We may hope that he lies, as indeed he might be proud to lie, in the great ship he had helped to fashion.

This radio play by the Ulster playwright Stewart Parker (1941–88)
owes something to Beckett's Waiting for Godot *and Stoppard's* Rosen-
crantz and Guildenstern Are Dead *and concerns the exploits on board*
the maiden voyage of a couple of shipyard workers killed during the
building of Titanic. *Danny and Hugh unwittingly conduct us on a voyage*
round the ship and bring to mind Dante's circles of hell. The word
'coffin-ship' takes on new meaning and the bogeyman stoker is an
unsurprising actor in the drama. The launch of Titanic *and the launch*
of Home Rule (both ill-fated) establish, through the characters of Thomas
Andrews and the ship's doctor William O'Loughlin, the political mean-
ings of the ship.

STEWART PARKER
The Iceberg

(Radio 3, 7 January 1975)

MINISTER: We have gathered here – in the opulent surroundings of
this lovely saloon – because of the gratitude in our hearts. I think I
can speak for everyone – certainly in the second-class accommodation
when I say that we are truly overwhelmed by the magnificence of
this vessel – truly a Titan amongst ocean-going craft – we give thanks
to her builders, to her owners, to those who go down to the sea in
ships, all of whom have made this maiden voyage such a splendid
one – particularly to Captain Smith and his officers whose expert
hands have guided us so safely and swiftly across the mighty ocean.

But above all we give thanks to Him who made us – whose hand
rocks us in the cradle of the deep – and to whom we address the
sailor's prayer – even in this triumph of the brain and hands of man
– oh Lord protect us – thy sea is so large – our craft is so small. And
so may God be with you, and cause his light to shine about you, and
to bring you peace. Now and forevermore, amen.

Murmuring, coughing, moving around

HUGH: Where now?

DANNY: I don't know. Onwards and upwards.

Crossfade refined background noise of first-class lounge

BANDMASTER: And now we make a magic journey by gondola along the dark romantic waterways of old Venice into the entrancing world of Offenbach's *The Tales of Hoffman*.

Smattering of refined applause

If you please, lads, and last one to finish buys the drinks.

Grams: orchestra plays Barcarolle from Tales of Hoffman

ANDREWS: One of your favourites, doctor.

O'LOUGHLIN: What's this, Thomas Andrews not working?

ANDREWS: Six days shalt thou labour.

O'LOUGHLIN: And on the seventh thou shalt merely look over some drawings.

ANDREWS: Ah, I've put away the drawings. She's as good as I can make her now.

O'LOUGHLIN: My dear Tommy, she's as good as any ship will ever be on this earth.

ANDREWS: No, doctor, you're talking about the next one – and I mean the perpetual next one.

(*Slight pause*)

You've got your Home Rule Bill launched anyway.

O'LOUGHLIN: Not mine, Thomas. Ireland's. Ours.

ANDREWS: Oh, not me. Besides, she's only launched, I doubt you'll find that she'll never make it into active service.

O'LOUGHLIN: There's good stuff in her. Four-fifths of the votes of the whole Irish people.

ANDREWS: It's her cargo I was thinking of. The powers of taxation invested in this putative Dublin parliament, for instance. You know as well as I do what's implied.

O'LOUGHLIN: Irish taxes for Irish services.

ANDREWS: Dublin taxes on Northern industry to prop up its own peasant economy.

O'LOUGHLIN (*exaggerating accent*): Ah, Thomas, sure you're terrible suspicious of poor peasants.

ANDREWS: We're simply rationalists up in the North, doctor. We look at Belfast today, a city close to half a million souls employed in manufacturing industries that can compete with any in the world. Yet what was it before the Act of Union made us part and parcel of Britain? A scruffy provincial village.

O'LOUGHLIN: Thomas, I never love you more than when you're earnestly assuring me of your rationalism and you sitting there with your eyes full of stars. Sitting in the biggest ship in the world which you built – in a country without a single raw material for the purpose – on a patch of reclaimed mud. No, we're far too sensible and workaday in the South – for the new Ireland to be complete, we'll need impractical wild dreamers like yourself and all those other mad Northerners.

ANDREWS (*laughs, then pauses*): You'll find that what we have we hold, doctor.

O'LOUGHLIN: Well, hold on to it tight, now – don't ever let it get a grip on your throat. (*Slight pause*) Ah, that's enough oul lip about politics for the one night. Here's to your ship, Tommy. I'm proud to be your country-man, even if you do disown me. Here's to your dream!

Fade out

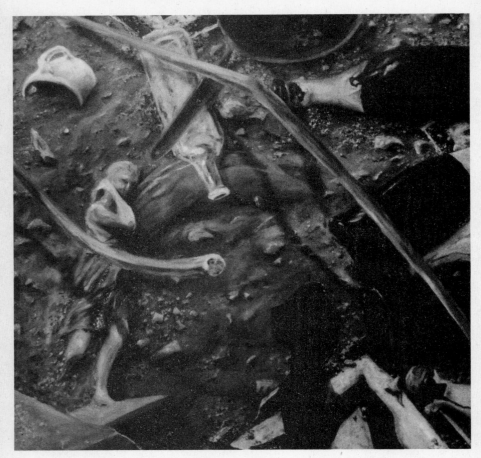

One of a series entitled *Vestiges of* Titanic, this painting by Canadian Steve Gouthro depicts a detail from the debris field.

12
The *Titanic* Effect

We'd rather have the iceberg than the ship,
although it meant the end of travel.
    Elizabeth Bishop, 'The Imaginary Iceberg'

The lessons shipbuilders, shipowners, boards of trade and ships' officers were supposed to learn from the Titanic *disaster implied that the ship had a series of transferable meanings. The public immediately found, and have continued to find to this day, innumerable meanings in the ship. The ship was the state, capitalism, humanity, technology, the hubris of the race, the social class system, an island of money, England, the Empire. Its lifeboats were Christian salvation (or the need of it, since the boats were insufficient in number); the surrounding ocean was the threat of abject poverty, of Godlessness, the habitat of man's helplessness. The iceberg was nemesis, retribution, pitiless nature. The proliferation of active metaphors has been perhaps the primary* Titanic *effect.*

*   Virginia Woolf wanted to write a full account of the tragedy, the hearings into which she and her fiancé Leonard attended. Her witticism in a letter to Ka Cox perhaps betrays a nervousness: 'Do you know it's a fact that ships don't sink at that depth, but remain poised half way down, and become perfectly flat, so that Mrs Stead is now like a pancake, and her eyes like copper coins.' (Mrs Stead was not on board.) Woolf was fascinated and frightened by the subaqueous, by isolation in crisis (in her first novel,* The Voyage Out *(1915), a character says: 'What solitary icebergs we are') and by the abyss (life she thought of as 'a strip of pavement over an abyss'). The collapse into solitariness, the failure to connect, which the* Titanic *disaster seemed to enact, depressed E. M. Forster whose novel* Howards End *(1910) captures the arrogance and the premonitions of impending calamity that* Titanic *realized. And the*

*image of the abyss was a common one in the literature of the time –
there in various guises in Gissing's* The Nether World *(1889),* Wells's
fictions of the 1890s, Charles Masterman's From the Abyss *(1902), Jack
London's* People of the Abyss *(1903).*

The contexts from which Titanic *metaphors spring are various but
the metaphors have flourished best in political and religious settings. The
simplicity of the metaphors has been a godsend to political cartoonists to
this day; one in particular, 'rearranging the deckchairs on the* Titanic',
*has become an over-versatile metaphor in times of political crisis and
an alternative to 'applying Band-aid solutions' and 'fiddling while Rome
burns'.*

The early advertisements that exploited the ship – for safety products,
insurance policies and aids to activities that required alertness and
attention – were also forms of metaphor. The discovery of the wreck
has given a new lease of life to the commercial metaphorizing of the
ship. In 1994 an 18-minute video, The Titanic, *was produced in the
USA by Standard Chartered at a trial in which that company sought
damages from the accounting firm of Price Waterhouse. The video
compares the firm to the owners and navigators of* Titanic *and alternates
information and graphics with footage from* A Night to Remember. *As
the liner slips under the waves, the narrator intones: 'Price Waterhouse
had numerous warnings United Bank was in troubled waters, but also
chose not to listen. Perhaps they too thought they were invincible.'*

This elegy for MacNeice's stepmother employs Titanic *as historical component and useful metaphor. The Ulster poet (1907–63) would have been four when he glimpsed the giant ship. The symbolism (here the personification) of the iceberg is a minor element in* Titanic *mythology and the American poet Elizabeth Bishop (1911–79) in 'The Imaginary Iceberg' pictured the iceberg as a dream of artistic perfection and the ship as flawed and foolish.*

LOUIS MACNEICE
'Death of an Old Lady'

(1956; from *The Collected Poems of Louis MacNeice*, 1966)

At five in the morning there were grey voices
Calling three times through the dank fields;
The ground fell away beyond the voices
Forty long years to the wrinkled lough
That had given a child one shining glimpse
Of a boat so big it was named Titanic.

Named or called? For a name is a call –
Shipyard voices at five in the morning,
As now for this old tired lady who sails
Towards her own iceberg calm and slow;
We hardly hear the screws, we hardly
Can think her back her four score years.

They called and ceased. Later the night nurse
Handed over, the day went down
To the sea in a ship, it was grey April,
The daffodils in her garden waited
To make her a wreath, the iceberg waited;
At eight in the evening the ship went down.

Titanic was not equipped with sufficient lifeboats because the ship herself was regarded as a lifeboat by its builders and indeed by those passengers reluctant to abandon its illusory safety and light and warmth for an open boat at night in mid-Atlantic. The unthinkable and the unsinkable were connected beyond rhyme.

KENNETH E. F. WATT
'The *Titanic* Effect'

(*The* Titanic *Effect: Planning for the Unthinkable*, 1974)

Many people are now saying we need to do something about the 'energy crisis'. Yet politicians who attempt to deal with the problem are discovering that the sentiment of the electorate is against any rise in energy prices as 'anti-consumer', and is also opposed to any public interest in the development of alternate energy sources at present, since that might lead to an increase in taxes. As a consequence of keeping prices down, high per capita use of energy will be encouraged and will thus continue to rise until the supply of energy runs out. And since the investment in finding substitute sources will have been inadequate, there won't be an adequate supply when we need them. In other words, the present public position is desperately short-sighted.

Yet this situation is by no means novel. History abounds with parallels of imminent disaster. Public warnings have been ignored when they were outside the range of past experience. Consequently, the appropriate countermeasures were not taken. The *Titanic* and other 'unsinkable' ships that nevertheless went down; the cities built on flood plains; Pearl Harbor and other military 'surprises'; hospitals and schools destroyed with great loss of life after repeated warnings of what fire or earthquake might do: these are some examples.

There appears to be a basic human tendency to ignore warnings about such possible enormous disasters as 'unthinkable'. We must understand this tendency and guard against it. That the world could run out of energy is 'unthinkable', and consequently it is difficult to interest people in ensuring that such a thing won't happen. Yet if we examine history, an important generalization, which might be called the '*Titanic* effect', can be discerned:

THE MAGNITUDE OF DISASTERS DECREASES TO THE EXTENT
THAT PEOPLE BELIEVE THAT THEY ARE POSSIBLE, AND
PLAN TO PREVENT THEM, OR TO MINIMIZE THEIR EFFECTS.

In general, it is worth taking action in advance to deal with disasters.
The reason is that the costs of doing so are typically inconsequential as
measured against the losses that would ensue if no such action were
taken.

To cure the growth disease, large steps are required. But the magnitude of the consequences that will ensue if those steps are not taken is
'unthinkable'. Thus, there is a real danger that nothing will be done.
Remembering the *Titanic* effect, we shall be on guard against such
thinking.

Born in 1905 in Bulgaria, Canetti moved to Manchester, England, with his parents when he was five. The effect of the sinking on the boy was profound as it must have been on a generation of British children. The word 'Titanic' is one of great power even for adults at this distance from the tragedy. The Nobel Prize-winning author remembers the mutual power of 'Titanic' and 'England'.

ELIAS CANETTI
Meadow, Island, Iceberg

(*The Tongue Set Free: Remembrance of a European Childhood,* 1979; from *The Memoirs of Elias Canetti,* 1999)

The two catastrophes that occurred in this period, and that I now realize were the earliest causes of mass public grief in my life, were connected with ships and geography. The first was the sinking of the *Titanic,* the second the death of Captain Scott at the South Pole.

I can't remember who it was who first spoke about the sinking of the *Titanic.* But our governess wept during breakfast, I had never seen her weeping before, and Edith, the housemaid, came to the nursery, where we normally never saw her, and wept with her together. I learned about the iceberg, about the terribly many people who had drowned, and the thing that had the biggest impact on me was the band that kept playing as the ship sank. I wanted to know what they had played and I received a gruff answer. I realized I had asked something unsuitable and started crying myself. So actually the three of us were weeping together when Mother called to Edith from downstairs; perhaps she had only just heard the news herself. Then we went down, the governess and I, and Mother and Edith were already standing there, crying together.

But we must have gone out after all, for I can see people on the street, everything was very different. The people stood in groups, talking excitedly, others joined them and had something to say; my little brother in the pram, who usually elicited an admiring word about his beauty from all passersby, was completely unheeded. We children were forgotten, and yet people spoke about children who had been on the ship, and how they and the women were saved first. People kept talking about the captain, who had refused to leave the vessel. But the most frequent word I caught was 'iceberg'. It stamped itself upon me like 'meadow' and 'island', although I didn't get it from my father, it was the third English word that remained charged for me, the fourth was 'captain'.

I don't know exactly when the *Titanic* sank. But in the excitement of those days, an excitement that endured for some time, I vainly looked for my father. He would have spoken to me about it after all, he would have found a soothing word for me. He would have protected me from the catastrophe, which caved into me with all its strength. Each movement of his remained precious to me, but when I think of the *Titanic*, I don't see him, I don't hear him, and I feel the naked fear that overcame me when the ship struck the iceberg in the middle of the night and sank into the cold water while the band played on.

Wasn't he in England? He sometimes took a trip. Nor did I go to school during that time. Maybe the disaster occurred during the holidays, maybe they let us off, maybe no one thought of sending children to school. Mother certainly didn't comfort me, she wasn't affected deeply enough by the catastrophe; and as for the English people in our household, Edith and Miss Bray, I felt closer to them than to my real family. I believe that my pro-English attitude, which carried me through the First World War, was created in the grief and agitation of those days.

An American feminist scholar sees the discovery of the wreck in an unusual light. The search for masculine metaphors may be a form of counter-metaphor. The Gipper is President Ronald Reagan; Iacocca is Lee Iacocca, once Chief Executive of Chrysler.

ANN E. LARABEE
'The American Hero and His Mechanical Bride: Gender Myths of the *Titanic* Disaster'

(*American Studies*, 1990)

The *Titanic* has come down to us as archetype of failed technology and legendary cornucopia of late Edwardian extravagance. In early myth, she is maiden or wanton, luring stoic Victorian men to destruction. Recently, with her rediscovery, she has become a feminine enigma, attracting marine cowboys and deep-sea wilderness men, who armed with light and scientific reason claim to love and loathe her. Marine geologist and *Titanic* explorer Robert Ballard, who found the ship in 1985, explained his obsession and his 'curse': 'Before you realize it, you're married to her. And let me tell you something: *There is no divorcing the* Titanic. *Ever.*'

She is, in sum, the mysterious, mechanical bride, an 'image of sex, technology and death' identified by Marshall McLuhan. In industrial age folklore, the mechanical bride is the car advertised as a 'dream date', the atomic bomb named for Rita Hayworth and the computer described by a math professor as 'the perfect wife – it cannot speak, does exactly what it's told, and works fast'. Jane Caputi explains that this conflicting image represents technological man's desire for a dead, artificial, ultimately male world, where no real women are present. In this metaphysical realm of opposites, the mechanical bride's inventor and owner is hyper-masculine: powerful, virile, heroic, individualistic.

The *Titanic* has received most media attention when traditional masculinity has been under reconstruction: in the 1910s, in the wake of the independent, sexually challenging New Woman; and in the 1980s – age of Rambo, Iacocca and the Gipper – after second-wave feminism and the Vietnam War had eroded American manhood. At such times, the *Titanic* has provided a symbolic framework for a politically useful revival of traditional male roles. In the first instance, conservatives upheld the industrial magnate's 'male chivalry', supposedly exhibited on the *Titanic*, as a lesson against suffrage. In the second, marine technowits allied with the Defence Department have presented themselves as macho deep-sea explorers to gain support for American technology. The continuity between the *Titanic* myth's invention and reconstruction lies ultimately in the manipulation of gender myths to bolster a power structure heavily invested in a masculine ethos . . .

But with unexpected disaster on the night of April 15, 1912, the image of the big, beautiful, obedient mechanical bride needed radical revision. She had suddenly become a technological golem, freed from male control. In his memoirs, surviving *Titanic* officer Charles Lightoller wrote:

> It is difficult to describe just exactly where that unity of feeling lies, between a ship and her crew, but it is surely there, in every ship that sails on salt water. It is not always a feeling of affection, either. A man can hate a ship worse than he can a human being, although he sails on her. Likewise a ship can hate her men, then she frequently becomes known as a 'killer'.

Old fears merged the independent, capricious machine and the rebellious, man-hating woman – both threatening to paternalistic, industrial man. The 'female' ship became a figure of wanton destruction, dragging her self-sacrificing men and their 'civilization' down into the icy ocean.

But this myth-building was based on more than fear: by animating the machine with a malevolent female spirit, men ducked responsibility for technological failure, shifting the guilt to a culturally resonant symbol. The *Titanic*, because of her human and particularly female flaws, subjected herself to 'fate', a 'combination of circumstances', or the 'mysterious will of God'. This myth persists in recent accounts; 'The fault lay not in her construction,' Ballard wrote 'but in *her* failure to avoid hitting an iceberg at almost full speed' (italics added) . . .

Titanic historians (almost exclusively male) have often identified hubris, blind faith in technology and conspicuous waste as lessons from the *Titanic*, but have blamed a gender-generic 'Western man' for these 'human follies'. Western man, they claim, must learn to contain his technological arrogance or be subject to nuclear annihilation. Accompanying this general cultural critique is the recurrent image of the mechanical bride and her heroic discoverer who in his quest restores masculinity and technology. Although the Edwardian businessman may have failed to control his technological golem, the modern American scientist/adventurer is able to resurrect and tame her through demonstrations of masculine prowess. 'Raising the *Titanic*', a recurrent dream of sea adventurers, would mean a massive display of technological force. Several serious proposals have been made, including salvage engineer Tony Wakefield's 'Vaseline scheme', a plan to pack the ship's hull with 180,000 tons of petroleum jelly which would presumably make the ship buoyant. In any event, raising the *Titanic* would prove American technological superiority over this relic, a cultural symbol of engineering's defeat.

In Clive Cussler's best selling novel, *Raise the Titanic* (1976), the U.S. military, interested in radioactive cargo, uses explosives to loft the ship two miles to the ocean's surface. Explicitly placing this project in the tradition of American technological chest-pounding, a government official remarks, 'If we can put men on the moon we can bring the *Titanic* up to sunlight again.' Cussler's book revolves around a secret government project to reclaim the *Titanic*'s cargo of the fictional radioactive element, byzanium, which is needed to power a Star Wars-like shield of soundwaves. Job pressures almost destroy several weak team members, one of whom desperately asserts, 'I created this project from nothing. My grey matter was its sperm. I must see it through to completion.'

Cussler's heroes are the hands-on men, engineers, preferably with combat experience. One of the manned submersible operators declares, 'The first men on the moon weren't intellectuals either. It takes the nuts and bolts mechanics to perfect the equipment.' These undersea engineers scrupulously shun emotional involvement with real women. Their emotions are saved for their machines and for the *Titanic* herself, a 'gorgeous bucket of bolts'. The project director whispers, 'Strange thing about the *Titanic*. Once her spell strikes you, you can think of nothing else.' The consummation of this metaphysical desire occurs when the *Titanic* rises like a technological Venus from the waves, shrouded in 'billowing rainbowed clouds of vapour'. Stunned, mesmerized, even tearful, the engineers murmur, 'She's up. She's up.'

Because of an intense, hostile confusion over shifting gender roles,

Cussler's novel places masculinity at a jarring intersection between nostalgia and high tech desire. Cussler desperately wants to return to an imaginary age when men were men (as so sublimely exhibited in *Titanic* legend), but his heroes must prove their manliness in a new arena of high technology. The engineers not only raise the *Titanic*, but a new masculinity ('She's up!').

The *Titanic*'s new, real-life technological hero is Dr Robert D. Ballard – a marine geologist who, under the auspices of the Woods Hole Oceanographic Institute, rediscovered the ship in 1985. Ostensibly, Ballard has used the *Titanic* in a public-relations campaign for science. Insisting that science is a 'contact sport', he has said many times that he wants to change the cultural stereotype of the 'nerd' scientist. Thus, Ballard presents himself as a very masculine adventurer/scientist, an image quickly adopted by male journalists. Explicitly associating himself with American technological progress and machismo, Ballard recounts that he was reading Chuck Yeager's biography when the *Titanic* was discovered. (Of the 'Right Stuff', Yeager was the first pilot to break the sound barrier.) . . .

The myth of resurrected masculinity played out in the *Titanic*'s rediscovery is now firmly embedded in America's patriarchal ideology. In a recent ad for *Fortune*, a businessman gloomily declares, 'The good news is they've made me captain. The bad news is I've come aboard the *Titanic*.' But the accompanying text reassures:

> An outsider is brought in at the eleventh hour to save a sinking ship. Turmoil turns to intrigue, as fast and furious changes ensue. Tough times call for tough managers who can rise to the occasion. And their tactics are logged in the ledger of Fortune.

Unlike the original *Titanic* hero who sinks into the sea, the new American capitalist 'rises to the occasion' and saves the ship. Thus the *Titanic* myth is again logged in the ledger of history, as American masculinity reconstitutes itself in an even more virulent form.

This complex little episode by a noted English novelist is at once polite revenge against class presumption (the irony being Beesley's second-class status on board Titanic)*; a self-deprecating reminiscence by someone guilty of the youthful snobbery of the rising middle class and given to intellectual presumption like the scholarship boys of the period; the debunking of a* Titanic *protagonist; and the contemplation of the elusiveness of history.*

JULIAN BARNES
Tragedy and Farce

(*A History of the World in 10½ Chapters*, 1989)

Fifty-two years before I met him, Lawrence Beesley had been a second-class passenger on the maiden voyage of the *Titanic*. He was thirty-five, had recently given up his job as science master at Dulwich College and was crossing the Atlantic – according to subsequent family legend, at least – in half-hearted pursuit of an American heiress. When the *Titanic* struck its iceberg, Beesley escaped in the underpopulated lifeboat 13, and was picked up by the *Carpathia*. Among the souvenirs this octogenarian survivor kept in his room was a blanket embroidered with the name of the rescuing ship. The more sceptical members of his family maintained that the blanket had acquired its lettering at a date considerably later than 1912. They also amused themselves with the speculation that their ancestor had escaped from the *Titanic* in women's clothing. Was it not the case that Beesley's name had been omitted from the initial list of those saved, and actually included among the drowned in the final casualty bulletin? Surely this was solid confirmation of the hypothesis that the false corpse turned mystery survivor had taken to petticoats and a high voice until safely landed in New York, where he surreptitiously discarded his drag in a subway toilet?

I supported this theory with pleasure, because it confirmed my view of the world. In the autumn of that year I was to wedge into the mirror of my college bedsitting-room a piece of paper bearing the following lines: 'Life's a cheat and all things shew it/I thought so once and now I know it.' Beesley's case offered corroboration: the hero of the *Titanic* was a blanket-forger and transvestite imposter; how just and appropriate, therefore, that I fed him false cricket scores. And on a wider scale, theorists maintained that life amounted to the survival of the fittest: did not the Beesley hypothesis prove that the 'fittest' were merely the most cunning? The heroes, the solid men of yeoman virtue, the good breeding stock, even the captain (especially the captain!) – they all went down nobly with the ship; whereas the cowards, the panickers, the deceivers found reasons for skulking in a lifeboat. Was this not deft proof of how the human gene-pool was constantly deteriorating, how bad blood drove out good?

Lawrence Beesley made no mention of female dress in his book *The Loss of the* Titanic. Installed at a Boston residential club by the American publishers Houghton Mifflin, he wrote the account in six weeks; it came out less than three months after the sinking it describes, and has been reprinted at intervals ever since. It made Beesley one of the best-known survivors of the disaster, and for fifty years – right up to the time I met him – he was regularly consulted by maritime historians, film researchers, journalists, souvenir hunters, bores, conspiracy theorists and vexatious litigants. When other ships were sunk by icebergs he would be telephoned by newsmen eager for him to imagine the fate of the victims.

Forty or so years after his escape he was engaged as a consultant on the film *A Night to Remember*, made at Pinewood. Much of the movie was shot after dark, with a half-size replica of the vessel poised to sink into a sea of ruckled black velvet. Beesley watched the action with his daughter on several successive evenings, and what follows is based upon the account she gave to me. Beesley was – not surprisingly – intrigued by the reborn and once-again-teetering *Titanic*. In particular, he was keen to be among the extras who despairingly crowded the rail as the ship went down – keen, you could say, to undergo in fiction an alternative version of history. The film's director was equally determined that this consultant who lacked the necessary card from the actors' union should not appear on celluloid. Beesley, adept in any emergency, counterfeited the pass required to let him board the facsimile *Titanic*, dressed himself in period costume (can echoes prove the truth of the thing being echoed?) and installed himself among the extras. The film lights were turned on and the crowd briefed about their imminent deaths in the ruckled black velvet. Right at the last minute, as the cameras were due to roll, the director spotted that Beesley had managed to insinuate himself to the ship's rail; picking up his megaphone, he instructed the amateur imposter kindly to disembark. And so, for the second time in his life, Lawrence Beesley found himself leaving the *Titanic* just before it was due to go down.

Being a violently educated eighteen-year-old, I was familiar with Marx's elaboration of Hegel: history repeats itself, the first time as tragedy, the second time as farce. But I had yet to come across an illustration of this process. Years later I have still to discover a better one.

Permissions

For permission to publish copyright material in this book grateful acknowledgement is made to the following:

Sheil Land Associates: from *The Discovery of the* Titanic by Robert D. Ballard and Rick Archbold (Orion Books, 1995), text © 1987, 1989 Ballard & Family; © 1995 Odyssey International; Random House UK Ltd: from *A History of the World in 10½ Chapters* by Julian Barnes (Jonathan Cape, 1969); W. W. Norton & Company for *Down with the Old Canoe: A Cultural History of the* Titanic *Disaster* by Steven Biel (1997), © 1996 by Steven Biel; James Lorimer & Company Ltd, Publishers: from *Voyage of the Iceberg* by Richard Brown (1983), © 1983 by James Lorimer & Company, Publishers; Stackpole Books: from *'Unsinkable': The Full Story of RMS* Titanic by Daniel Allen Butler (1998), © 1998 by Stackpole Books; Farrar, Straus & Giroux, LLC: for 'Little Mary, The Sinking of the *Titanic*, Captain Scott' from *The Tongue Set Free: Remembrance of a European Childhood*, from *The Memoirs of Elias Canetti*, trans. Joachim Neugroschel, © 1999 by Farrar, Straus & Giroux, Inc., translation © 1979 by The Continuum Publishing Corporation; Stephen Deuchar: for 'The Case for the National Maritime Museum' from Titanic *International* (1994); Suhrkamp Verrrlag: for 'First Canto' and 'Fourth Canto' from *The Sinking of the Titanic. A Poem* by Hans Magnus Enzensberger, trans. the author (Houghton Mifflin, 1980), © Suhrkamp Verlag Frankfurt am Main 1978; translation © 1980 by Hans Magnus Enzensberger; Sheridan House: for *Titanic Survivor* by Violet Jessop, ed. John Maxtone-Graham (1997), © 1997 by Sheridan House Inc.; University of Pittsburgh Press: for 'Dark Prophecy: I Sing of Shine' by Etheridge Knight from *The Essential Etheridge Knight* (1986), © 1986 Etheridge Knight; Ann E. Larabee and *American Studies*: for 'The American Hero and His Mechanical Bride: Gender Myths of the *Titanic* Disaster' from *American Studies*, 31:1 (Spring 1990); Aldine de Gruyter: for 'Shine' by Bobby Lewis from

Deep Down in the Jungle: Negro Narrative Folklore from the Streets of Philadelphia by Roger D. Abrahams (Aldine Publishing Company, 1970); David Higham Associates: for 'Death of an Old Lady' by Louis MacNiece from *The Collected Poems of Louis MacNiece*, ed. E. R. Dodds (Faber & Faber, 1966), © The estate of Louis MacNiece 1966 and 1979; Quartet Books: from *A Life to Remember* by William MacQuitty (1991), © by William MacQuitty, 1991; Derek Mahon and The Gallery Press: for 'After the *Titanic*' from *Collected Poems* by Derek Mahon (Gallery Press, 1999); Alexandra Cann Representation: for *The Iceberg* by Stewart Parker (first broadcast on Radio 3, 7 January 1975), reprinted in *The Honest Ulsterman*, No. 50 (Winter 1975); University of Toronto Press: for lines from 'The *Titanic*' (1935) from *Complete Poems. Part 1* by E. J. Pratt, ed. Sandra Djwa and R. G. Moyles (University of Toronto Press, 1989), © University of Toronto Press, 1989; Public Record Office: for testimony by J. Bruce Ismay and Charles Lightoller from the report of the Board of Trade enquiry, in *Shipping Casualties (Loss of the Steamship* Titanic*)*, 1912 (Cd 6352), facsimile limited edition, PRO Publications, 1998; and the Statement issued by the Executive of the Dock, Wharf, Riverside and General Workers' Union on the loss of the *Titanic* (BT 9/920, no. 19) (signed by Ben Tillett); The Society of Authors: for 'The *Titanic*: Some Unmentioned Morals' (*Daily News*, 14 May 1912) and 'Beating the Hysterics' (*Daily News*, 22 May 1912) by George Bernard Shaw from *Agitations: Letters to the Press 1875–1950*, ed. Dan H. Laurence and James Rambeau (Frederick Ungar, 1985).

Every effort has been made to trace or contact all copyright holders. The publishers would be pleased to rectify any omissions brought to their notice at the earliest opportunity.

Illustrations

Preparation for launch
Courtesy: Ulster Folk & Transport Museum. Photographic Archive. Harland & Wolff Collection

Machine art: aft propeller brackets
The Shipbuilder: A Quarterly Magazine devoted to The Shipbuilding, Marine Engineering and Allied Industries, ed. A. G. Hood (Volume VI, Midsummer 1911. Special Number)

Grand Staircase
Courtesy: Vancouver Maritime Museum

Advertising dream that became a nightmare
The Illustrated London News (6 April 1912)

Titanic as she left Queenstown
E. E. O'Donnell (ed.), *Father Browne's* Titanic *Album: A Passenger's Photographs and Personal Memoir*, Wolfhound Press, Dublin, 1997 (published in USA as *The Last Days of the Titanic: Photographs and Mementos of the* Titanic *Maiden Voyage*)
Photographic © Father Browne SJ Collection/The Irish Picture Library
Courtesy: Wolfhound Press

Harold Bride in the Marconi room
E. E. O'Donnell (ed.), *Father Browne's* Titanic *Album*
Photographic © Father Browne SJ Collection/The Irish Picture Library
Courtesy: Wolfhound Press

Cartoon: 'Unsinkable' by Chopin
San Francisco Examiner (17 April 1912)

Cartoon: 'The Helmsman' by Johnson
Philadelphia *North American*

The most sung about ship
Peter Boyd-Smith, *Titanic: From Rare Historical Reports* (Steamship Publications, 1994)

Survivors' stories
Courtesy: Vancouver Maritime Museum

Saved from the Titanic (1912)
Paul Heyer, Titanic *Legacy: Disaster as Media Event and Myth* (Praeger, 1995)

A Night to Remember (1958)
Rank Film Distributors of America, *Exhibitor Campaign Manual*
Courtesy: Vancouver Maritime Museum

Vestiges of Titanic, Steve Gouthro
Courtesy: Steve Gouthro